Studies in Local History
Effingham Common

Studies in Local History
Effingham Common

Edited by

Susan Morris, Christopher Hogger & Bryan Sherwood

Effingham Local History Group

MMXI

Published by
Effingham Local History Group
c/o The Parish Room, 3 Home Barn Court, The Street
Effingham, Surrey KT24 5LG
http://www.surreycommunity.info/effinghamparishcouncil/local-history

First Edition 2011

ISBN: 978-0-9570076-0-4
British Library Cataloguing in Publishing Data

Data available

Printed and bound in the United Kingdom by
The Blissett Group
London
Paper from wood grown in sustainable forests

CONTENTS

Acknowledgements   vii

Introduction   1

1   What is a 'Common'?   3
Susan Morris

2   The Parish Council and Effingham Common   9
Susan Morris

3   Picturing the Common   12
Various contributors

4   Mapping and the changing landscape of the Common   19
Bryan Sherwood

5   The pond, the pound and the Common Keeper   28
C. Edward Crouch, Antony Page & Bryan Sherwood

6   Gypsies and the Common   33
Hilda Brazil and Susan Morris

7   'An account of the sad, splendid lawsuit of William of Effingham'   38
Susan Morris

8   William the 1st, William the 2nd, and Adrian   73
Martin Smith

9   Memories of the Common – oral histories   81
Doreen E. Hemus
Michael S. Waller
C. Edward Crouch & Jessica Page
Ivor Gillespie

Booklist   101

Websites   101

List of illustrations   102

Sources   104

Editorial Notes

There are many variants of spellings for some names used often in this publication. For instance, Leebrooke, Leebrook or Lee Brook? Slaters Oak or Slater's Oak? Brickfield or Brick Field? In these situations we have had to make a choice and we have tried to stick with the same version throughout. We hope this will not cause too much of a problem for readers accustomed to a different version.

The web address of the Effingham Local History Group's home page is

> http://www.surreycommunity.info/effinghamparishcouncil/local-history

The book occasionally cites particular pages on the website and does so using an abbreviated format. In every such citation, for example

> .../research-projects/manors-of-effingham/

the prefix '...' stands for the full home page address as shown above.

We have done our best to ensure that the contents of this book are based on information that has been checked for accuracy both of detail and of interpretation. However, new material yet to appear might throw a different light, or reveal mistakes or other problems. For these or any other failings we apologise in advance. We warmly encourage readers to bring any corrections to our notice. There is much still to tell about the Common – we have barely scratched the pre-nineteenth century – and thoughts of a second publication are already being whispered.

Acknowledgements

This book would not have been possible without the help of many people.

Members of the public who came to Village Day in July 2010 or to Commoners' Day in September 2010, or who made contact with the Effingham Local History Group in other ways, have contributed memories, photographs and documents calling Effingham Common's past back before our fascinated eyes.

The past and current owners of the four properties with Commoners' rights have firmly supported efforts to make the Common more widely understood and appreciated.

Others have worked on Effingham's history for many years and their ground-breaking researches have given the Group's more recent efforts a flying start. Outstanding amongst these is Mary Rice-Oxley, who has made her major collection of historical sources on Effingham representing 'a lifetime's work' freely available to us. She also contributed to the main extant reference work, Monica O'Connor's book *The History of Effingham*, which has been an invaluable resource.

We must acknowledge the unstinting enthusiasm of Adam Owen who since 2003 has been the Trees and Countryside Manager of Guildford Borough Council, which owns and manages the largest sector of the Common. He has taken care of the Common in accordance with the highest standards of best practice and research and has made sustained efforts to inspire and involve residents. Adam has been a prime mover behind events which led to the first project of the Group. His explanation of aspects of the past management and ecology of the Common has opened many people's eyes to what the Common once was like and the changes wrought by time.

Yvonne Shaw, through her keen work on recording and transcribing oral histories, has brought to light historical detail about the Common, besides much else, that would have been undiscoverable by other means. For this we owe much both to her and to the many people she has interviewed.

Eddie Crouch, Jessica and Tony Page and others have repeatedly ransacked their memories, photographs and personal memorabilia to help this project. They have provided many clues to the main lines of research, all with the great generosity and quantities of good humour that have helped to make this first project so enjoyable for everyone involved.

The shaping and planning of the book was assisted by the other members of the editorial team: Hilda Brazil, Keith Cornwell, Liz Hogger and Jane Pear.

To all the above and to our other colleagues who have authored articles in this book, we offer our most sincere thanks.

The Editors

Introduction

Effingham Common lies on the far northern boundary of Effingham parish, yet this land has played a central role in the history of Effingham and in the lives of the people of the village. In this first publication of Effingham Local History Group, we explore the Common's history and landscape, based on maps, official records, photographs, and, most importantly, the recollections of local people whose memories of the Common stretch back nearly 100 years.

Anyone using Effingham Junction Railway Station, or driving down Effingham Common Road to and from the A3 and M25, will have drawn pleasure from the vista of open grassland fringed with trees which stretches south of the station and south west of the road. On a summer day cricket matches on the club ground offer an idyllic scene with the Common as a beautiful backdrop. Walkers, riders and cyclists use the Common's footpaths and bridleways, and naturalists appreciate the plants, insects and birds to be found in the Common's grassland, pond and woodland.

In years past, the Common was more than a pleasant place to visit. Since medieval times, many ordinary village people relied on it to graze their animals and gather firewood. Although the land was owned by various Lords of the Manor, some villagers had rights to use the land, and these commoners' rights have been fiercely defended by local people down to the present day. Finally in 2003 most of the Common passed into public ownership when it was acquired by Guildford Borough Council, ensuring that ordinary people will be able to continue using and enjoying this land into the future.

In these pages, we offer a variety of insights into the history of the Common.

We set the scene with an explanation of what a 'common' actually is, and what is meant by 'commoners' rights'. We then sort out the complicated relationship between the 'manors' of Effingham and the Common.

The Parish Council Minutes begin in 1895 and give a vivid picture of the council's early interest in the affairs of the Common, an interest which continues to this day.

The first map of the Common currently known to us was produced in the middle of the eighteenth century. This and other early maps were followed by a succession of Ordnance Survey maps which reveal how the landscape of the Common has changed. We can see how it was affected by early uses including brick-making, and the impact of the coming of the railway in 1880.

The pond and the pound were significant features on the Common in the past, and we shall visit them in these pages. From early times, the Lord of the Manor appointed a Common Keeper to 'police' the land, whether to protect grazing rights from outsiders or to wage war on litter, a battle still waged in modern times!

Gypsies were regular visitors to the Common in the past; then, as now, they were welcomed by some and vilified by others. Other nomadic visitors included the artist Augustus John.

The core of this publication is the account of William of Effingham and the legal battles which ultimately preserved Effingham Common for future generations to enjoy. Read on to discover that the said William was a rather unusual warrior in the cause of Commoners' rights.

Finally we offer some eye-witness views of life on the Common over the last century, from recordings made by our oral history working group. It will become clear that Effingham Common was home to several larger-than-life characters, and we hope you will enjoy meeting them in these pages.

Effingham Local History Group hopes this publication will delight and entertain as well as record some of the very many reasons why Effingham Common is special.

What is a 'Common'?
Susan Morris

From medieval times and even earlier, most villages across the country had a common which was an essential source of sustenance for villagers. Commons were owned by the Lord of the Manor, but usually the soil was in some way unsuitable for tillage so it could not be rented out like other fields. Instead, depending on what the land was like and what it could offer, villagers were permitted to use it for other purposes such as grazing for animals (horses, cows, sheep, geese etc.), allowing pigs to forage for acorns (known as 'right of pannage'), collection of fallen wood for fuel ('estovers'), turf ('turbary'), fishing ('pescary'), and so on. Households allowed to make use of the common in this way greatly valued their 'commoners' rights' because they represented such an invaluable supplement to their diet and domestic economy.

In early Effingham there were several manors, and different areas of Effingham Common were owned by each: Effingham Manor, Effingham East Court Manor, Byfleet Manor, Effingham La Legh Manor and Effingham la Place Manor (there may have also been others). This is why there were/are several manor houses in the parish, including Lee House (now the moated site Scheduled Ancient Monument), Effingham House (now the Golf Club), Effingham Hill House (now St. Teresa's School), Browns, etc. (On the web-site at .../research-projects/manors-of-effingham/ there is an article *Manors in Effingham* by Susan Morris which explains in greater detail what manors were and their role. It also gives a more detailed list of the owners of the different Effingham manors from the earliest records to the twentieth century.)

In the late eighteenth century when the great national drive to improve the yield of agricultural land began, large numbers of landowners completely reorganised the way village land was farmed (the enclosure movement). Many commons across the country were taken into private farming use and, despite protests, thousands of villagers lost their customary commoners' rights.

This did not happen in Effingham. By then, several of the smaller manors had been subsumed by the bigger ones and disappeared so that Effingham Common was now divided between only two lordships: the Manor of Effingham, and the Manor of Effingham East Court. The lords of both these manors

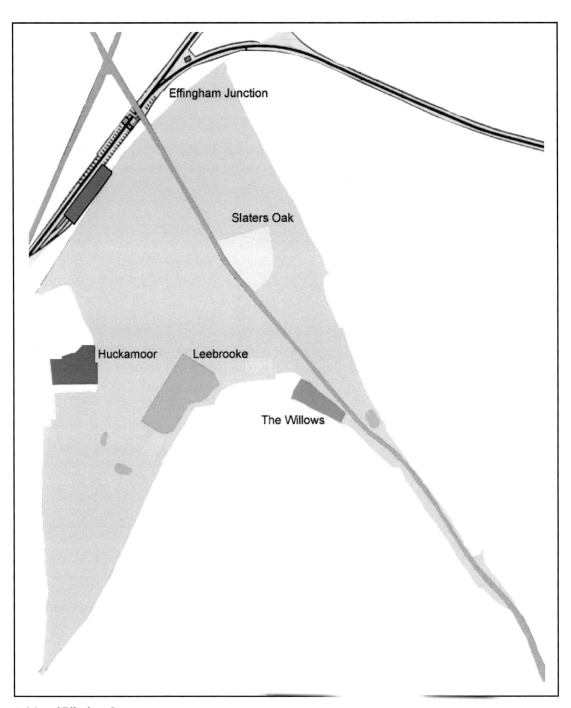

1. *Map of Effingham Common.
The Common is the green area.
The yellow, blue, pink and orange
areas represent land belonging to the
four properties having commoners'
rights.*

introduced Enclosure Acts for their cultivable fields but these did not affect the relatively impoverished ground of the Common. However, there was a great village battle over Effingham Common still to come.

By 1965, there was national concern that remaining commons were being sold off for one purpose or another, or being built on, so that historic green spaces were being lost and villages spoiled. An Act was passed which allowed villages to register not only their commons, but also any surviving commoners' rights. This would ensure a common was preserved from development for ever, and the commoners' rights could never be taken away from them.

By this time one family owned the land of both Effingham manors. Effingham residents wanted to register Effingham Common, but the Lord of the manor(s) opposed this, feeling, perhaps understandably, that as he owned it, it was his private land to do with as he wished. A village campaign was started and residents contributed a considerable amount of money to pay for the legal work needed to challenge him. Many ancient documents and proofs were exhaustively researched, examined and discussed to assess their legal status. Finally, in 1976, the Commons Commissioner announced his finding. The Common was registered, and four Effingham properties had successfully proved their entitlement to commoners' rights. These are now preserved in perpetuity. Much more is told in Article 7 of the epic battle to secure them.

The Commoners

The four properties which today have registered commoners' rights are:

> Huckamoor (formerly Brickfield Farm), Orchard Close
> Leebrooke, Effingham Common
> Slaters Oak, Effingham Common Road
> The Willows, Effingham Common Road

and their locations can all be seen in Illustration 1.

Commoners' rights on Effingham Common

Table 1 shows in simplified form the rights held by each of the four properties. Because these rights are now registered, they cannot be inadvertently 'lost'. It is not strictly essential to exercise the rights regularly, but if this is not done it could substantiate future arguments for changing the appearance or use of the Common in some way – but, as things currently stand, that would require a major change in legislation.

You can find more information and photographs of past Commoners' Days on the web-site at .../commoners-days/

Table 1.

	GRAZING FOR HORSES	PONIES	DONKEYS	COWS	SHEEP	GEESE	ESTOVERS
EAST COURT							
Slaters Oak	2	12	10				
Huckamoor							
Leebrooke					1	15	Yes
The Willows	1						
HOOKE COMMON (5 acres at north)							
Slaters Oak	3		1	2	10		
Huckamoor			24	12			
Leebrooke	1			4	20	15	Yes
The Willows	6*			6*			Yes
HOOKE COMMON (remainder)							
Slaters Oak							
Huckamoor							
Leebrooke					1	15	Yes
The Willows							

* Either 6 horses or 6 cows, but not both

The Commons Register
Effingham Common is Unit CL24 on the Commons Register for Surrey. The Register shows the definitive boundary and lists the specific rights. The Commons Registration Authority is Surrey County Council, which has a Commons Registration Officer to maintain the register and answer queries about boundary issues, rights etc.

The lordships of the manors today
As explained above, until the early years of the 20th century the two manors, and the titles of Lord of the Manor which went with them, were owned by separate families. But eventually both Effingham Manor and Effingham East Court were acquired by the same family – the Calburns. The Calburns sold up their last holdings in 2000-2002 and today the *lands* are owned by several freeholders. But the titles 'Lord of the Manor' remain. They are a 'commodity' which may be bought and sold separately from the land. Currently the titles are still held by descendants of the Calburn family.

Effingham Common today: what it is, and what it is not
The word 'Common' can be very misleading. It is easy to mix up the phrases 'the common man' and 'the general public' and

2. Huckamoor, exact date unknown but thought to be the late nineteenth or very early twentieth century. This was originally a hand-tinted photograph, and traces of the colours can still just be seen. Currently we do not know the names of the people.

conclude that 'common land' is somehow ownerless and/or belongs to everyone. But this is not so. 'Common' does not necessarily mean 'Open to the general public as of right'. So, for the record:

Effingham Common is ALL privately owned land. At present there are 28 owners of various areas, some small and others large, of the Common. Guildford Borough Council owns by far the largest expanse. Two areas are charitable assets of Effingham Village Recreation Trust, held in trust for the residents of Effingham and managed by the Trustees. (Effingham Parish Council holds the freehold). The remaining pieces are owned by individuals. Some are Effingham residents, some are not.

Thus the general public does NOT have the right to do anything it wants on private land, but it can certainly do a lot.

Some freedoms and restrictions
The general public may, as pedestrians,
- walk on the marked public Footpaths and Bridleways, and on GBC's permissive paths;
- roam ON FOOT across the whole area, but NOT when the signs are up during the nesting season (to protect endangered ground-nesting birds);

- walk dogs, but ON LEADS ONLY when the signs are up during the nesting season (to protect endangered ground-nesting birds).

Horseriders and cyclists may
- ride horses or cycles on the marked public Bridleways and on GBC's permissive paths but NOT on the public Footpaths; and NOT across open ground. (Because there is no Section 193 Deed of Declaration on Effingham Common, the provisions of the 2000 Countryside and Rights of Way (CROW) Act do NOT apply, so non-pedestrians do not have the right to roam).

Commoners may
- (as occupants of the four properties with commoners' rights) exercise their rights on the relevant registered areas only.

Persons must NOT
- use metal detectors on any land without obtaining advance permission of the owner(s) of that land.

  The largest area of the Common is owned by GBC Parks and Countryside Dept. GBC is very interested in the historic value of its land and in any information that could be added to the 'cultural database', but would never give permission for 'casual' detectors on any land it owned. It would permit metal detecting if it was part of a significant historical research project and there was a demonstrable case for its use as a tool in that project.

Owners of the Common must NOT
- create any obstacles or set any structures on it which detract from it being uninterrupted open green space.

  (The Cricket Club is on the Common. Although the pavilion is a built structure which would not normally be permitted on a common, it has been there a very long time with consent – it was originally given to the cricketers by the Lord of the Manor perhaps as far back as the 1850s. Commoners have considerately not exercised their rights over the cricket field in living memory.)

The Parish Council and Effingham Common
Susan Morris

Effingham Parish Council came into being on 4 December 1894 when, in accordance with the provisions of the Local Government Act 1894, all electors in the parish convened to nominate and vote in their representatives. From the start, Effingham Common was firmly on the agenda.

The first Parish Meeting took place on 25 March 1895 and was held in the schoolroom. It was presided over by Charles Edward Lambert, the Council's Vice-Chairman who was apparently standing in for the Chairman Francis Muir. Mr. Lambert was the tenant of Effingham House/Manor (today's Golf Club) and one of the richest and most socially important householders in the village. Mr. Muir was also a wealthy man, owning The Lodge on Lower Road (which he later sold to Mr. George C. S. Pauling). Proving its central importance to the village, the subject of Effingham Common was the **very first** (and only!) item of business raised at this meeting by residents:

> Proposed by Mr. Edward Davis seconded by Mr. Charles Whittington that the Parish Council use its influence to compel the owners of Cottages situated on Effingham Common to provide their tenants with proper drinking water – and also that the Parish Council do not be at any expense to make a main foot-path across the Common.

These themes, of safe drinking water and footpaths on the Common, would come up several times more in early Parish Council meetings. Meanwhile, the new electorate knew their stuff. Before 1895 was out they had 'requisitioned' a second Parish Meeting, on 23 September. The first (and only) item of business was once again Effingham Common. Of the two gates which had formerly barred the northern and southern ends of the track across the Common – perhaps to keep animals from straying, or to collect a toll from road-users or to show the extent of the Common owned by the Lord of the Manor – the southern one had been removed. We don't currently know why this had been done. It may have been because the track was seeing a lot more traffic to and from the village since Effingham Junction station had opened in 1880.

The Minutes record the petition:

> We the undersigned Parochial Electors request that you as Chairman of the Parish Council will call a Parish Meeting to

enter a Protest against the Common Gates having been removed –
Signed
Frank Hills
Edward Davis
Andrew Bonsey
Edward Setchell
John Carpenter
George Burton

About 50 Electors present.
Mr. F. Muir in the Chair

3. *A historic postcard from the early 1900s showing Effingham Common Road, looking south from the railway bridge. You can see the northern gate, in place across the track although standing open. The southern gate had been near a pair of cottages, now gone, named 'Common Gate', on the site of the property now called Tollgate Cottage. The cottages on the right of the picture were for station or railway staff. They were demolished to make way for the station car-park in the late 1970s or early 1980s.*
Currently we do not know the names of the people shown.

We know a little bit about some of the residents who signed this petition. All of them came from the Effingham Common area. Frank Hills who lived at Indian Farm was one of the Parish Councillors voted in at the first election, and several of the other names on this list went on to serve on the Parish Council in the not-so-distant future. Edward Davis, farmer, tenant at Lower Farm, stood for the first time in March 1896 and during two long terms went on to serve over a period of nearly 30 years. Edward Setchell was a farmer at Norwood Farm. Andrew Bonsey lived at Effingham Common. He went on to become a Parish Councillor in 1896 (only). John Carpenter was described as a fruit-grower in *Kelly's Directory* for 1913. He lived at the

Effingham Common.   Pub. by W. Richards, Effingham.

farmhouse then called Carpenters, but later called Leebrooke. At the 1909 Annual Parish Meeting, Bonsey and Carpenter appeared again, this time to ask the Parish Council to look into the state of the footpath 'from Bookham road across the fields to Effingham Lane on to the Common and station'. George Burton also lived near the Common, at one of the properties whose address was given simply as 'Effingham Common'.

Here is the resolution arrived at by the meeting:

> Proposed by Mr. Edward Davis seconded by Mr. Andrew Bonsey that this Meeting approve under safe conditions having a Gate erected in lieu of the one which has recently been removed from the South end of the Common, they venture to ask the Highway Authority and the Lord of the Manor of Effingham East Court to consent to a [gate] being erected, the cost thereof being defrayed by the Copyholders and when erected such gate to always be kept open from 7 in the morning until 10 in the evening, and that an undertaking be given by several of the Copyholders on behalf of the whole that a person shall be employed at their expense to open and close the Gate at the times mentioned, and if requested a light should be placed on such Gate. It was further resolved that in the event of the required permission being granted, the other Authorities should be applied to for similar permission with regard to the Lower Gate.

The Copyholders were the tenants of the Lord of the Manor who would be using the Common – more than just the four properties which later succeeded in registering their rights.

At the time of writing, it does not seem as if the above resolution was ever brought into being. The replacement gate seems not to have appeared. Be that as it may, down the years, Effingham Common itself has gone on being a subject of great importance to the village and thus to the Parish Council. Such diverse incidents as hardcore being laid, foot-and-mouth disease, desire to create a station car-park, the wartime need to grow more food, a plan to build a housing estate, the activities of model aircraft hobbyists, the future of the skylarks versus the future of the Dartford warbler and many many other topics, have regularly called upon councillors' debating and decision-making powers. There is no sign that it will ever be otherwise!

Picturing the Common
Various contributors

Seeing how the everyday scene, so familiar today, is different from what it was even a short time ago sparks immediate interest in many people. In Effingham we are fortunate to have a variety of photographs showing what the Common was like about a century ago. These allow us to see such details as how the road and tracks or the shapes of buildings have changed; how landmark trees, now full-grown, looked when they were younger; how changes have occurred even in the relative dampness of the ground and in the types of plant life.

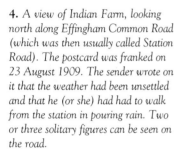

4. *A view of Indian Farm, looking north along Effingham Common Road (which was then usually called Station Road). The postcard was franked on 23 August 1909. The sender wrote on it that the weather had been unsettled and that he (or she) had had to walk from the station in pouring rain. Two or three solitary figures can be seen on the road.*

Many of these photographs were taken by or on behalf of Mr. William Richards. Born in Finchley in 1852, he moved from Hertfordshire in about 1879-1881 to The Street in Effingham. Here, for many decades, he ran the 'Baker, Confectioner and Corn Dealer' shop which until it was demolished stood on the site of the current property Westmead. He served as a Parish Councillor from 1898 to 1907. He published at least two early series of picture postcards of Effingham, presumably for sale in

Indian Farm, Effingham Common.

his shop. The earliest date we have (so far) for these postcards being on sale is 1904.

One of his series bears headings printed in characteristic red lettering, of which there was an example (Illustration 3) in the previous article.

The next four views were also photographed by or for Mr. Richards in the early twentieth century. You can see that their headings are not all printed in the same style which implies they are from two different series and therefore of different dates, but we don't yet know which was the earlier. They concentrate their interest upon the group of houses on the west side of Effingham Common Road, approximately opposite its junction with Lower Farm Road. We are grateful to Martin Smith for identifying in each case the position and viewing direction of the camera, as shown in his diagram (Illustration 9) based upon a map of 1930. (The situation at this location today is very different, as there have been substantial changes to properties and boundaries.)

The first (Illustration 5) in this group of four is the earliest one. It was taken from position A in the diagram and is looking towards a clump of pollarded willow trees that stood at the point where the track now designated a Public Footpath (FP114) meets the track connecting Tyrrells to the road. In the image, the entrance to Tyrrells is on the right. The pale thin band

5. *Looking eastwards across Effingham Common Road from near the entrance to Tyrrells.*

Effingham Common.

Pub. by W. Richards, Effingham.

6. *Looking south-west across Effingham Common Road towards Rose Cottage (now Squirrels).*

7. *Looking westwards towards Willow Cottages from near the entrance to Tyrrells.*

The Common, Effingham.

8. *Looking southwards towards Tyrrells.*

running from left to right at some distance behind the trees is the road, then little more than a dirt track. Of the five main trees shown, the one second from right had been felled by the time the other three photos in the group were taken – in the diagram it is indicated by the tree symbol shown as just a green outline.

These other three (Illustrations 6, 7 and 8) were taken later, and all on a single occasion, judging by their common portrayal of the delivery boy with horse, cart and cart-driver, seen from different viewpoints. We know these postcards were also sold by Mr. Richards because his name is printed on their reverse sides.

Illustration 6 was taken from position B, looking southwest. Sheep are grazing the ground nearby, but the rush shows how damp the area was at that time; it is much drier now. This photograph, and other copies of it we have seen, was evidently doctored slightly during preparation for printing, to improve the 'legibility' of the image. This was quite frequently done if the level of contrast that the camera was capable of registering was not sufficiently sensitive to make paler areas stand out. Here, the outlines of the roof ridges have been artificially darkened to render several properties more visible. The houses shown are, from left, The Willows (at far left, behind trees and before it was rebuilt), Rose Cottage (now Squirrels, at centre), Nos. 1&2 Willow Cottages (now Willow Cottage and Willow Barn) and (at far right) Nos. 3&4 Willow Cottages (now Wytecot and Burcot). The house Tyrrells is not visible, being a little to the right of Rose Cottage but set further back and obscured by trees. The horse and cart are at position H1 on the diagram and are standing on the road. The more prominent white band behind them is the track leading off to Tyrrells. The group of pollarded trees mentioned earlier is in the background behind the cart.

Illustration 7 was taken from position C. Prominent in the foreground is the track leading (leftwards) to Tyrrells. The lesser track leading away from it through the pollarded trees gives access to Willow Cottages. The horse and cart are here in a different position, H2 (this would not be possible for them nowadays, as the land at this location is completely given over to scrub). Behind them is the property Wise Folly, but wholly obscured by trees.

Illustration 8 was taken from position D, looking southwards. We now finally see Tyrrells fully revealed, although the photographer has artificially outlined the roof lines and the chimney breast. Note the very high fence shielding the property on its east side. The horse and cart are again at position H2.

The next view (Illustration 10) is from a postcard published by 'W. H. A.'. The latter was almost certainly W. H. Applebee

9. *Estimated camera positions for the previous four photographs.*

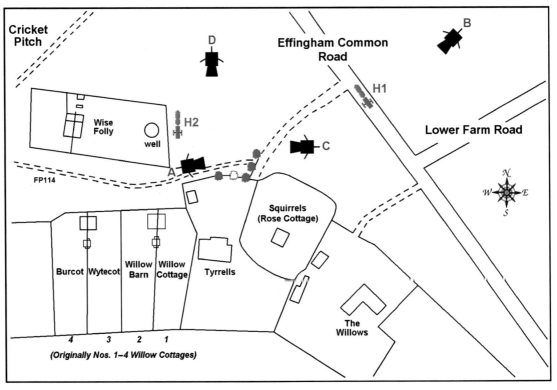

10. *Effingham Common Road, looking from the north towards Indian Farm and the village.*

who, based in Ashford, Middlesex, printed postcards for numerous photographers in the south-east during the approximate period 1912–25. Who the photographer was in this particular instance we cannot say. The view is along Effingham Common Road, looking from the north towards the south. A timber wagon is making its way to the village. The road ahead is a steady haul uphill to the village, but the wagon has just gone down the small dip in the road at this point. The photographer has taken advantage of this and is standing on the higher ground nearer the entrance to Lower Farm Road.

The stamp on the reverse is franked Effingham 26 February 1918. It is addressed to Mrs. Fletcher, 15 Beauchamp St., Shaw Heath, Stockport, Cheshire and the message reads:

Monday

Dear Mother
Just a line to say I arrived here at 9am this morning, it was a long journey and I felt about [sic] tired out, but I am all right again. This is a view of where I am showing the farm, all on its lonesome. Isn't it a pretty spot. With fondest love to all from your loving son

Jack

11. *The man is scything the verge, rather than the crop, in the course of seeking the route of the gas main. The crop in the field is corn, establishing that part of the Common was ploughed in this period. The last crop was harvested in 2002.*

Moving on nearly two decades, Illustration 11 shows part of the Common in 1936, clearly being used for crop growing.

Finally, besides studying the history already recorded long ago, it is important to record relatively recent events, as these will become 'long-ago' history for future generations. Illustration 12 captures just such an event, one that is – and will surely ever remain – unique in its nature.

12. *On 24 October 2003 the final flights of the three British Airways Concordes took place, and were staged such that people viewing them from specific locations could be kept advised of progress by live TV and radio coverage. They were scheduled to arrive together at London Heathrow at 16.00 for a spectacular three-aircraft back-to-back landing, with all three in the sky over London at the same time prior to landing. The first Concorde to land, coded Alpha-Echo, flew from Edinburgh; the next, Alpha-Foxtrot, flew from Heathrow for a VIP trip around the Bay of Biscay, whilst the last was BA002 from JFK airport in New York, performing the final transatlantic Concorde flight. This photograph taken on Effingham Common by Diana Smith, and described here by her, shows BA002 Concorde, circling on the Ockham beacon while the landing formation of all three was being synchronised.*

Mapping and the changing landscape of the Common
Bryan Sherwood

The Tithe Commutation Act of 1836 led many land owners to call for the Ordnance Survey to produce large scale maps of the country, added to which further pressure was then put on by the railway companies during the building boom in the 1840s.

Over many decades prior to this, a succession of small scale maps had been published with or without all the villages between 'Guldford and Darcking' [sic] being marked. Where they did appear the exact location seemed more to do with the skill of the engravers fitting in the names, than any attempt at topographic accuracy. The first detailed map was produced by John Rocque around 1759/62 and was shortly followed by the first series of the Ordnance Survey in the first part of the 19th century. It was, however, not until 1871 that Effingham Common appeared in the first large-scale County Series (Illustration 13). By this time surveying techniques had improved and this map is the first to depict the area accurately.

This map is also particularly interesting as it gives a good indication of what went on in the past as well as the situation at the time of the survey. By the time of this map the major route north across the Common was from Lower Farm, west of Slaters Oak, and on to what became Effingham Junction. From there the various paths were consolidated to a formal cross roads showing a north-east – south-west route between Stoke d'Abernon and the Horsleys and a direct route north-west to Ockham. These tracks follow, very much, the modern roads we have today.

What is more significant are the numerous, less well-defined, paths you can see across the Common, which reflect the earlier traffic of goods and people in the area. Chief amongst these are remnants of former well-used paths: one from north of the brickfield which went south to join the main path over the common at Lower Farm, with others linking it to the Horsleys and Bookham. Another path, from the pair of Leewood Cottages (which no longer exist), went to Lower Farm and on to Effingham village. A third path from north of the brickfield ran across the Common and along a field boundary on Norwood Farm to Bookham. Although these paths are still being indicated on the 1871 map, apart from the link between Effingham and the station, they were largely redundant, it seems, by the turn of the 19th century. What are no longer visible

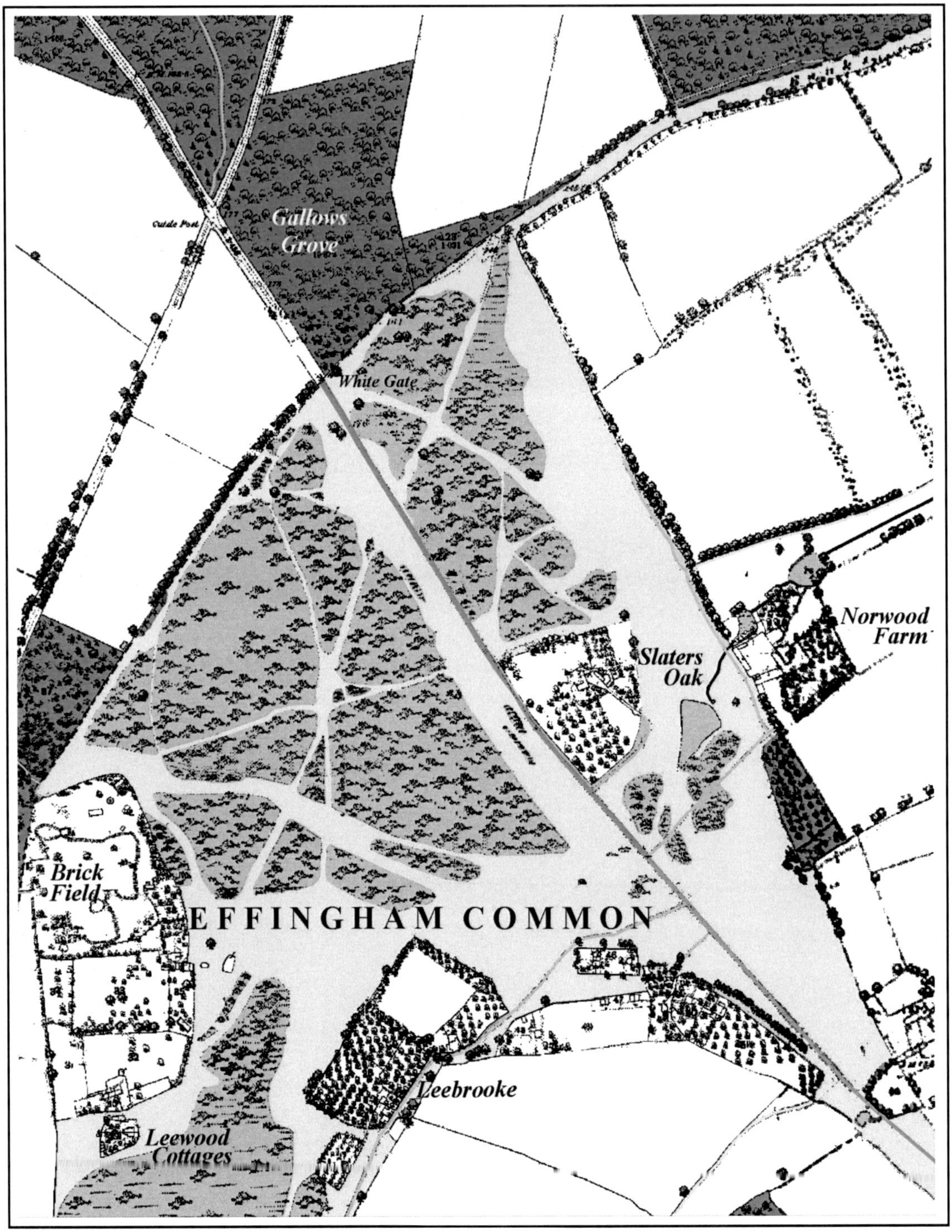
Gallows
Grove
White Gate
Norwood
Farm
Slaters
Oak
Brick
Field
EFFINGHAM COMMON
Leebrooke
Leewood
Cottages

13. *The 1871 Ordnance Survey Map. Adapted from the 1871 O/S map of the north Common. The trackways are shown in a lighter tint.*

by 1871 are the original track from Lower Farm to the northern boundary of the Common and a complex arrangements of paths leading away from the edges of the Common. Most of the latter disappeared as the result of changes in field boundaries and land use.

Whilst most of the major changes in land use took place between the 1750s and the 1850s, there was one development that was going to drastically alter everything – the coming of the railway.

In 1880 the London & South West Railway built the track between London and Guildford. This missed the Common and ran through an adjacent field between the north of the Common and the crossroads. At a similar time they and the London Brighton & South Coast Railways also had stations in Leatherhead and the line of the latter ran on to Horsham via Dorking. It was not long before a link to the Guildford line was wanted. The most direct route would have taken the track past Polesden Lacey and bring a service to the villages of Bookham and Effingham. However, it is said anecdotally that Queen Victoria, who disliked railways, objected to this connecting link passing so close to the Polesden Lacey estate and thus it had to be routed in a wide arc meeting up with the Guildford line in the field alongside the Common at Effingham – the line that is there today. In doing this it clipped the edge of Bookham Common and divided many farm fields. The rail link was in place by 1885 and a station named Bookham & Effingham was built on the edge of Bookham Common. Three years later in 1888 a new station was built at Effingham Junction, with minimal facilities for passengers. Both stations were some distance from the villages they were expected to serve. At the Junction a bridge had to be constructed and three cottages were built for the station staff. Two of these were semi-detached and had entrances directly onto the stretch of made-up road extending from the station to the northern edge of the Common. The third, built for the stationmaster, was some distance away and could be accessed either from the platform or from a path along the edge of the field. These cottages are first shown on the 1897 O/S map (Illustration 14a). Shortly afterwards, and before the railway shed was built, a second pair of semi-detached cottages was built between the existing cottages. These also had their entrances on the extended path (Illustration 14b). This path still exists and now marks the edge of the Common. Although the rail service was quite frequent, the staff living out in this field must have felt socially very isolated.

The arrival of the station meant a significant increase in traffic, not just of people but also of goods and livestock. The

14. *Locations of the Station Cottages:*
a) The 1897 map shows the three
original cottages built for railway staff.
The single cottage to the south was for
the stationmaster.
b) The 1914 map shows the additional
middle pair of cottages.

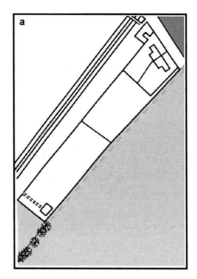

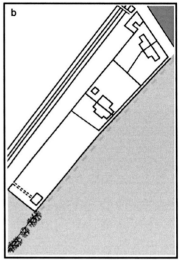

track from the station to the village became the main artery across the Common, giving way to the modern road we have today.

After the First World War it was decided that the Junction would be a suitable place to construct railway sidings. In addition a large building was erected at the eastern end of the station cottages. The cartographer who drew the first maps after its erection in 1920 labelled this 'Engine Shed', a name which is still used today. To be strictly accurate it never was an engine shed. The track inside did not occupy the total length of the building, which was actually a carriage shed, as recognised on modern maps. The building of the shed provided an additional source of work for local, mostly female, residents of Effingham, as carriage cleaners and the like. Whilst this shed was built in the same field as the station it was so close to the hedge line of the Common that it appears the railway company encroached slightly onto common land to provide access alongside the building. This had an impact on the Common's edge – it could not have gone unnoticed – but there was probably no complaint, as the railway was by now an important part of the economy of the village.

Following the railway, houses were built along the north side of Forest Road and these formed the hamlet of Effingham Junction, in East Horsley Parish. On the south side of the railway, the Common effectively prevented much of the 'ribbon development' you would expect to see near a station. Houses were built along the Common road from the village northward up to Lower Farm, along Lower Farm Road and, more recently, around the original unmade road to Leebrooke, but the

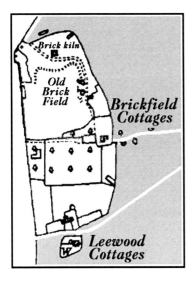

15. *Brick Field in 1871.*
This map shows a brick kiln (or the former site of one) inside the enclosed area. This continues to be marked but unnamed on maps up until 1961, although there was nothing visible on the ground in the 1950s.

Common itself was largely unaffected. The only exception was the construction of a private entrance to Banks Way Farm, constructed after French actress Yvonne Arnaud and her husband purchased the farm in 1937. Most of this road follows the old northern edge trackway of the Common and first appears on the 1961 O/S – the first post-war map.

Of the early history of the Common the only activity that has still left its mark today is the brick works: one of several that came and went in the surrounding area. Brickmaking was very much an itinerant business and for the most part took place at the location of the raw material. The works on the Common was it seems an exception. Starting around 1570s it flourished for about 200 years. We know this was still in existence in the 1760s, when it was shown as a building with kilns on what was then open common land. By the 1871 O/S map an area had been enclosed and formally called Brick Field, although by then it was no longer in production. A brick kiln is identified inside the grounds (Illustration 15) on the 1871 map, and then appears on all the maps up to 1961. But there was no building there in the 1950s and by 1961 it was most probably a site, rather than a physical construction. Brick kilns were usually simply constructed by stacking dried bricks on a bed of combustible material, which was sealed with an outer clay wall. It was presumably the results of digging that created the ponds inside the Brick Field property which during the 1950s were home to wild duck. Traditionally clay was dug during the autumn and winter months and allowed to 'weather': the brickmaking season in Surrey began in mid-April. The other important ingredient for brickmaking was sand as this stopped the clay sticking to the moulds. Presumably the Effingham brickworks obtained their sand from the same sources as others in the area. The nearest was Ockham and this could explain why the tracks from the field to this village were important for so long.

Two modern tracks have come into existence both of which can, in part, be attributed to the effect of the railway. The first of these is the precursor of Forest Lane. It came about because the original main exit from the brickfield was north-west across what became Forest Road and on through Barnthorns Wood. But this route was severed by the building of the original railway track, so a new exit had to be created onto Forest Road beside the railway bridge, in the adjacent field between the brickfield edge of the Common and the railway land. Between the Wars this track up to Brick Field Cottage entrance was developed for housing. It could not have been long before people on the Horsley side of the bridge discovered that by using Forest Lane and skirting the Common behind the engine shed they had a

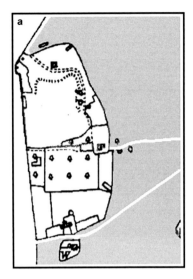 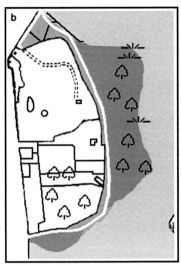 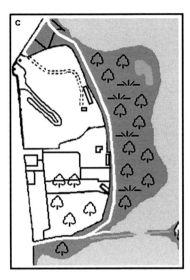

16. *Paths around Brick Field.*
a) The early paths across the Common to Lower Farm.
b) By 1974 the main route was behind Brick Field, as it is today. However, the trees have started to encroach on the open common and the land is becoming waterlogged.
c) Today the gap between 'North Common' to the north and Hooke Common to the south is almost closed off by a hedge. Water draining from the brickfield and other property causes temporary and more permanent ponds among the trees.

short cut to the station. Up until the 1870s a similar track seems to have existed in part, but this was simply following the hedge line along the edge of the Common, and was of little significance. A similar situation occurred with the second track, which first appears on the 1970s O/S maps. As housing developed west of Hooke Common it was realised that a path from Heathway, round the eastern side of the brickfield, could also provide a useful link to the station (Illustration 16). The need for this was now greater than for the existing path to Norwood Farm and the village. As a result the latter path disappears off the post-war O/S maps, only to be reinstated more recently (as Footpath No 114). The obvious and direct route from Heathway to the station – diagonally across the common – was prohibited, probably more by the farming activities than by any conservation concerns.

The successive post-war maps show other more recent changes on the Common and locate sites that were more ephemeral. Good examples of the latter include the pound by Lower Farm, discussed in Article 5, and farm buildings, which have come and gone. Examples of the former include the filling in of the pond on the west side of the road opposite Lower Farm to build a pumping station and the disappearance of Leewood Cottages in the late 1960s. The best example, however, is perhaps illustrated by the station cottages and the station car park.

After the Second World War very few people had private transport; most residents and visitors relied either on the bus service between the village and the station, or used a taxi service provided by the garage at Effingham Junction. There was no parking provision at the station so it was not long before car

17. *The Station Cottages.*
The last two cottages to survive were the pair on the roadside.
(This is a detail of the postcard shown earlier in Illustration 3).

owners discovered they could park on the east side of the Common at the bottom of the slope from the bridge. A roadside drainage ditch and hedge prevented direct entry onto the common land, so drivers would turn into Banks Lane and park up on what was then open grassland between two semi-mature oaks. This served them well in the summer but became muddy in prolonged periods of bad weather and during the winter. These enterprising drivers therefore started bringing ashes and gravel to form an unofficial hard standing between the trees.

Inevitably as car ownership grew and commuting to larger local towns and London increased, the space on the Common became too small to accommodate all the vehicles. After much discussion the railway agreed in 1965 to build a car park on the ground then occupied by the station cottages. This was not done in one operation, but slowly the houses were removed and the car park grew outwards from the discrete area by the engine shed until finally all the cottages were demolished (Illustration 17). As the single stationmaster's cottage at the far end was the first to go, an entrance had to be constructed across the edge of the Common onto the railway land. This also explains why the entrance was (and still is) not directly off the main road as one

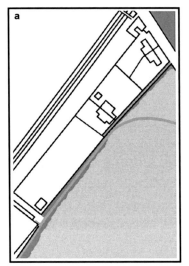

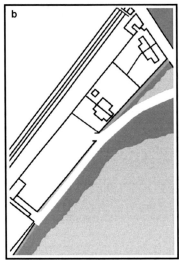

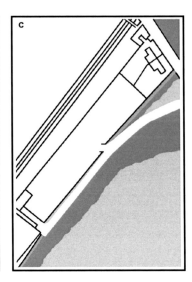

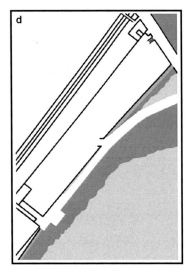

18. *The station car park
(modified from the 1961 O/S map).*
*a) The five station cottages there on the
1961 map.*
*b) By the 1971 map the most westerly
cottage had gone, and the car park had
been constructed with a new entrance
road across the Common.*
*c) By 1977 the middle cottages were
demolished and the car park extended.*
d) The modern map shows all the cottages demolished and the car park extended, as it is today.

would expect. The first car park was finally opened in 1968. It soon became obvious that it was not going to be large enough for the volume of commuters using the station, but it took another ten years for the railway to extend the area. This it did by demolishing the middle cottages, as shown on the 1977 map. It must have been about this time that the pair of cottages by the road (Illustration 17) were also evacuated, for in 1985 the Parish Council complained to the then British Rail (BR), that these cottages were empty and in a dilapidated condition. However, despite continued pressure, it was not until 15 January 1988 that BR wrote to say that they expected to begin demolition 'in four weeks'. These changes are well illustrated in the succession of O/S maps (Illustration 18a-d).

Finally one must make some mention of the environmental changes that have taken place on the Common. Although these are hinted at, their full impact cannot be assessed from maps alone.

From at least the 18th century until well into the 1970s the Common was more or less open ground, with some patches of scrub. During this period a small number of oaks grew on the periphery and in hedgerows, but the land was used mostly for grazing and more recently as a site for recreation. It was used for walking, riding and as a large open playground for the children of both Effingham Parish and Effingham Junction. Owing to different ownership of the land on either side of the road, these areas evolved in totally different ways. The east side north of Slaters Oak has largely, due to lack of any intervention, now become totally scrubbed up. The short grass has given way to bracken; the trees and the understorey are now so dense as to be almost impenetrable in places.

The west side had a very different recent history. There are no maps between 1934 and the 1960s so there is nothing to show the farming activities that took place during the late 1930s or at the end of the War. Farming and some degree of soil improvement has left this side of the Common as an area of inundated grassland which, despite many recent ditches, does not drain readily in winter but bakes and cracks in periods of warm weather. This has affected the mix of vegetation we see today. The growing of spring corn, temporarily at least, caused the west field to support a small population of lapwings, and skylarks were frequently seen over the Common. The lapwings disappeared in the early 1950s with the change in land use. The skylarks and other birds are still there, but on the whole in much reduced numbers. In addition there has been a slow encroachment on the open ground by the woodland fringe. Most marked is the area along the track around the eastern side of Brick Field (Illustration 16). This perhaps has not been all bad, as it has increased the diversity of habitats for plants and wildlife. A full assessment of species using the Common started only when the Guildford Borough Council took ownership in 2002 and thanks largely to Adam Owen (Trees and Countryside Manager since 2003), some baseline surveys have been undertaken. This, with ongoing recording, should result in a better understanding of the biodiversity of the Common and help dictate future management.

In this article I hope to have shown something of how the resident population of Effingham has impacted on the land, as reflected largely in the changes shown on the maps. The remainder of the book covers the real story of the Common – the lives of the everyday people who lived and worked in this changing landscape.

The pond, the pound and the Common Keeper
C. Edward Crouch, Antony Page & Bryan Sherwood

5

The pond

There are in fact several ponds on Effingham Common, but the one with which most people are familiar is the one beside Effingham Common Road, between the property called Willow Pool and the driveway to Lower Farm. This is the pond previously seen in Illustration 10, in which the view is from the north to the south.

A different view of the pond, looking from the south to the north, can be seen in Illustration 19.

Mrs. Lena Bridger, late mother of Mary Rice-Oxley, lived in the village from 1932. In a recording of her memories, made by Mary in Autumn 1971, she mentioned that 'by Willow Pool was a pond with magnificent frogspawn'. Originally the pond was (and still is) fed from a source about half a mile to the west, roughly Hooke Common, but the exact whereabouts of this source (and of the 'Lee brook' itself) are still unclear. However, a major source of supply since the road was properly surfaced and drained is surface water drainage from the slope rising to the south (Effingham Common Road, The Street and Beech Avenue). Terry Driscoll has explained for us how the current water-flow system of this pond operates: when the water level in the pond rises high enough, it flows out over a cill set in its eastern bank into a stream which runs along beside Lower Farm, and then into the three lakes Pikes Pool, Herons Reach and Mallards Mere which are south of the eastern end of Lower Farm Road. The outlet from Herons Reach joins a stream from Bookham Common north of Bank's Farm, and flows north. Along with several other drainage ditches it then joins the River Mole between Emlyn Lodge and the Sports Ground at Stoke d'Abernon.

Bryan Sherwood relates that the western side of Pikes Pool was originally a natural pond, but in the early 1970s (before 1974) it was enlarged by excavating the pond's eastern side; Herons Reach was originally boggy ground, lying a little way to the east of that pond, which was dug out in the late 1960s to form the current lake; Mallards Mere is a totally artificial lake, created at the same time as the work on Herons Reach.

Over the years, if left to itself, the Effingham Common pond can (and has) become overgrown almost to the point of extinction. In 1976 the Parish Council took the lead in seeking

Effingham Common.

19. *The pool by Effingham Common Road, in another postcard produced or published by William Richards. Could it be the photographer's bicycle leaning up against the small white barrier fence between the pond and the road?*

Skating on the frozen pond in her childhood in the 1920s has been described vividly by Doreen Hemus in Article 9.

to have the pond properly dredged (with due regard to the clay sub-soil), and unwanted vegetation removed. This thorough job cost about £3,000, raised by private subscription and a contribution from the Parish Council.

It is very much up to the village whether it wishes to preserve this amenity; the enthusiasm for doing so varies in proportion to the proximity of villagers to it. It is however a natural feature to the many who use the road across the Common.

The pound

Not far from the pond there is a flat area of Common between the frontage of Lower Farm and the road; this was once the site of a *pound*. A pound would have been a relatively small structure, probably constructed of sturdy wooden hurdles or suchlike. It would have been a very important feature of the Common when the latter was in use as a shared grazing area – in other words, for centuries. As agreed with the Lord of the Manor, each cottage household had the right only to pasture certain numbers and types of animals on the Common. This ensured that there was no overgrazing, that is, no more animals than the land could sustain. If anyone tried to abuse this and graze more than they were entitled to, the extra animals could

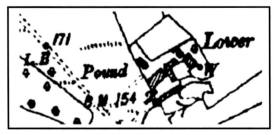

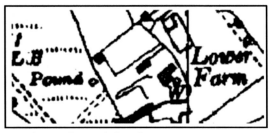

20. *The pound as marked on the 1919 Ordnance Survey Map.*

21. *The pound as marked on the 1934 Ordnance Survey Map.*

be 'impounded'. Also, animals which appeared to be wandering unsupervised, including dogs, could be fenced in until reclaimed. Sometimes fines were payable.

The first Ordnance Survey map to identify the pound was apparently the 1919 one (Illustration 20). If so, the pound could have been set up at any time between 1897 (the date of the previous map) and 1919. Similar structures may well have existed on other areas of the Common down the centuries before the 1919 map, but never considered as sufficiently permanent to record. The pound is marked again on the 1934 O/S map (Illustration 21) and now appears as a small square just to the right of the label. The 1961 O/S map depicts the situation identically but is not very reliable – it was based on older data that had not been thoroughly checked for changes before publication. People who knew the Common very well in the 1950s do not remember even traces of the pound existing at that time, so it had most probably disappeared before then.

Perhaps the known location, near Lower Farm, was chosen because this was conveniently near where the Common Keeper lived? Speaking of which …

The Common Keeper
The Common Keeper was an official appointed by the Lord of the Manor to 'police' the use, and users, of a common. One of his responsibilities would be control of the pound for the purposes described above. Another is described in a *Surrey Advertiser* article of 1 May 1909: Mr. Batt, described as Common-keeper, 'armed with permission to impound' rushed out with about twenty commoners who together 'secured about nine Gypsy horses from an encampment that had appeared on the Common'. The horses would have been eating the grazing intended for Commoners' animals.

As late as 1923 Effingham still had a Common Keeper. He would have been appointed by Robert Calburn who was by that time Lord of the Manors of both Effingham and Effingham East

Court. This is alluded to in the Minutes of the Parish Council, when the Common Keeper was 'volunteered' in his absence to deal with a local nuisance causing aggravation at the time. The issue began in the previous year, 1922:

Minutes of Parish Council Meeting, 19 June 1922
Attention was called to the state of Effingham Common, on the previous Wednesday after an Excursion Party from Wimbledon. It was decided to approach Mr. Calburn and Capt. Searle in the matter, and the Clerk write a formal letter to Capt. Searle.

Judging by a later reference as this issue wound on, it is possible that the Parish Council believed Capt. Frederick John Searle, to be Calburn's Common Keeper. Capt. Searle and his wife had lived at Norwood Cottage until at least until Autumn 1921 but, according to the electoral register for Spring 1922, they were no longer resident in the village. The Minute book continues:

Copy of Letter to Capt. Searle
I am directed by the Effingham Parish Council to invoke your assistance in calling the attention of those in charge of Excursions Treats as to the desirability of impressing upon all Members of their parties that it is unfair both to the residents of Effingham and also to the Visitors to leave paper and other litter about on the Common. A little care and consideration for others in this respect will it is thought in no way interfere with the enjoyment of the Country-side, and will maintain unspoiled beauties and Amenities of the Common.

The issue seemed to be resolved for the time being:

Minutes of Parish Council Meeting, 3 August 1922
Re litter by Excursioners Effingham Common
Decided to take no further action for the present.

However by the following year it had returned:

Minutes of Parish Council Meeting, 31 July 1923
Re paper and other litter by excursionists on the Common
The Chairman read a letter from the Common Preservation Society about making a scheme [believed to mean a system of regulations to govern use of the Common, to prohibit the dropping of litter, etc. – like byelaws]. Miss Gradwell proposed that a letter be written to Mr. Calburn and that **his Common Keeper** might be instructed to clear up the waste paper and other litter left by the excursionists on the Common. Capt. Botterell seconded. The question of the Regulation Scheme adjourned until next meeting pending further enquiries as to cost by Miss Gradwell.

Minutes of Parish Council Meeting, 16 October 1923
Scheme for Common – Miss Gradwell reported she had been unable to obtain the information. Adjourned until next Meeting.

Minutes of Parish Council Meeting, 20 December 1923
Scheme for Common
Miss Gradwell said she had nothing further to report.

Ah well.

Perhaps Miss Cecil Gradwell, who lived at Slaters Oak, had decided on other priorities, or had given up on this one. She was a woman of some importance in Effingham's feminist history. Women had had the right to stand for election as County Councillors only since the Qualification of Women Act 1907 (most women did not even have the right to vote until 1918). By 1922 Miss Gradwell had become Effingham's Rural District Councillor, having succeeded Mr. Ponting probably at the election of March 1922. She is first mentioned in the Effingham Parish Council Minutes in December 1922 in connection with the route of, and obstruction of, footpaths on Effingham Common. She was subsequently invited to fill a vacancy on the Parish Council, was elected thereto on 10 May 1923 and signed her Declaration of Acceptance of Office on 31 July 1923. She stood down in 1925.

Gypsies and the Common

Hilda Brazil & Susan Morris

Since the 1930s, in Effingham there have been 'settled' Gypsies living on their own properties just like any other resident. This article however is mostly about nomadic Gypsy and Traveller communities (which moved from place to place) and how they connected with the history of Effingham Common.

Surrey is home to the fourth largest Gypsy and Traveller community in Britain. According to *Gypsy Roma and Traveller History Month* research, today this is about 10,000 people, of a national total of about 300,000. Since the sixteenth century at least, Gypsies have been Surrey's largest ethnic minority group.

The arrival of nomadic Gypsies has not always been welcome to settled communities. This was as true for Effingham as for anywhere else. Yet, Mr. Adrian Estler, who lived at Leebrooke from 1935 to 1990, certainly had a great deal of time for them: at one time he sold them a piece of his own land on the Common. Much more is told about him in the next article.

In their journeyings Gypsies had to be on the lookout for open green spaces, not just for the tranquillity of the countryside (the isolation and the mud could be very grim, especially for the women and children) but for the sake of their horses. Wherever they went, the horses which drew the caravans needed water and grazing. Anywhere in the country, commons were a likely stopping place for them.

Often, the horses pulling the caravans were not the only ones travelling with the group. Horse-breeding, training and dealing was, and remains, a central component of Gypsy culture. Effingham's proximity to Epsom racecourse and thus to the Epsom Derby, Britain's richest horse race first staged in 1780, meant that it was one of the many local villages through which Gypsies and Travellers would regularly pass. Derby week is in early June each year. Gypsies and Travellers would set up camp on the Downs in readiness for the week. For many years they were a famous and colourful part of the Epsom race scene. Just before Derby week each year, Gypsies and Travellers were the annual heralds of what would become a steady stream of traffic through Effingham. We have evidence for this in the memoirs of Mrs. Bridger recorded in Autumn 1971:

> Talking of horses, [in] Derby week, Gypsies travelled through some time before – about a week before, they used to come in

[to Mrs. Bridger's shop] and buy their provisions, on their way.

Following the Gypsies, once the race-days had started, a further wave of traffic was caused by the hopeful race-goers and the returning ones. Mrs. Bridger recalled this too:

> And [on] Derby Day, sitting on the wall opposite the White House to watch the traffic going past, the children calling out "Throw out your mouldy coppers". They picked up quite a bit there, it was quite a day there ...

The White House, on the south-east corner of the crossroads at the top of The Street, was the property now called Crosslands. Opposite it, along the north-east side of the main road, was the flint wall, long since demolished, on which the children had been sitting. It is clear this annual event was a long-established tradition, also recorded locally by a much older lady. Agnes Mabel Conisbee of East Horsley (1862-1945), who lived in the Horsleys from about 1894, records it in her *Memories of our Village and W.I by An Old Inhabitant* which she wrote down towards the end of her life, the first of two booklets she published to raise funds for the war effort:

> Another excitement was the Derby, when nearly every one who didn't go to Epsom went up to the "Duke" Corner [Duke of Wellington public house, on today's A246] to see the people returning home with different coloured streamers to their hats and making a noise with anything they could make a noise with, throwing coppers out to the children, if they had had a good day.

Returning to our evidence for Gypsies travelling through Effingham, we are fortunate to be able to present an early postcard (Illus. 22) demonstrating this. It was produced by William Richards for his postcard series. This particular one was kindly lent to us by Ann Wilson who had obtained it from a lady in Alabama; that lady did not know how it had come into her possession! It bears a stamp that was franked on 5 October 1904, the earliest date we have so far for any of Mr. Richards' known postcards. It shows the dirt-track Effingham Common Road in the foreground and eight horse-drawn caravans in the background, together with a small carriage at the far left. Two of the caravans are at the centre, one directly behind the other. It has been suggested that the encampment was located on the eastern side of Effingham Common underneath an oak tree that stood virtually opposite the station; that area was all open grassland at that time and had not yet gone over to the scrub

Effingham Common.

22. *This postcard was put in the post in St. Albans on 5 October 1904 addressed to a Mrs. Spittle, 41 Manbey Rd, Leyton Rd, Stratford, E [East London] and the message simply says 'You may expect me to morrow Thursday Cannot tell you the time'.*

that covers it today. So in this interpretation the station would be to the left of the scene. We believe the suggested location would have been the most likely one since it was usual for Gypsies on a common to use an inconspicuous corner (which this one was) to avoid drawing attention to themselves.

Mr. Richards and presumably his customers may well have been viewing this scene as a picturesque one. Since the mid-nineteenth century there had been great interest in the seemingly romantic Gypsy lifestyle. It had come to represent freedom from the petty demands of the everyday world, and the undoubted ugliness of urban living. For instance, in 1853 Matthew Arnold published a much-admired poem *The Scholar Gypsy* about an Oxford student who successfully turned his back on the boring demands of academia and immersed himself in Gypsy life. This view did not disappear quickly. Nearly 80 years later in 1930 D. H. Lawrence wrote the short story *The Virgin and the Gypsy* about a girl escaping from an oppressive family. The Gypsy image appealed to artists as well as to writers. Not many people perhaps realize that 'bohemian', which is a word often used about an unconventional artistic lifestyle, derives from a term for 'Gypsy' as explained on the Wikipedia website:

> The term Bohemianism emerged in France in the early 19th century when artists and creators began to concentrate in the lower-rent, lower class Gypsy neighbourhoods. *Bohémien* was a common term for the Romani people of France, who had reached Western Europe by way of Bohemia.

A biography of the famous portrait artist Augustus John (1878-1961) provides further evidence of a Gypsy presence in Effingham in the early 1900s (but not necessarily on the Common). In his youth Augustus affected a very *avant-garde* lifestyle for the time, unquestionably 'bohemian'. He was very interested in Gypsies – their freedom, their ethos, their family structures – and for a time he travelled around from place to place with his growing family in caravans, trying to live in the Gypsy way. Some of the Surrey journeying made by Augustus in early 1909 is described in the 1997 book *Augustus John* by Michael Holroyd, published by Vintage Books and reprinted here by permission of The Random House Group Ltd.:

> By April 1909, having put his affairs in order, Augustus was more than ready ... to exchange "the flockbed of civilisation for the primitive couch of the earth".

... the caravan which Augustus was buying from Salaman had lain gently disintegrating on Dartmoor. But recently he had moved it up and anchored it strategically at Wantage, where it was given a lick of fresh paint. A brilliant blue, it stood ready for adventurings. On his first expedition, he took along John Fothergill, architect and innkeeper, as companion. They trundled off on 1 April. "I called on [Roger] Fry at Guildford and found him in a state of great anxiety about his wife who had just had another attack", Augustus reported to Ottoline ...

Lady Ottoline Morrell had become a friend of Augustus two or three years earlier. His report to her, dated 8 April 1909, about his visit to Roger Fry at Guildford continued:

"He [Fry] sent off his children that day [because of his wife's illness]. I was sorry as I wanted to take them on the road a little. Fry came down and we sat in the caravan awhile. Next day I hired a big horse and proceeded on through Dorking and up to a divine Region called Ranmore Common ... I called at the big house to ask for permission to stop on the common and was treated with scant courtesy by the menials who told me their man was out. So on again through miles of wild country to Effingham where, after several attempts to overcome the suspicion attaching to a traveller with long hair and a van, I got a farmer to let me draw into one of his fields. At this time the horse was done up and my money at its last."

So he left his van in the field, along with the sleeping horse and the sleeping Fothergill, and caught the milk train up to London. He had covered eighty miles on the road and it had been highly satisfactory.

He had made what passed for elaborate preparations ... To the sky-blue van still stationed at Effingham he added another of canary yellow and a light cart, a team of sturdy omnibus horses, a tent or two, and eventually Arthur, a disastrous groom. They mustered at Effingham – a full complement of six horses, two vans, one cart, six children, Arthur, a stray boy "for washing up", Dorelia [his partner], and her virginal younger sister Edie. "We are really getting a step nearer my dream of the Nomadic life," Augustus told Ottoline ... Their camp was like a mumper's, only, he boasted, more untidy. Undeterred by the scorn of the local gypsy, the convoy moved off to Epsom, where Augustus hit the headlines by protesting against the exclusion of gypsies from the racecourse on Derby Day.

So, from the last extract, we know there was a 'local' Gypsy apparently residing in Effingham in April 1909, but we are not told precisely where.

7 'An account of the sad, splendid lawsuit of William of Effingham'
Susan Morris

24. *Mr. Estler, very formally attired in a context and location unknown.*
He was born on 4 February 1909 and appears here to be beyond his twenties, so when this photograph was taken he would (we believe) have already bought his smallholding on the Common.

This intriguing and poignant promise is the title of an article which appeared, without naming its author, in *The Economist* for 21 March 1959 (p.1050). I came across it as a typed transcript amongst Parish Council papers. It is lightly humorous, written in the gentle, sardonic style of the day much used by writers for *Punch* and the like. 'Delightful' probably captures it.

The article recounts how the simple needs of one Effingham animal, William the horse, tested the English legal system to the limit. Having previously never heard of William, I was amazed. But when I mentioned this to other Effingham residents, they said 'Oh *William*, yes we knew *William*. He pulled a little cart up and down Effingham Common Road, and his owner used to let all the village children have rides. He used to graze on Effingham Common *until he was denied his rights.*' Really? 'Yes, but' (and here the light of battle flashed joyfully in their eyes) 'THEN *we went to court, and* GOT THEM BACK!'

So this is the delightful story of an Effingham character who should not be forgotten.

Setting the scene

In 1916, the manor of Effingham East Court was acquired by Mr. Robert Reitmeyer Calburn. In 1922 he also acquired the separate manor of Effingham Le Legh. This meant that amongst his holdings was the area of open ground called Effingham Common. And, in 1935, a Mr. Adrian George Estler aged about 26 bought a smallholding of 5.5 acres at the edge of the Common. This incorporated land that had formerly belonged to both these manors.

In this period it just so happened that the legal position affecting common land was changing in a very significant way. On 1 September 1926 the provisions of section 194 of the Law of Property Act 1925 had come into force. From that day forward, to 'enclose' any land subject to commoners' rights would require the consent of both the Ministry of Agriculture and Fisheries and the County Council. 'Enclose' means a whole variety of activities involving permanent structures or changes, such as laying areas of hardstanding, buildings, walls, ditches – not just fencing around the edge of an area.

By itself this provoked no problems in Effingham but soon afterwards the 1932 Town and Country Planning Act required

District Councils to prepare a Planning Scheme. Thus it came about that Guildford Rural District Council (GRDC) 'zoned' (identified) Effingham Common as *'public open space' subject to rights of common*. In other words, it was the GRDC's view that some properties around the Common had inherited ancient rights to pasture their animals or gather firewood etc. on it. The Council didn't know for certain that these rights existed, nor, if they did exist, what specifically they were. But it was enough for GRDC to record the fact that rights were believed to exist. It would be for another body to determine the question one way or another.

When GRDC submitted its Draft Planning Scheme to the Ministry of Health for approval in 1937, Mr. Calburn objected. He believed Effingham Common was his own private land, not public open space, and that any commoners' rights which may once have existed were long since extinguished. He had already generously given Banks Common to The National Trust in 1925, so by 1937 he may justifiably have felt he had already done his bit for public open space and as will be seen presently, his objection at this time did not bring to an end his role as village benefactor. Various investigations and researches followed. It transpired that the property called Slaters Oak looked as if it would be able, should it be necessary, to prove commoners' rights recorded on its deeds since at least 1907 (but these still had not been tested in court). Furthermore, Mr. Estler had been actually exercising the commoners' rights which belonged to his property Leebrooke and which went as far back as anyone could remember.

25. *Leebrooke, on Effingham Common, as it was (we believe) in the 1970s.*

Mr. Calburn seems to have wanted to illustrate his right to do what he wanted.

In 1937 he put in a planning application to develop the whole of Effingham Common for housing. The application was refused by GRDC. Then a year later, in 1938, Mr. Calburn's objection to the Draft Planning Scheme was heard at Public Inquiry. The result was a compromise reached between himself and GRDC. Mr. Calburn agreed to drop his objection, and GRDC agreed to drop the reference to commoners' rights. Crucially, neither side abandoned their views – they just agreed not to write them into this document.

But time was now against the Draft. Nothing had been finalized by the time the War broke out in 1939. It still hadn't been concluded when the 1947 Town & Country Planning Act made major alterations to planning procedure, consigning the earlier Draft to oblivion.

In 1948 there was a brief difference of views on another front. Effingham Parish Council hoped to have an area of the Common set aside for games, which they could do with GRDC's blessing under provisions of the Commons Act 1899. Because of Mr. Calburn's sustained opposition, however, this also was not pursued. In 1954, Mr. Calburn objected again to a description of the common as 'public open space', this time in Surrey County Council's Development plan. Again, it was agreed to drop this wording in the document, although, again, this had no effect on whether commoners' rights actually existed or not.

In 1954 Mr. Calburn began discussions with the Parish Council about giving an area of land on the Common traditionally used as a cricket pitch, and another small area intended to be a carpark, to Effingham's King George V Playing Fields and Hall Charity. This gift was completed in 1955. In 1954 he made a Deed of Gift carried out by his executors in 1961 by which he gave the then stunningly beautiful Beech Avenue trees to the County.

The action warms up …

After stewing slowly over many years, matters finally came to a head in the person of William.

In 1955 Mr. Calburn let a large part of the Common to a Mr. Archibald Murrells. Mr. Murrells lived at Lee Wood Farm and was a Surrey County Councillor. Calburn leased him some land for grazing. The upshot was that Mr. Murrells fenced off a very large expanse, either on Calburn's orders or with his permission. But this was enclosure! And without the necessary consent of the Min. of Ag. & Fish! The Parish Council, the District Council (GRDC), the County Council and the Open Spaces

26. The cricket pitch on the Common. This match was played during the 'Celebration of Effingham Common' event held on 26 September 2010.

Society all objected with vigour. Secret night sorties were made to cut the wire. And now the commoners themselves began to stir – Major H. V. Hughes and Colonel C. W. Hughes, (owners of Slaters Oak), Miss P. M. Meacock (The Willows) and Mr. Estler (Leebrooke) instructed a firm of solicitors. In December 1956 the solicitors wrote to GRDC requesting it to take all necessary steps to protect, maintain and preserve their clients' commoners' rights on Effingham Common. On 3 January 1957 GRDC discussed this and agreed it must act. On 20 March it duly applied, as it must, for permission first from Surrey County Council to pursue this under section 26 of the Local Government Act 1894, because it would entail the spending of public money in court. On 30 April 1957, Surrey CC gave approval.

... and now it begins in earnest

Later, it turned out to be extremely fortunate that due process had been followed and all this apparently dull decision-making by committees had cited the proper powers. It was not only fortunate, it was in the nick of time.

Only a few days later (*The Economist* article stated) 'on or about 2 May 1957, Mr. Murrells took possession of the horse named William belonging to Mr. Estler' and impounded him.

27. *William with Denis Harvey, a friend of Mr. Estler.*

Apparently this had happened on several previous occasions 'thereby not only interfering with his life's work, but also keeping him away from the Guildford pageant, where he was booked to make an appearance in person'. But this provocation meant that, finally, the investigation that all had been tiptoeing around for so long – did commoners' rights exist, or did they not – would be researched, tested and determined in court. GRDC set out, as its Clerk later explained in a Statement to the District Auditor, to 'take proceedings in the name of Mr. Estler for the recovery of his horse William, and for damages, the purpose of the proceedings being to establish the common rights of Mr. Estler and others, and only incidentally to recover the horse' (shame!).

William at law (1)

The case was heard by Judge Gordon Clark in the County Court at Dorking on 8 May 1958. Mr. Calburn put in a counter-claim, that William was 'damage feasant'. This legal term is a corruption of the French words 'faisant dommage', meaning 'doing damage'. It is usually applied to the harm that animals belonging to one person do upon the land of another, by feeding there, treading down grass, corn, or other 'production of the earth'. Mr. Calburn claimed £30 damages – and won his case! When the judgment was given on 1 July, Mr. Estler was ordered to pay £20 damages and the costs of both parties.

William at law (2)

'But, being a man of spirit, Mr. Estler went to the Court of Appeal', reported *The Economist*.

In his judgment Judge Clark had remarked that the case considered Mr. Estler's rights only over the 'Hooke Common' part of Effingham Common, which related to the manor of Effingham Le Legh, whereas Mr. Estler claimed rights over Effingham Common in the manor of East Court *as well*. Judge Clark had pointed out that this was still undecided. Counsel were consulted. Using a barrister usefully called Mr. Owen Stable, Mr. Estler launched an appeal against the County Court judgment in the Court of Appeal in London. It was heard on 9, 10 and 11 February 1959 by Lord Justices Hodson and Willmer and Mr. Justice Wynn-Parry.

Sadly, Mr. Estler's appeal was also dismissed, although Lord Justice Willmer had clearly enjoyed himself enormously and recorded his appreciation for being given 'a refreshing expedition through what is becoming a rather obscure branch of the law'.

The gist of the case turned upon the amount of land William needed, under a provision called 'Common of pasture appurtenant'. *The Economist* helpfully explains and takes up the tale:

> But if appurtenance was to be the winning card counsel must deal very carefully with levancy and couchancy. To an uncultured mind levant and couchant sound rather like a French version of bed and breakfast; but that is not their true meaning. They denote, in fact, a means of deciding the number of beasts that a man may graze on a particular common. It has been settled since 1799 that there must be a limit to the number, and levancy and couchancy are the agents that decide it.
>
> How do they fix the limit? What do levancy and couchancy do? Well, first they ascertain how many acres of a claimant's land have the right of pasture appurtenant to them. Then they make enquiries about what happens in the winter, finding out how many beasts the claimant can feed during the winter months on the produce of his land. If he can keep seven beasts fed in the winter, then he can turn out seven to

graze in the summer. If three, then he can turn out three and so forth.

Now to feed one horse in the winter takes a ton of hay; and to produce a ton of hay you need about three acres of land. So a smallholder with three acres of the right sort has the right to graze one horse throughout the summer. That looked good for Mr. Estler with his five and a half acres. They should surely give him everything he wanted for William with a good margin to spare.

But things did not work out like that – and for a very subtle reason connected with levancy and couchancy, which are not so simple as they sound. When it comes to the common of pasture appurtenant, levancy and couchancy will only take note of land that was copyhold [held on agreement from the lord of the Manor] until 1926. Anything that was freehold before that year means nothing to them. They do not recognize it. And unhappily only two of Mr. Estler's five and a half acres were ever copyhold. The others have been freehold all the time. So levancy and couchancy made their calculation of his rights on two acres only. And two acres would give him a right to two-thirds of a horse. To graze two-thirds of a horse being physiologically impossible Mr. Estler lost both his case and his horse. Moreover he must pay £20 for the damage William did.

Involved in this litigation have been one county court judge and three judges in the appeal court, at least three learned counsel, a firm of Solicitors in Guildford, and two particularly eminent firms in London. The costs have been estimated to be £1,000. The case lasted for three days in the Court of Appeal and while it must, of course, enhance our respect for the majestic simplicity of the English law, it may also make us wonder what it is that drives ordinary folk to go to law on such terms as these. Of the principal figures in the case the most intelligent, it may be thought, was William.

But William and the legal system are not done with each other yet, not by a long way.

William at law (3)

At this point Mr. Murrells may have wanted to dance on the ashes of Mr. Estler's case.

He wrote to the District Auditor and challenged GRDC's Statement of Accounts for the financial year ending April 1959. His objection was that GRDC had wrongfully paid some £580 of rate-payers' money to solicitors whom they had instructed to act on Mr. Estler's behalf in the second 'William' case. In other

COLONEL'S CAR DAMAGES

"TOOT" AT 50 COWS

After evidence in which reference was made to a dispute over grazing rights on Effingham Common, Judge Lionel Jellinek yesterday awarded £36 15s. damages and costs to Colonel Charles William Hughes, of Slaters Oak, Effingham, Surrey, in a suit at Epsom County Court for damages to his car which he alleged were caused as he passed a herd of cows.

He sued a Surrey County Councillor, Mr. Archibald E. Murrells, of Leewood Farm, Effingham, and his son, Frank, of Effingham Common Road, Effingham, for £7 10s. damages and £100 general damages, arising out of the alleged incident. The Murrells counter-claimed £100 damages, alleging that the colonel ran Mr. Frank Murrells down.

Colonel Hughes, aged 63, said that when he came up behind the cows on November 25, the drover did nothing to assist him to get through. "I gave one toot on the horn. The drover immediately turned round and hit my car on the wing as hard as he could with the stick in his hand, then came nearer and hit it less hard on the bonnet. I recognized him as Frank Murrells."

On passing the cows, his car was hit or kicked by Archibald Murrells, he said.

"NO GOOD WILL"

In cross-examination Colonel Hughes said it was right that he bore no good will towards Mr. Murrells, senior. He had nothing to do with a dispute between the Murrels and local people about grazing rights on the common, although his sympathies were with the commoners. His ill-feeling arose from the fact that on one occasion he did not, when asked, stop the noise of a hay cutting machine to allow the colonel's seriously sick mother to get some rest.

During the lunch adjournment, the judge, barristers, and parties went into a yard behind the court where the judge listened while the colonel revved and idled the engine of the car. At the judge's request the colonel gave a toot on the horn.

Frank Murrells, aged 30, who is in partnership with his father at Leewood farm, said he was at the back of the herd of 50 and his father in front. The car came up so close behind him that it touched his gum-boots. "The engine was revving up and down and the hooter was being continuously sounded." He shouted: "Wait a minute," and swished his stick behind him, hitting the car once.

"When I swished, I was annoyed. The noise was not only stopping me doing my job, but was upsetting the cows."

"TRESPASS" FINDING

Mr. Murrells, senior, aged 59, said he signalled the car to slow down. It went straight at him and he jumped on to the grass verge. The hood brushed his left arm. "If I had not jumped out of the way he would have run me down. He came at me like a flying bullet."

He agreed with Mr. Michael Eastham, for the defence, that there was ill-feeling between the Lord of the Manor and the former commoners about his farming part of the common. It was true that on the instructions of the Lord of the Manor he had impounded "a fairly celebrated horse" called William and that he won the resulting case which went all the way to the Court of Appeal.

Deciding that the Murrells were Guilty of trespass against the Colonel's goods by deliberately striking them, the judge awarded damages of £31 15s. against Frank Murrells, including £6 15s. special damages and £5 damages against Murrells senior.

The judge observed that it was clear there was ill-feeling between the parties. "There has been trouble over the common which has involved the defendant who cultivates the common. The defendant takes the view that Colonel Hughes has taken an active part in making trouble in regard to this, although Colonel Hughes tells us he had done no such thing."

The counter-claim for damages for assault was dismissed with costs.

28. *This article from The Times, 23 June 1959, some three months after the High Court judgement, shows how the issue of commoners' rights was suspected of causing bad feeling more widely.*

words, public money should not be used for the benefit of a single individual.

The District Auditor, who was rather satisfyingly called Mr. Eagle, summoned a Public Hearing of the Objection, at which Mr. Murrells was invited to explain his complaint more fully. This he did, and alleged that GRDC's action was 'unjustified, unnecessary and reckless'. Mr. Eagle ruled that the objection would, if true, be valid so the matter must now be gone into more deeply. There would have to be a Public Inquiry. This was duly held at the Council's offices in Guildford on 24 February 1960. Reporters from the *Surrey Times* and the *Surrey Advertiser* were invited to attend.

The Clerk of the Council prepared a detailed statement which admirably described the history of the Common and the dealings between the Lord of the Manor and the Council from the beginning of the century (he was later complimented on its clarity and helpfulness by the Auditor). He was able to make clear that the Council had not briefed solicitors to act on behalf of Mr. Estler. Mr. Estler was only temporarily the owner of Leebrooke. Leebrooke had been owned by many people before him and doubtless would be owned by many people after. It was the *rights of common* attached to the *property* which were the subject of the case, and GRDC had been concerned about these for some twenty years already. So GRDC had been acting quite correctly under Section 26 (2) of the Local Government Act 1894 'to aid persons in maintaining their rights of common' and, as required, it had very properly obtained confirmation from Surrey County Council that it could spend money in this cause *before* doing so. The expenditure had gone to GRDC's own solicitor, not to Mr. Estler or to his solicitor.

Objection overruled. Case closed.

29. *William, perhaps taking a rest from legal matters ...*

William at law (4)

In *Letters from London* (published by Pan Macmillan, 1995), author Julian Barnes describes how between 1989 and 1995 he wrote for *The New Yorker* magazine as their London correspondent. It was his job to contribute essays on aspects of contemporary British life, in a way that would make them intelligible to American readers. The appeal of Test Matches, and of Mrs. Thatcher; the qualification of Norman Lamont to be Chancellor of the Exchequer – that sort of thing.

I quote this because in his *Preface: On Author*, Barnes describes a truly formidable group of people, the fact-checkers who were part of the editorial team of *The New Yorker*. The fact-checkers demanded from journalists the very highest standards of factual accuracy, beyond anything he had ever experienced before:

> Making a statement on oath before a judge is as nothing compared with making a statement before a *New Yorker* fact-checker. They don't mind who they call in their lust for verification. They check with you, with your informants, with their computerized information system, with objective authorities; they check to your face and they check behind your back. When I interviewed Tony Blair at the House of Commons, I was impressed by the elegant door hinges of the Shadow Cabinet room. My Pevsner guide told me they were attributable to Pugin, or rather, 'Augustus W. N. Pugin'. Pevsner states: 'He designed, it can safely be said, all the details in metal, stained glass, tiles etc., down to door furniture, ink-stands, coat-hangers and so on.' Half-wondering if the department of verification would swallow the phrase 'It can safely be said', I ascribed the hinges to 'Augustus Pugin' in my copy and awaited the fact-checker's call on this and related topics. 'Could we leave out "Augustus" so as not to confuse him with his father?' was the first shot. Sure, no problem: I'd only put 'Augustus Pugin' because I fancied American style prefers 'John Milton' to 'Milton' (the truth also is that I didn't know Pugin had a father, let alone that my suppressing the initials would cause genealogical havoc). Then I waited for the next question. It didn't come. Semi-satirically, and with my Pevsner open at the page before me, I asked, 'You are *happy* that the hinges are by Pugin?' 'Oh yes,' came the reply, 'I checked with the V&A'.

This intense scrutiny of detail was bad enough for issues which could be proved by reference to some tangible form – an existing item or a text for instance. But here is my point. Barnes goes on to describe the frenetic efforts of fact-checkers trying to verify information which *existed only in memory*. He writes '... trying to confirm that dream about hamsters which your grandfather had on the night Hitler invaded Poland – a dream never written down but conveyed personally to you on the old boy's knee, a dream of which, since your grandfather's death, you are the sole repository', the fact-checkers would admit defeat *only* if they had 'had all your grandfather's living associates up against a wall' and had 'scoured dictionaries of the unconscious without success'. They would then make clear that *The New Yorker* could not be held responsible for any inaccuracy conveyed to readers, by covering themselves with a footnote stating that this text was 'on author'.

The first reason for mentioning this is because it makes me laugh, and the second is that everyone who remembers that era should read the book. But the *real* reason is that one wonders whether older residents of Effingham may have been subject to something of the fact-checkers' attentions in the period 1971-76. Even so much as to *think* the words 'Effingham Common' could lay them open to days of intensive questioning. 'When did you see that? How old were you then? How many geese, do you think? Why do you think it was that number? How can you be sure that they were geese and not ducks? Draw on this map *exactly* where you saw them. Now sign and date it.'… and so on.

But here I am ashamed, because though this description is not so very far from the truth of what had to be done, it is unworthy to cast in a humorous light the years of gruelling effort contributed by Parish Councillors and volunteers. To save Effingham Common from being designated just 'land in the Green Belt', and to have it registered as common – in other words, preserved as open space for the commoners to use and the residents to enjoy for ever – they were faced with rescuing from the past a truly mountainous body of densely detailed evidence which would withstand challenge in court.

In fact many, many people contributed to the ensuing campaign, with information or time or money. All should be remembered and thanked by every Effingham resident who has ever enjoyed the Common (or even the idea of the Common). But chief amongst campaigners, to whom an enormous debt is owed for their selfless service, were: Cllr. Tony Page, parish councillor from 1965-97 and Chairman from 1969-80 (apart from a gap of a few months), Cllrs. Derek Hubbard, Dora Worthington, Edie Wilson, Ron Allen, and Col. Peter Tyrwhitt-Drake; Mr. Eddie Crouch, Clerk to the Parish Council; Mr. Seymour Plummer of Warren Field, Beech Avenue. There will be more to say about their contributions in the section below on William at law (5).

Opportunity presents

The campaign actually started in 1965. This was the year in which the Commons Registration Act passed into law. It had been preceded by the usual consultation, Report, White Paper, Bill etc. and its progress down the years had been keenly watched. In 1959 when the first 'William' court case took place it was at the Report stage. After reading the article in *The Economist*, Mr. A. O. B. Harris of the Commons, Open Spaces and Footpaths Preservation Society wrote in to the subsequent edition (28 March 1959): 'If Parliament shelves this admirable report it will only have itself to blame for repetitions of the kind of laws which your article described'. So perhaps William had helped the Report blossom into the Act – who knows?

30. *Effingham Common today, a place 'to enjoy for ever'.*

The new Act presented communities up and down the country with an opportunity to save much-loved open spaces from being turned over to development by their owners.

The Act laid out a clear timetable. It would be a long haul. On 1 January 1967 Surrey County Council, the new Commons Registration Authority for this area, would open a register. Up until 30 June 1968 individuals and/or communities could submit their claims detailing the land they believed should be registered as common. Then, from 1 October 1968 to September 1970, there was a period when counterclaims and objections must be submitted. Commoners' rights *not* registered at all by 2 January 1970 would lapse forever (however the period for claims was in fact subsequently extended). The Commons Registration Authority would collate all the evidence and in September 1970 register any common where there was no dispute. Turning next to disputed claims, they would weed out any obvious non-fliers, but where applicants were convinced they had a case, and Surrey County Council was also persuaded of this, Surrey could be asked to submit details to a higher authority, the Commons Commissioner. A hearing would be held. This would finally determine the issue. The land would either achieve lasting peace in the Commons register or not, as the case might be.

As we have seen, the Parish Council had been alive to issues affecting the Common for many years, and so had GRDC. It was clear to them from the start that the opportunity to register Effingham Common should be seized. As a 'relevant authority' under the terms of the Act, GRDC confirmed (in letters dated 9 January 1968 and 19 June 1968) that it intended to register Effingham Common and it urged the Parish Council to encourage commoners to register their rights. This would mean *really* challenging the Lord of the Manor full on. The Lord of the Manor was now Mr. Charles Calburn. His father Robert had died in November 1961. Like his father, Charles was Lord of *two* Manors: Effingham Manor (or Effingham La Legh) and Effingham East Court.

Robert had been a generous benefactor to the Effingham area, so for the Parish Council to follow GRDC's urging while maintaining cordial relations with the Calburn family would require footwork of the most exquisitely diplomatic kind. The crux of the matter, grasped by the Parish Council but difficult to convey to residents, was the need to prove that *commoners' rights* over the land had existed in the past, *and still existed*. If this could be conclusively proved, there could be no question that the land was indeed common.

Gathering up the data

The first and most basic step was to identify who 'the commoners' might actually be. This was not so easy as you might think. Details of property ownership were kept much more private, even secretively so, than now. The Parish Council circulated an explanatory leaflet about the Registration process to the owners of 'likely' properties in the vicinity of the Common. This was later followed by a letter encouraging folk to consider very seriously whether they could make a claim, describing the benefits to the village of preserving the Common, and pointing out the vital need to disinter relevant documentary proof.

The response was lukewarm at best. Some people thought they had rights but didn't know if they could prove it. Some of the people the Parish Council was sure did have rights, and *could* prove it, were not exactly enthusiastic. Ten properties were felt to be 'in the picture'; the owners of two responded positively. This was hardly surprising. It was a complex and challenging venture, with very little prospect of a good time along the way. The Parish Council did not give up. It continued to write, advise and encourage people to get to grips with the idea. As folk warmed to it, members of the Parish Council searched out, copied and catalogued every piece of evidence

31. *Slaters Oak on Effingham Common, as in the early 1970s.*

they could find to ascertain what claims there were, and how firmly based.

Eventually the claims to rights of four properties – Slaters Oak, The Willows, Huckamoor and Leebrooke – seemed to have the best chance of success and the claims were duly registered by the owners. In the lull before the next stage, the claimants were strongly advised (in letters dated 12 September 1968 and 27 February 1970) to actually exercise their commoners' rights in public. But it was necessary to wait and see what Mr. Calburn would do.

In early 1970 news arrived. Surrey Commons Registration Authority sent a formal letter, copies of which had to be affixed 'in the case of a parish council on or near the principal door of each church or chapel in the parish' to comply with a circular from the Ministry of Housing and Local Government dated 8 July 1968. Mr. Calburn had contested all four claims. It was now open to the claimants to back down, or show that they meant business, legally speaking. The Parish Council metaphorically rolled up its shirtsleeves, led from the front and formed a Commons Sub-Committee to debate strategy.

Part of the difficulty facing the Parish Council arose from the fact that it would have to prompt and support others to take the necessary action. It could not itself prosecute a legal case on behalf of any individual claimant. What it *could* do was help to find and collate all the evidence of rights. In this way, it could advise and support the *solicitors* of these residents *as a group* through the course of a *joint* action. Hopefully, in this way, the individual claimants would all support each other's cases, not unwittingly sabotage them by contradictory evidence. The Parish Council felt this plan was the only way of assembling a coherent case without unfeasibly high legal costs falling to individuals and thus discouraging them. On 22 October 1970 it wrote again to the commoners to find out if they were agreeable to this plan, and if they would supply the Parish Council with copies of their evidence and proofs.

On Friday 13 August 1971 the Parish Council Sub-Committee had a meeting at County Hall with a Surrey County Council Highways Officer to discuss the fact that the County had rather surprisingly objected to the Effingham claims. SCC had bought strips of the Common when they had wanted to widen Effingham Common Road. The maps of the area over which the commoners had claimed rights included these strips. SCC said that because the strips were acquired for Highways purposes, this had extinguished the commoners' rights. The Parish Council felt this was a complication from which they would have to draw back and the objection was resolved. (In fact, as the freeholder / custodian trustee of two pieces of land on the Common, the Parish Council itself could conceivably have stood as an objector! Both pieces of land concerned were registered with the Charity Commission as assets of the King George V Playing Fields and Hall Charity. In March 1975 the Charity Commission wrote to the Parish Council for confirmation that the Parish Council was objecting to the claims for commoners' rights over these lands. In this it was to be disappointed.)

Although it was annoying that Surrey had not previously brought up this issue of the strips, the meeting itself served a useful purpose. The Parish Council Sub-Committee members returned from it both sobered and motivated by the insights they had gained from contact with an officer closer to the registration process. In their report on the meeting they wrote:

> We feel even more after the interview that it is going to be a battle and if we are to help the claimants, a lot more work has to be done, particularly in recording the testimony of those who have lived on or near the Common for long periods.

Old ladies in Kensington and Fetcham, old gentlemen in cottages and council houses were exhaustively tracked down and interviewed and invited to hand over their paperwork. A tattered piece of paper in the files says:

Mr. Crouch

A Mrs. Worthington called.

She says that Mrs. Garnett, Brickfield Cottage claims that she has Common Rights. Her daughter is Mrs. Amos, 20, Canonside, Fetcham. Mrs. Worthington suggests that you should deal with the daughter in this matter, as Mrs. Garnett is over 80.

Carefully preserved is the attached note pencilled in large shaky writing: 'Mrs. Amos, 20 Canonside, Fetcham'.

The practical difficulties of assembling the proofs should not be underestimated. Acquiring copies of reliable maps which showed property boundaries, for instance, required persuasion, promises or purchase, and, always, grim persistence. Enormous amounts of information had to be 'extracted', which means identified as useful and then transcribed word for word and / or redrawn by hand on visits to archives. Some historic documents (for instance Enclosure Awards) had to be borrowed, professionally photographed and printed up from negatives because parchment deeds or bound volumes were either physically too large for the 'reprographic machines available at County Hall' or too much at risk of damage.

By April 1972, through its solicitors whom we shall refer to as 'Legal', the Parish Council had sought and retained a suitable Barrister ('Counsel') specialising in this area of the law. Miss Sheila Morag Clark Cameron had been recommended by The Commons Preservation Society 'as being an expert in this particular field'. This did not prevent periodic bouts of anxiety about whether she was the best person for the job (she was relatively young), as will later be seen. Her first job was to give an *Advice* on the case – that is, to look over what was known so far and suggest what evidence would need to be found for the case to have a chance of succeeding. Also through Legal there was contact with GRDC, which confirmed that the two councils would work jointly towards the registration of the Common. Effingham Parish Councillors would contribute research and information at local level. Legal would not estimate the costs of Counsel for a contested case until the brief had been drawn up, but there then followed a very English tricky moment. GRDC volunteered to contribute two-thirds of Counsel's fees. But

GRDC were not aware that Miss Cameron had already been retained, and preferred a different (25% more expensive) Counsel, Mr. Gerard Charles Ryan. This put Legal 'in some difficulty'. The first suggestion was a sort of compromise: if Miss Cameron 'was not acceptable to us' there would be a get-out moment after the delivery of her *Advice*. But in the event, Legal found a supremely diplomatic solution. They ventured the perfectly normal reason of bringing an additional client (GRDC) into the case as changed circumstances that justified them approaching Mr. Ryan to take the lead, while suggesting that Miss Cameron might of course also be kept on, and accepting that she might wish to be released. Fortunately she did not.

In April 1973 the Parish Council rather pointedly encouraged Legal to get a move-on with briefing Counsel so that 'the case would be prepared and returned well before the legal holidays, and at least by the end of June next' ... 'unless progress is reported on getting the Case to Counsel at our next meeting on May 1st [1973] the fur will fly'. Accordingly, on 21 May 1973 Legal sent Mr. Ryan a document laying out the gist of the case for his consideration. This usefully shows the extent of the Parish Councillors' foragings so far. The list of items which 'Counsel is sent herewith' includes:

1. Location and brief history of Effingham Common.
2. Map and notes thereon.
3. Historical notes (2).
4. Index of Registrations under 1965 Act.
5. Registrations under 1965 Act (8).
6. Objections to Registrations.
7. Observations by Mrs. D. L. Worthington on matters in issue.
8. Copy Deeds and correspondence re Slaters Oak.
9. Copy correspondence etc. re Huckamoor.
10. Copy Deeds and correspondence re Lee Brooke.
11. Copy Deeds re The Willows.
12. Copy Notices of Objection re The Willows.
13. Observations of Mrs. D. Worthington re Hammer Farm, Cranleigh.
14. Statutory Declarations by:-
D. L. Lake
M. M. O'Connor
M. A. Boxall
W. G. Ranger
H. E. Tyrrell
A. H. Kelland
J. Boxall
W. A. Roberts
B. A. Ayres

J. H. Hughes
Mrs. Mathews
Miss Stilliard
Miss Newton
Mrs. Munnery
Mr. Munnery

15. Two Questionnaires – O'Hagan & Bretherton re Common Rights 1949
16. Photographs.
17. Previous Proceedings re Lee Brooke Estler v Murrells
18. Proceedings Rates' Appeal Murrells and Guildford RDC
19. Copy Correspondence and Documents from file of Commons, Open Spaces and footpaths Preservation Society 1936 – to date.

In the gap while we wait for Mr. Ryan to respond, we could take a moment to note that in February 1973 Mr. Calburn put in a second planning application (the earlier one having been in 1937) to develop the Common for housing, this time to build 150 houses on it. The Effingham Residents and Ratepayers Association (ERRA) circulated the village with a flyer to encourage objections (Illustration 32). GRDC received 200 letters of objection (and one – anonymous – letter of support). As one of the objectors who copied their comments to the Parish Council perceptively wrote, the planning application if granted 'would almost certainly destroy the amenities of the Common'. The application was refused. In the following year, Mr. Calburn caused more consternation when he ploughed up a large area of the Common instead.

In the event Mr. Ryan proved too busy and could not deliver. Despite another review of who should hold the brief at a later stage, from now on Miss Cameron handled the whole case through to the end. Despite the great quantity already sent, she requested yet more copies of maps, of deeds, of the Commons registration document, before she would start. 'Next June next' was when the Parish Council eventually received the *Advice* – June 1974.

Not good enough
The *Advice* made it horribly clear that the research and compilation phase was far from over. For the case to succeed, the elderly residents who had made statutory declarations would now need to make sworn affidavits of a forensically detailed nature. Each affidavit should be accompanied with a fully marked-up map or plan, but people who didn't 'do' maps should make clear descriptions mentioning any landmarks. Here are

February, 1973.

Have you heard of the application (number 77/1/73/EFF) to

BUILD 150 HOUSES ON OUR COMMON

in the area from Slaters Oak to the Railway Station, on either side of the road ?

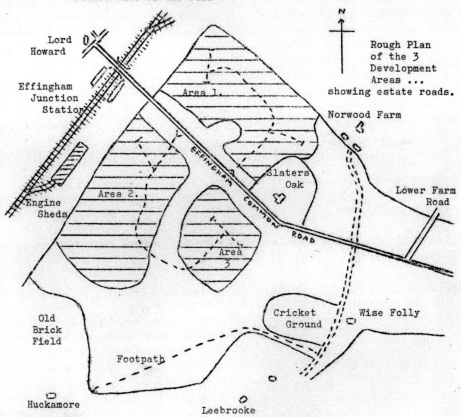

Area: 80 acres   Open Space: 26.73 acres   Cricket Pitch: 3.27 acres
Area for Development: 50 acres   Number of houses: 3 per acre
Assumed house type: 1600 Sq Ft   Outline Application: 150 houses

If you wish to object, please write before 27th February, to
The Clerk to the Council, Guildford Rural District Council, Millmead House,
Guildford, Surrey.

Grounds for objection could include "Green Belt" and "Common Land".

32. *The Effingham Residents and*
Ratepayers Association (ERRA) flyer .   E.R.R.A.

some examples of the information Miss Cameron said was required:

Beatrice Alice Ayres
(i)   Indicate site of Leewoods on plan.
(ii)   Date of her marriage.
(iii)   Between what years did she visit her parents at Leewoods?
(iv)   Colonel Hughes did not register a right to graze donkeys (see her paragraph 4). Did he graze any ponies, sheep, a cow or geese?
(v)   Did she see sheep, geese, cows or ducks on the common? If so where and when?

Annie Boxall
(i)   In which year did she cease to live at Huckamoor, formerly Brickfield Farm?
(ii)   Name the properties occupied by Mr. Carpenter, Mr. Peter Ranger and Mr. Bonsey.
(iii)   Approximately how many sheep and geese did her father graze on the common?
(iv)   What varieties of animal have been grazed on the common during the last 30 years?
(v)   Did the occupants of Huckamoor collect wood from the common for fires, repairs etc.?

Charles Edward Monnery
Break down the period from 1934 until 1971 into smaller periods, say 1934 to 1939, 1939 to 1945 and 1945 to 1971. Say which types of animals were grazed during each period and whether the numbers varied during each period.

It reads like one of the worst ever History examinations, and there are 15 further sections beyond the three here! But thousands of pounds of public money was going to be laid out and the Parish Council was not prepared for it to be wasted by inadequate preparation. The evidence must be watertight. A meeting of the Commons Sub-Committee on 12 July 1974 noted:

> The Clerk to be asked to write to those persons who had given the statements, thanking them for their help, and saying that we hoped that they would not object to Mrs. Worthington calling upon them to obtain further information.

As to how much time was available to achieve all this, Cllr. Dora Worthington wrote as follows to Legal on 6 August:

> I have heard from the Commons Commissioner who as I expected confirms that there is no statutory [time] limits

within which the County Council can make a reference to the Commons Commissioner, it is in the Council's discretion. I further understand there are many hundreds of references to be heard and if the reference was made immediately it could not be heard until January 1975 at the earliest. Even that is too early so far as we are concerned.

The detectives set out. One of the claimants had died, so Ray Davies, the new owner of Slaters Oak, had to be gently alerted to the nature of the problem and the pressing need for his involvement. He calmly and generously agreed to support the cause.

Still not good enough

Having tracked down and submitted all of the above, in due course the Parish Council sought another meeting with Miss Cameron so that she could deliver *orally* her preliminary *Opinion* on whether the evidence was good enough and the case had a chance of succeeding. A two-and-half hour meeting took place on 4 November 1974.

It was a turning point. From now on, the game was truly afoot. Miss Cameron's verdict was that 'the case was well worth pursuing' (remember that the Parish Council has been

33. *The cover of The Kinks Are The Village Green Preservation Society, released in November 1968; a 'concept album' inspired by Ray Davies' time spent in rural Devon, well before he came to Effingham and actually helped with the cause. This photograph of the band was taken on Hampstead Heath. From left to right it shows Ray, his brother Dave, Mick Avory and Pete Quaife.*

'pursuing' this for nine years already!). But they were nowhere near ready yet. As Cllr. Derek Hubbard reported back to the Chairman following the Sub-Committee's meeting, on 6 November 1974:

> On detail there was considerable exchange of information. It seemed that historically we were well covered, but the time between the 30s and 1968 was at present a weak period. Further specific statements [no! surely not!] giving as much detail as possible were required for these years ... Mr. Allen and Mrs. Worthington have notes of information required and actions to be taken … She [Miss Cameron] did not think that there was any mileage in trying to dispute the William case over again even with new evidence.

This time, it was not re-affirmation of the existing declarations, it was a case of trawling again, and yet further afield. The Parish Council wrote to all claimants:

> Advice was given in conference … of the nature of further evidence to be sought and enquiries in that direction are being rigorously pursued by and on behalf of the Council. In that connection the Council is making enquiries of a number of organizations in the district to discover people who are able to help with information as to the use of the Common, either by grazing of animals or taking wood, bracken etc., and also seeking the loan of photographs. We wonder if you can put us in touch with persons or relatives who may be able to assist for any period up to 1966/7, in which event the Council's representative, Mrs. Worthington, would be pleased to interview the person concerned.

'*In conference*' meant that Miss Cameron had given her view verbally, but was still to write up and send her formal 'written' *Opinion*.

As well as to the commoners, the Parish Council wrote to Effingham Junction Women's Institute, Effingham Cricket Club, East Horsley Parish Council, East Horsley Preservation Society, Surrey Naturalists' Trust, The Ramblers' Association and Effingham Residents & Ratepayers asking them to grill their members for memories of the use to which the Common had been put (grazing, taking of wood, turf etc.) or the loan of photographs.

There was the distinct feeling that it might soon be possible to ask Surrey to send the case forward for a hearing by the Commons Commissioner. It was likely to be six months from the submission date to the hearing, although impossible to say for

34. *Mr. Estler's letter confirming he will appear at the Inquiry.*

Lee Brook
Effingham
Surrey

2ⁿᵈ January 1975

Dear Mr Crouch,

Thank you for your letter of 11ᵗʰ December. I should be glad to appear before the Commissioner at the Inquiry.

Yours truly

Adrian Estler

A. ESTLER

sure; and the hearing might take seven to ten days. The owners of the four properties were made to promise that they would move heaven and earth to attend the hearing in person, given the amount of public money being committed. For Mr. Davies of Slaters Oak, there could be great difficulty if he happened to be away on tour with his band, but he was particularly supportive and keen to help. Mr. Estler wrote simply (and feelingly, one imagines), on 2 January 1975, 'I should be glad to appear before the Commissioner at the Inquiry. Yours truly Adrian Estler'. William does not seem to have been invited.

Then in March 1975 Miss Cameron's written version of her *Opinion* arrived. Sixty-nine paragraphs on thirty-two pages. Unbelievably, *eighteen more* detailed questions. A selection:

> 26 [Para 26 of the Written Opinion] Deeds of Flower Cottage to be checked to see if it was copyhold of the Manor.
> 33 Evidence required of grazing from Slaters Oak during the tenure of Cecil Gradwell and Octavia Richardson 1907-27 and Sir Guy Meyrick Mallaby-Deeley 1927-47 [sic]

50 Further evidence required on practice of Commoners, whether there was a Common keeper, who kept the money and whether there is any record of how the liability for each Commoner was worked out

55 Evidence of Mr. Boxall to be checked where he refers to Brickfield Cottages, whereas Mrs. Boxall refers to Brickfield Farm

The Parish Council pressed on. Still largely in the dark about likely eventual costs, they began to think about asking GRDC to pay two thirds of *all* costs, not just of Counsel, and, in support of this, they stressed the amount of money that had been saved by councillors themselves doing so much of the research and copying work needed by the lawyers. GRDC agreed. Effingham set up a fund-raising body distinct from the Parish Council, namely the Effingham Common Preservation Committee (Patron: Sir Barnes Wallis) which calculated that it probably needed to raise £1,500 minimum or £1,750 to be on the safe side. The Parish Council began to broach again the tricky question of whether Mr. Ryan or Miss Cameron considered themselves retained for taking the case to court. On 25 July 1975 a member of Legal wrote to the Parish Council:

> For what it is worth I had a word with the Clerk to the Commons Commissioners concerning both Mr. Ryan and Miss Cameron. He [the Clerk] told me that Miss Cameron was often before the Commissioner and that she was well-known to the Tribunal, particularly as she does a lot of work for the Duchy of Lancaster. He observed that he did not know Mr. Ryan so well.

On 31 July the same person provided further assurance because now GRDC in its turn became anxious about whether Miss Cameron was a safe choice:

> I am told that she acts for both the Duchy of Cornwall and Lancaster and has appeared on Inquiries from the North of England down to Devon. The Clerk said she is very experienced, that the Commissioners, including Mr. Squibb [Mr. G. D. Squibb, QC, the Commons Chief Commissioner], who will hear the case, are much impressed by her and that he feels we could not do much better. I am told she knows what she is doing and what the Commissioner wants.

On 23 July 1975 the submission was at last with the Commons Commissioner, and on 25 July the date for the hearing was confirmed to be 2 December; to be held at the Council Chamber at Millmead in Guildford; forecast to last ten days. It seemed like all the research was over, and minds turned to activities designed to raise money. It was decided to hold a Public Meeting with raffle on 7 October, and in August, to advertise this, the committee sent a letter to all residents explaining again the action the Parish Council was taking and why this was in the village interest:

> As early as 1971 Effingham Parish Council decided that it was their duty to do all they could to try and preserve the Common. A huge amount of research both into the memories of those who have knowledge of the Common and into documents has been carried out by voluntary labour and at no cost; however, for a case to be successfully prosecuted legal knowledge is essential and so solicitors and Counsel have been consulted. It seems to the Committee that there is likely to be a shortfall of some £2000 in costs which it is hoped to collect by public subscription.

There was a special extension to the letter for people whose houses bordered the Common, appealing to their self-interest:

> May we remind you that by preserving the Common, preventing enclosure and keeping the open space you are both preserving the value of the property and the enjoyment of your family of a village heritage.

Other activities were also planned. Barbara Henry ran a Bring-and-Buy coffee morning which raised £246, Richard Smith ran a Race Nite which raised £306, and Enid Edsall's sponsored walk raised £698 (all as recorded in the ERRA Chairman's Report for 1975-76). In the end the Preservation Fund was able to present the Parish Council with £2,800 towards the legal costs.

At the Public Meeting Cllr. Hubbard spoke with great feeling about the incredible quantity of research that had been amassed. Remember, reading this today, we know the outcome. He and the audience, coming to the end of almost eleven years of effort (so far), did not. Having ventured hours of their lives and a very great proportion of public money indeed (so failure would surely bring a very bitter reckoning) on this mission, their hopes hung in the balance. Cllr. Hubbard said

> it seemed to the Parish Council that only by doing the work ourselves, using local knowledge, could we build up a case and keep the cost within our means. We could have left the case to the Claimants themselves and to the legal department of the then Guildford Rural District Council to submit their individual cases but we considered it to be

essential to submit a co-ordinated case. Moreover we thought that the amount of time that the Rural District Council could devote to the case would not allow such deep research as we considered necessary. The work which has been carried out at almost nil expense by a considerable number of people has been most time consuming, but it has proved possible to consult village memory going back over many years. Old documents and maps have been read and where necessary photographed which in itself was often a very tricky operation because of their shape and age. Statements have been taken and in many cases this meant several visits to those whose evidence was thought to bear on the case to ensure that the statements were accurate. As I have said all this and more was carried out by volunteers who made no charge for their time or their expertise ... We are now confident that Counsel representing the village claimants of Common Rights, Guildford Borough Council and Effingham Parish Council as a concerned authority will present a united, meticulously prepared and reasoned case to the Commissioner of Commons, supported by documentation so painstakingly obtained. As a result we hope the Commons of Effingham will be established as Commons for all time and safe from any alterations to Green Belt policy which may emerge from the Surrey County Council Structure Plan ...

Afterwards, the Council was congratulated on having put the case 'with such firmness from the public side, but with such fairness as to the other'. Someone who knew Mr. Calburn

35. *Wild flowers adorn the entrance to the Common, opposite the cricket pitch.*

explained that he [Mr. Calburn] had found the whole issue extremely difficult but 'I am very sure that your words will have made him very happy too'. It was also very touching that Mr. Faulder, the manager of Effingham Manor Estates which was Mr. Calburn's property management company, had attended the Public Meeting, won a prize in the raffle (in other words, he had contributed to the fund-raising) but he gave the prize back so that it could be re-raffled to make more money. Reporting the Public Meeting afterwards, the *Surrey Advertiser* tried to fan a mood of confrontation between the contenders just as the *Leatherhead Advertiser* had previously done following a Parish Meeting on the same subject in 1971; but neither side was having any of it.

More information needed

On 18 November (two weeks to launch and counting), Miss Cameron sent her *Advice on Evidence*. Staggeringly, it contained another stupefyingly long list of questions to which she wanted detailed answers, and of documents for which she needed copies:

> I have not yet seen a proof of evidence from Mr. ...
> I require one before the hearing.

> Copies of these [20] letters should be placed in a paged bundle and if possible agreed with the objectors.

> [Copies of] the following [Parish Council documents, 24 in number] should be placed in a bundle and if possible agreed with the objectors.

> Two points arise out of my examination of the Parish file:
> (i)   Enclosed with his letter of 22nd January 1949 the Clerk of the Parish Council sent to the Clerk of Guildford Rural District Council 7 completed forms of questionnaire in relation to rights of common. This was acknowledged on 28th January 1949. Copies were subsequently sent to Mrs. Joyce Bristow by the Deputy Clerk to Guildford Rural District Council on 22nd June 1953. Where are these forms now? I should like to see them.
> (ii)   In the letter of 4th June 1956 from the Clerk of Effingham Parish Council to the Clerk of Guildford Rural District Council it is said that the question of Effingham Common is raised at every Parish Council meeting. Are there minutes of the meetings showing this? If so, the minute book must be disclosed and copies of relevant entries must be prepared.

She also required: 5 more maps such as the 1842 Tithe Map for Effingham, several sets of original title deeds, an affidavit from a commoner who could not attend, dates of death of two original witnesses to be notified to the objector's solicitor and their original documents to be produced.

Miss Cameron included an equally long roll-call of 21 mostly elderly persons she said must be transported to the hearing (presumably not on William's cart!) to be available as witnesses if needed.

The solicitors and Dora Worthington went into hyperdrive. Everything was duly arranged, seen to, completed. The hearing started in Guildford on Tuesday 2 December and closed on Wednesday 10 December. On 12 December Legal wrote to the Parish Council:

> A great deal of documentary evidence was submitted to the Tribunal on behalf of the Claimants and additionally oral evidence was given by three Claimants (Mr. Davies being in the U.S.A) and some thirteen witnesses who gave evidence of the circumstances surrounding the Common for a period from before the First World War to date.

One of the witnesses had his statement taken in the departure lounge at Heathrow. Cllr. Hubbard recalled that another witness, Mr. John Hughes,

> ... was at that time involved in saving Aintree Racecourse and the Grand National threatened with closure. John found time to come down to give evidence of his trips as a boy on his bicycle to his Uncle at Slaters Oak and his memories of various activities there then. After his evidence the Judge thanked John and wished him well with the Grand National.

On 26 March 1976 the decision was received. Miss Cameron and Mr. Squibb did not disappoint.

You knew all along, of course, that the commoners would win. But here is the extraordinary reason that they won. After *all that*, it was not by virtue of the weight of assembled evidence!

Calburn's legal team had made an error. They had omitted to object to claims for rights over one particular small area, some 5 acres. This was in the middle of the Common and completely continuous (no fences) with the rest. The documentary evidence proved beyond doubt that commoners' rights of grazing sheep and geese attached to Huckamoor, and these applied to the area of this 'island'. However, the animals had always wandered freely, without objection or hindrance, in and out of 'the island' and the surrounding land, and other commoners' animals had done the same in reverse. If the 'island' was incontrovertibly common, this gave crucial support to the claims that everything around it was also common.

In 2010 Jessica Page, who with many others had been present at the hearing, described the scene with pleasure undiminished by the passage of time:

> Miss Cameron had spotted that the other side had failed to object to rights over one area. We were all sworn to deadly secrecy. When the moment came she said "I note you do not contest that rights exist over this particular area?" The opposing Counsel became very flustered and angry and red around the gills. He asked to see the papers and was very put out because it was obvious he had made a mistake which defeated his whole case. You can imagine how much we enjoyed this!

The judgment also confirmed Leebrooke's rights over land on *both* Hooke and East Court Commons (i.e. land of both manors), so, crucially, William's right to graze on more than two acres.

It may be supposed that William flicked the mane out of his eyes, shook a hoof, nonchalantly took all three thirds of himself over onto the Common, and began to graze.

William at law (5)

Keeping up? Quick resumé:

(1) Murrells v Estler (and William)
  Civil case heard in the County Court at Dorking, 1958.

(2) Estler, (William) and GRDC v Murrells and Calburn

Civil case heard by the Court of Appeal at The Royal Courts of Justice, the Strand, London, 1959.

(3) Murrells v GRDC (and William)
  Public Inquiry held by the District Auditor at Guildford, 1960.

(4) GRDC, (William) and others v Calburn
  Public Hearing held by the Commons Commissioners at Guildford, 1975.

Twenty years in, the finale:

(5) Effingham Parish Council (and William) v Legal, determined by The Law Society at The Inns of Court, 1978.

The next subject of contention in the battle to preserve the Common arose even before the Commons Commissioner's decision was received. Legal had first been instructed by the Parish Council in January 1971. In January 1976, since their work was now complete, Legal sent a bill for the third and final installment of their fee to the Parish Council. Which was thrown into mounting consternation.

Right from the outset the Parish Council had been concerned that it must reach for the very highest standards of probity in its dealings on the Common case. It was obviously essential that public money should be committed only after the fullest possible assessment of the risk that the case might not succeed and all the money lost. The spending of every penny must be recorded clearly and transparently, to satisfy the Public Auditor. These were statutory constraints affecting any project, any time. But it was recognized from the start that this particular campaign might demand a very large amount of money indeed. Early on, as we have seen, it took advice to help assess whether it had a case at all and whether it was likely to win. Legal were asked to provide clear estimates of how much the eventual costs would be.

Added to that, there was a further complication. Two of the then Parish Councillors were actually employees of Legal. As Parish Councillors, they contributed their services to the village for free, but on this project they might be highly paid, leading to accusations that they were lining their own pockets.

The Parish Council made great attempts to protect itself from a possible future charge of impropriety. It took advice on the position of the two Councillors, and also of the Clerk, because through his main employment with estate agents Cubitt & West he also occasionally was involved with Calburn's company Effingham Manor Estates. It was assured that, as long as bills from Legal to the Parish Council were very clear about how much time had been spent, and on what exactly, and how much the time cost per hour, and that regular bills were submitted so there should be no nasty surprises, there should be no problem. In fact, the Parish Council would benefit from the specialist local knowledge and doubtless enthusiasm that these gentlemen would contribute to the casework. Because they would inevitably contribute time at home for free, this would also cut the cost and improve the care taken over the case. Legal agreed that they would be happy to work very closely with other Parish Councillors and residents who had volunteered to do a vast amount of the research themselves, to cut the cost even further.

For the first stage of the work (i.e. the assessment of whether the evidence was good enough to sustain the case), the Parish Council paid Counsel and Legal almost £1,200 in fees and costs.

In August 1975, when it was known the case was actually 'on', Legal provided another estimate that the cost from that point forward would be approx. £3,750. This was the point at which the fund-raising from the public began. GRDC agreed to contribute two-thirds of all future costs to a maximum of £2,000 (plus VAT). The Effingham Sub-Committee set about raising a minimum of £1,750 to which the Parish Council contributed some £800 from the precept over the two years 1974-76.

As we have seen there were raffles, a sponsored walk, coffee mornings, a bring & buy sale and a Race Night. There were straightforward begging letters to current residents of Effingham, former residents of Effingham (even living overseas), commercial organisations and likely charities or interest groups. The owners of the four properties with commoners' rights all contributed. In the Parish Council files is preserved a postcard from the owner of the property Raveloe, Lower Road, who wrote:

> My house is the last one in the Effingham postal district and the first one to pay rates to Leatherhead [ie outside the civil parish of Effingham and Guildford Borough, in Mole Valley]. Effingham did such wonderful work against the M25 which would have been right on my doorstep that this cheque [£50] is partly in view of this. All good wishes to the appeal.

An accounts sheet by the Treasurer records that the total raised so far included 'the proceeds of a sponsored ride by a 7, an 8 and a 9 year old'. In the event, almost £2,700 was assembled.

36. *In the years that followed the success of the campaign for registration, it became the custom for those enjoying their newly-confirmed commoners' rights to exercise those rights openly each Autumn. We have come to call such events 'Commoners' Days'. Mr. Estler, with his horse and cart, featured prominently in these events for the rest of his life. Here is Mr. Estler (carrying a log) with friends on East Court Common (part of Effingham Common alongside Lower Farm Road) on Commoners' Day in 1986.*

37. *Ray Davies with his donkey on the Common on Commoners' Day in 1996.*

Unfortunately,

(i)   The production of an *estimate* is difficult. Legal made it clear at the time that they had had to employ 'a crystal ball'. From the very beginning they had been under constant pressure from the Parish Council to provide reliable estimates, and they constantly reiterated how difficult this was to do for a contested case.

(ii)   The production of a solicitors' *bill* is difficult. As Legal said, 'apart from copying out the whole file, any bill could be said to be inadequate ... you would be obliged to write a book not a bill'. But there were demonstrable errors in the first bill. It included work which either Mrs. Worthington had done or inaccurate secretarial services which had needed correction by Parish Councillors. From then on bills were treated to intense scrutiny.

(iii) As we have seen, very late in the day there was a sudden intense scurry to organize the last documents and the witnesses, occasioning a very great deal of work in a short time.

(iv)   Finance was made more complex by both the introduction of VAT and the roaring inflation of the 1970s. The time the case took to come to completion pushed costs up.

When the final bill came, it was approximately £550 more than estimated – a significant percentage increase on £3,750.

This was a serious shock. There followed a great deal of internal consultation and worry:

> 'These figures seem to be monstrous.'
> 'Most of us have to make estimates and stick to them – why should Legal be exempt?'
> 'We should face up to criticism and support our colleagues.'
> 'The deficit [the writer meant the fact that it was known more money had been collected than the original target] is none of Legal's business – we didn't raise the money to cover their error of judgment.'
> 'From a practical point of view they [Legal] acted as a post office, and the only real work was to collate information and work which [Dora] provided.'

It seemed impossible to account for because so much of the period covered by the third bill was simply time spent waiting – no activity. Some Parish Councillors questioned whether Legal was charging for work which had been actually done by Mrs. Worthington and others as volunteers. Several members of the council and the fund-raising committee had a go at number-crunching. Depending on whether they included the whole period or just the second stage, VAT or not, installments already paid or not, they all reached different figures but the bottom line remained the same – why was the bill so high? This then was the nightmare scenario – payment of a large amount of public money, to a firm where Parish Councillors worked. One can imagine how difficult and painful these discussions between friends and colleagues must have been, especially for the two 'in the middle'.

The Parish Council resolved to grasp the nettle, and challenged the bill. Politely but firmly, the Chairman wrote to Legal explaining the need for everything to be above board and above reproach, and that he must ask for further clarification. Legal explained that in fact they had *undercharged*; if everything had been charged for, and at the appropriate rate, the bill would have been much higher. An impasse. Eventually at the end of March 1976 the Parish Council agreed that neither side would persuade the other and accepted Legal's suggestion of asking The Law Society for a 'certificate of reasonableness' – in other words, to review the solicitors' bill and adjudicate on whether it was justified.

In March 1977 the Parish Council wrote again asking for the papers to be submitted for analysis. In July and in October they wrote again. In January 1978 the papers were finally submitted by Legal, and in February The Law Society asked for the Parish Council's comments on Legal's submission; this was supplied. The Parish Council stressed how Mrs. Worthington among others 'had done many hours of devilling as an unpaid helper' on the vast majority of the research, had checked and re-checked Legal's work, had attended key meetings, and had been vital support for Miss Cameron in court during the actual hearing.

In July The Law Society wrote back. They found the bill reasonable. The Parish Council Minute of 25 July glumly records 'The Law Society upheld Legal's case and the council reluctantly settled the account.'

Luckily the money raised from the generous public exceeded the target. But this was not actually a defeat, and was not seen as such. The Parish Council had fought an honourable battle to ensure that not a single penny of public money was wrongfully spent, and that not a single elected member could have their character impugned. Perhaps this was the most difficult, and the most admirable, battle of all, considering what it must have cost in stoicism and forbearance. Effingham residents were truly well-served by this voluntary adherence to the highest ethical standards.

Aftermath

Most people visiting the tranquil open spaces of Effingham Common today are probably completely oblivious of the massive collective output of energy, effort, vision, memory, money and – well – slog, by so many people, sustained over twenty years, which allows them to enjoy it now. 'Due process' is perhaps boring and it is certainly slow, but it exists to protect and enable all sides, and participation is incredibly energizing for those who are fired up. You perhaps have your own ideas on what drives community-minded or 'public spirited' people and projects. If so by all means write them up for homework.

And should anyone tell you 'the law is an ass', you may say 'yes, better it were a horse.'

Postscript

Will the *real* William step forward?

In the interests of accurate historical record, we were keen to present readers with photographs of William, our warrior for Commoners' rights. But the waters were muddied by the fact that Mr. Estler treated 'William' as a sort of generic name for his current horse!

We first acquired a photograph of 'William' harnessed to Mr. Estler's cart in a photograph dated 1981. Could *this* William, a much-loved creature very fondly remembered by residents, possibly be *that* William who was the subject of the first court case in 1959? Could a horse be that old?

Some said yes; others thought no. Investigations followed. Friends of William came forward to explain what they knew. Quite unnervingly more Estler-connected horses, in different colours, and even of the opposite sex (a Camilla), suddenly began to emerge from the mists of memory.

Along with several other Effingham residents, Barbara Henry attended the Commons Commission hearing and was present when Mr. Estler was asked about earlier contention between him and the Lord of the Manor over his claim to be able to graze horses on the Common. Barbara described her vivid recollection of the exchange. 'What', the Commissioner asked, concerning one particular incident, 'was the name of the horse?' 'Thisbe' was Mr. Estler's reply. The Effingham residents and the court generally appeared not to have been expecting this distinguished name for a horse, and gales of laughter broke out. Sad to say, no more has been heard of said Thisbe thus far.

Perhaps Mr. Estler had been indulging here in a little bit of verbal horseplay ...

Martin Smith has heroically sifted the evidence and explains in the next article that there was more than one William. The grey horse seen in Illus. 27 and 29 was the real William of the court case, but a subsequent William stepped into his horseshoes and continued exercising the rights of Mr. Estler to graze a horse on the Common. He also deserves our recognition. So read on to learn about William 2nd, also known as Bill ...

William the 1st, William the 2nd and Adrian
Martin Smith

8

In December of 1977 I moved into a small cottage on Effingham Common. Having a fondness for natural history and the countryside it was a good move as I am still here 33+ years later.

That first winter passed and Spring arrived with the dawn chorus starting the day; but in the sounds of the morning was another sound, one I had not heard before, a metallic ringing, the sound of metal on metal.

In those days we had a Rough Collie 'Tara' so before work a walk was in order. On our way to the other side of the cricket pitch, we came upon this solidly-built skewbald horse. He was attached by a length of chain looped around his head and then fixed to a metal stake driven into the ground accompanied by a bucket of water and another loose stake. This was my first encounter with William (the 2nd) but better known to us in future as Bill.

38. *Bill.*

As I got to know the Common I would see Bill staked out at various locations. The ringing was of course Bill being staked out by Adrian Estler, the second stake being used to drive in the fixed stake. I guessed a mallet would be too valuable to leave around. My meetings with Bill carried on whenever I walked the dog to where he was tethered.

Bill was a powerful and headstrong horse and I saw this demonstrated on a couple of occasions when Adrian would move him to a new site. Bill did not always want to go where Adrian wanted so we were treated to the sight of Bill either refusing to go in the desired direction or trotting off with Adrian clinging to the chain, hurling all sorts of curses at Bill.

40. *Bill being fed a snack.*

In the summer of 1982 we had my partner's nieces staying. They thought we lived in the wilds of the countryside. Adrian got wind of their stay and brought Bill down to the small bit of common adjacent to our house and tethered him almost outside. The girls were enthralled and Bill got plenty of tidbits.

My wife is a dentist and one of her patients was a farrier by the name of Steve Icke (Steve unfortunately died this year). We were fortunate to be offered a gas supply to the house for a reasonable outlay. This meant we had a bunker full of anthracite left over when we converted to gas. Steve got wind of this during a visit to the Dental Surgery and was keen to take it off our hands. When Steve found out where he would be collecting from, he told us that he looked after Adrian's horse Bill and was able to give us some information.

To give some history on the picture below, it was taken by Denis Harvey and was given by way of thanks by Steve to my wife for the anthracite. We can only assume this was in turn given to him by Denis. The picture was taken in 1986.

41. *Bill grazing, with the caravan behind.*

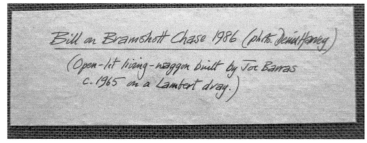

Bill on Bramshott Chase 1986 (photo. Denis Harvey)
(Open-lot living-waggon built by Joe Barras
c. 1965 on a Lambert dray.)

42. *The label on the back of the original photograph shown in Illus. 41.*

43. *Bill, as seen on the cover of Denis Harvey's book.*

According to Steve, Bill did not belong to Adrian, but holidayed on the Common for much of the time. Occasionally he would be collected by his owner and hitched up to a Gypsy open-lot living-wagon and spend time on the road. So the question is, who did Bill belong to?

You might think the story ends there, unanswered owing to Steve's passing. But using the internet I discovered that in 1979, a Denis Harvey had published a book called *The Gypsies: Waggon-time and After* and I was able to track down a copy on the internet. The small picture shown on the website looked very much like Bill. I had to have the book. I ordered online from a supplier in Vancouver and it was sent from their warehouse in Las Vegas! When I received the book it confirmed that the dust cover did indeed feature the same horse, Bill.

So, did Bill belong to Denis or to Adrian?

The book contained many photographs some of which featured Bill and were credited to *Daniel* Harvey so I tracked down a 'Dan Harvey' in Dorking who, when contacted, confirmed that he was indeed the son of Denis.

Dan is an artist and working with his partner on an installation for the 2012 Olympics. When I explained that I was trying to get as much history on Bill as possible, he agreed to take time out from his hectic schedule and invited me to his studio. What a fortunate discovery this was.

On meeting, he confirmed that his father Denis and Adrian were friends, and Bill belonged to his father, who had bought him from Travellers in 1967/68. Although acquired by Denis, Bill was worked and cared for by both men.

Denis was also a prolific photographer and Dan still had many of his father's photographs, more importantly some of almost priceless value for the history of Effingham Common. As well as the book, the information that follows is thanks to the Harvey family.

44. *Adrian's house Leebrooke.*

45. *Another view of Leebrooke.*

46. *Adrian, probably at Leebrooke, holding a painting of some sheep.*

Adrian lived with his brother Mervyn in Leebrooke. As the pictures show, the property is somewhat overgrown with Adrian's passion for cultivated plants and in later years it almost disappeared beneath them. More importantly Dan had two pictures of the man himself.

When Adrian died in 1990 Denis wrote a tribute to Adrian for one of the papers, and Dan has allowed me to include the clipping.

Bill went on to live another four years and died just before Christmas 1994. He was buried in Powys, Wales.

So what about William 1st?

Well, once again Dan came up trumps confirming that there had been an earlier William owned by Adrian. This horse, a grey, was William 1st and he was the key player in the Commoners' rights issue narrated in the previous article. The pictures of him in that article are just two of several that we fortunately have of him.

Dan kindly phoned his mother Rita who now lives in Wales and she confirmed these facts, adding: "How sad it was when William [1st] was released having been kept locked up for

'Tree surgeon extraordinary' dies at 80

ADRIAN ESTLER — an American-trained tree expert of Anglo-European descent — died on Tuesday last week aged 80 at Rosehill Nursing Home, Dorking.

Mr Estler began working in Surrey in the late thirties at a time when the American styling of "tree-surgeon" was almost unheard of in England and even considered a satirical joke. He never used the term; Estler was in fact Tree-Surgeon Extraordinary, being not only a technically skilled expert, but also one who was much concerned with fostering a graceful form in a tree, and with creating visually attractive tree-relationships and vistas in a landscape. "Treescaping" was an art he liked to practice.

He rapidly established a reputation not only locally but also among the landed gentry generally and at stately homes throughout the Home Counties and further.

He did also work for the Royal Horticultural Society, for Kew Gardens, the Royal Hospital Gardens at Chelsea, and in London parks. Closer to home he was employed by Lord Beaverbrook, Dr Marie Stopes, and the old Dorking urban council, as well as at Leeds Castle, Kent.

Mr Estler lived on an island site on Effingham Common comprising meadow, wood and orchard. Here, with a horse, bantams, a house-cow and an annual crop of hay and damsons, he nurtured many rare and exotic plants and trees in a garden that appeared at first sight to the uninitiated to be a barely-controlled jungle, but was in fact carefully tended.

A great champion of the Common Rights movement in the Fifties he got into an expensive legal tangle, like many another luckless commoner, by trying to recover his grazing rights on the common that had been ploughed up during the war.

He was a keen horseman and rider-to-hounds and for many years until recently, in the lanes ad highways around Effingham, it was a familier sight to see him trotting a harness-horse with ralli-trap or four-wheeled dog-cart phaeton and even, one memorable winter of heavy snow, a one-horse open sleigh.

Though a natural loner, Adrian will be remembered fondly and sadly missed by a great many people.

D.H.

47. Denis Harvey's obituary to Adrian, published on 12 April 1990.

months until the trial. When Adrian managed to get him back his muscles had wasted away ..." She could not remember if Adrian had him put him down or if he just died shortly after.

49. *William 1st pulling Adrian and the phaeton trap.*

Bill (William 2nd) was named as a nod to William 1st.

Memories of Effingham Common: oral histories

Doreen E. Hemus, Michael S. Waller,
C. Edward Crouch & Jessica Page, Ivor Gillespie

Effingham Local History Group decided very early on that one of its main concerns was to capture as much information as possible about village life in earlier times from current or former residents. So far these recordings have been made by and transcribed by Yvonne Shaw with help from Chris Hogger, often launching into action at a moment's notice if an unmissable opportunity presents! The Group has plans to record many more residents, and if you have any suggestions for people to speak to, please get in touch.

We are extremely fortunate that memories of Effingham Common captured so far come from an interesting variety of perspectives: different generations, different sexes, and different experiences of those who actually live (or lived) by the Common, compared to those who knew or visited it for other reasons.

The accounts below are extracts from longer recordings which can be read in full on the website. Although often less flowing than a written account would be, the spoken form of the interviews has been retained.

Doreen Hemus was born at her grandparents' home, Norwood Farm, in the 1920s and has lived on or near Effingham Common most of her life. Her recording was made on 2 August 2010.

Michael Waller was born in 1934 and lived in a cottage on the very edge of the Common until 1965. His recording was made on 15 September 2010.

Eddie Crouch MBE has lived in the village since 1946. As Parish Clerk effectively since 1951 then Parish Councillor and Chairman of the Parish Council, he has known of the Common and the many debates and campaigns surrounding its future and its management for over 60 years. His recording was made on 15 June 2010.

The parents of Jessica Page née Harrold returned to settle permanently in the village just before the Second World War when Jessica was a child, and she has lived in Effingham ever since. Later, as Guildford Rural District Councillor then Borough Councillor, Parish Councillor and then Chairman of Effingham Parish Council, Jessica, like Eddie, played a considerable part in debates, decisions and campaigns about the Common down the years. Her recording was made on 15 June 2010.

Ivor Gillespie has lived at Hooke Farm since 1968, and nearby in East Horsley before that. His recording was made on 5 July 2010.

Doreen E. Hemus

I was born across Effingham Common in a very nice farm called Norwood Farm. My Grandfather moved there in 1912 with his family. They worked very very hard. My grandfather was a farmer and my father was the son, but he didn't really want to take on farming; it was too much hard work, getting up at 4 o'clock in the morning and milking the cows, and [these days] they don't have to milk them by hand you see, and they've got lovely hot water and everything laid on; and the farmhouse was facing the farmyard, and the cowsheds were along the side. Grandfather was very fussy and he did keep them nice and clean or rather his employees did. He employed quite a lot of men from Effingham village. I went to school in Effingham village, to the Church school and the headmaster was Stewart Adams and his wife was the Governess. I was in the Governess' class and they were there for 25 years. They had no children [of their own]. I suppose there were about 30 [children in the school] and they had several classes and a great big fire grate and big lumps of coal like they used to have on the railway with those steam [engines] – puffin' billies we used to call them, they were so big.

It was a lovely farm and it had five bedrooms but of course like all farms in those days they had a well to get their water for drinking, pumping well, no sanitation at all but they had a double one; a little one for the children and a bigger one but of course in those days, farm toilets were called earth toilets. They used to put special stuff in; they were at the end of the garden.

It was really wonderful! Outside the back door was a great big tree and it was full of walnuts when the season was on and they would hit your head – oh they were lovely. They had a nice lawn.

Grandfather went there in 1912 with his wife and his family, my father being one of the sons and he was there for 16 years. He moved from there in 1928, he still loved farming so he moved to Ockham – Guileshill Farm. This was a modern farm, it had a proper toilet you see. As the years went on things got a bit more modern and at Guileshill Farm there was a lovely little church in a field, that's where I was christened.

There was a great big Common, Effingham Common facing Norwood Farm. There was a great big pond facing Grandad's farm and when it was bad weather and ice (silly thing to do really) but all my father's brothers and sisters including him and me because I was the first grandchild we used to go skating on there, so you can see what severe weather we had then because we didn't fall in. And I can remember when I was about 6 trying to skate on there not knowing what I was really doing, but it was fun for Grandad's sons and daughters. It was in the grounds, it must still be there. But it is covered with a lot of bushes, hawthorn bushes now but Grandma and Grandad in their bedroom when they looked out, they could see the main road because the trees on the Common hadn't grown then. The pond was between the house and the main road. It was quite a big farm really and when he walked along the little road to get on to the main road, the pond was facing his farm and well all the boys and girls liked skating there in the severe weather but I suppose they were safe. None of them fell through!

Grandma used to get up early in the morning and Grandfather would always make a big fire and make toast with a big toasting iron but Grandma would always take one of the boys with her and go out in the field, early hours of the morning, and pick mushrooms and then come back and after the milking session had finished they went indoors to have bacon and fried mushrooms. She loved going out there every day but she always took someone with her.

[Going to school] My mother used to have a bike and at the back of it there was a seat, a carrier, and I had a cushion and the feathers came from Grandad's chickens and mother used to cycle with me at the back to Effingham School for years. There wasn't a lot of traffic in those days and the first bus was a green one. So once they started running the bus, it only ran about once an hour, it was the most old-fashioned bus I've ever seen, then I packed up. So once the buses started to run, Mother didn't want to take me any more, it was hard work for her. When I was about 10 or 11 Father bought me a second hand bike from Cobham from a garage for twenty-five shillings, and I had that for years and I had to cycle. Oh the wind used to blow across that Common, and it was so cold! I was only about ten when I started cycling, and then my mother gave me a lovely job! Just before it was dark, she would say 'Will you go on your bike and do a bit of shopping?' And I'm glad she did because up to this day, up to this day, I love shopping. I used to love to do that and I had an old fashioned straw basket and I think they were only about five or six pennies (new ones) with a handle and I used to throw it over the handle bars full of shopping, and I loved that! Come home from school going shopping in Cobham. It was an easy life then, it really was an easy life.

When the War came in 1939 of course with my age I had to

join up. Well I had such a homely home here, and I'm not really a good mixer, I didn't really want to go into the Forces or anything so I had to join, so I joined the Land Army. My sister said, 'You were a good Land Girl', although I never worked on the land, I was lucky there, I did a milk round.

I had a black horse that walked all the way round with me; I was frightened of it but it wouldn't trot, it was too old, and an open float; I used to get drownded. I did a round round here so I knew all the customers and they liked me and I liked them. They used to give me lovely Christmas boxes, about 2/6d, some five shillings and one gentleman always gave me £1.00 – that was a lot! And I was in uniform, and I did the milk round for four and a half years. The dairy was in the middle of Effingham village, where the little chapel is and opposite the little chapel, it was called Home Farm. And I was there for 13 years. I did the milk round for four and half years and I'd had enough of it. To be honest, I liked the milk round, I liked the customers, at Christmas time they used to give me lovely Christmas boxes. One farmer across Effingham Common he was a tree surgeon – Mr. Estler – well he was very nice and his wife was like a lady and they had a little boy and girl, [Giles and Susan] she dressed them beautiful and every Christmastime, he wouldn't give me a tip or anything, he gave me a lovely joint of venison – is that deer? I brought it home and I said 'Mother, here's a beautiful roast joint you can do. I've got a piece of venison' and she said 'Oh show me', but every year he gave me a lovely piece for Mother to cook, that was my Christmas present.

The dairy was kept by two nice brothers, their name was Curtis. William Curtis he did all the farming at Home Farm and they were all Jersey cows and they used to go out in the fields with all the buttercups – it was a pretty sight, and his brother Charles, Charlie, he did all the machinery that went wrong for the bottling department, he organised to see all the bottling was done properly. They also had a beautiful shop in Church Street, Bookham, next to the telephone exchange and he had it built and it was the Dairy Shop and sold groceries and milk. But they didn't have any cows and that, we had the cows in Effingham village and it was good trade for them.

Mallaby-Deeley had Slaters Oak and one side of the house was a field and they had donkeys for the children to play on. He did have a title, he was Sir Mallaby-Deeley and his mother was an old fashioned lady and she always wore a black ribbon [round her throat] and I do believe she was Lady Mallaby-Deeley and they had a simple boy and the mother lived there as well and they used to walk this poor simple boy up to the station, it was so sad. I suppose he might have been about 14 or 15, but they were titled. And they had one side of the house as a great big garden and they made into an orchard and it was the most beautiful sight in the spring, full of daffodils, oh it was beautiful! They were kind to me because they had quite a long path to get down from the road to the big house and they used to say to me, just open the gate by the side of the road and put our milk behind a tree, which was nice.

I delivered to Mr. Estler and he had a housekeeper and I suppose I ought not to say this, but he had a most attractive wife, she was like an actress, and a little boy and girl about 4 or 5 and she made up nicely and dressed beautiful, but he dressed for the farm and something went wrong and she left him. She left him for an officer in the Second World War and took her children with her. He spoke beautiful, he was a tree surgeon and I do believe he was something or a relation – there was some German blood. He had a brother.

Michael S. Waller

I lived at 2 Station Cottages from 1934 until 1965. The first thing I remember about the war years is that in September 1939 on September 3rd I remember my mother crying because the First [World] War hadn't been over for 20 years. My neighbours at Station Cottages were named Mr. and Mrs. Pottswood. They had two daughters, Vera and Enid, and they took on two evacuees from London, Rita Simmons and Sheila Brown, who I became friendly with as a child; we used to play on the Common and get up to all sorts of things. The Common was on either side of the cottages, we used to play cricket and rounders and we used to climb trees and generally enjoy playing on the Common. At that time of course it was double British Summer Time during the War and so we had light evenings. I had to go bed at 7 o'clock, and I could hear everybody else still playing on the Common and I was very annoyed about that because I wanted to be out there with them! Schooling, I went to Effingham, St. Lawrence I think it's called now, Primary School when I was five and from what I can remember it was quite a happy period of my childhood then. Stewart Adams was the headmaster and his wife was the Governess. I remember also that they had a stuffed lion on a plinth in the corridor of the school. I don't know if it's still there! There were outside toilets in the playing fields and I had a real problem one day, I got stuck in the toilet outside. It was freezing cold and a teacher, Miss Parker, had to come out and fetch me in. The other teachers there were Miss Dixon and Miss Hardiman. Stewart Adams didn't do a lot of teaching that I can remember. He did the lessons with physical observings like weighing bits and pieces – weights and measures – and he used to get volunteers from us kids to help him with his garden; so if we could get out of arithmetic lessons everybody put their hands up and special ones were chosen to go and weed his garden. I was also chosen by him to fetch his cucumbers from Mizens the market garden just down the road.

Still in the Primary School, The Lodge opposite the School had allotments and we used to grow vegetables [there is a photo of this in Mary Rice-Oxley's book] and we were taken for walks in the fields and we had sports day playing cricket etc. in a field up past Curtis' Farm, at the back of Curtis' Farm. We used to go up there to play cricket from the school. There was also a big yew tree in the grounds which I notice is not there now. We had a playing field which opened in the spring and on a fine summer day we would sometimes go outside and have lessons sitting on the grass in the field which was all very pleasant.

The classes were divided into As and Bs. I went from 1A and 2A which I think was the top junior class and then there was a B class B1 and B2. Stewart Adams was a character: he used to wear a trilby hat and he used to tell us all sorts of anecdotes, he was a bit of a comedian. He generally was quite a pleasant chap. I know he had a Morris car which we all envied and sometimes when we had lessons he spoke to us about the fact that he had visited every county in England, I think he used to say. Generally I quite liked him and his wife too was very pleasant and I enjoyed the school there. My mother used to take me on the carrier of her bicycle and take me to school from Effingham Junction which I suppose was about a two mile bike ride and also I used to walk back home from the school which was a pretty good walk on short legs and sometimes a car wouldn't pass me – there was no traffic at all. My cousin who worked for Bowmans Bakery had an Austin van, a white van, and as I was walking along I'd suddenly see him appear with his van and he would give me a lift back to the Junction.

I moved on to Effingham Central School – I must have been ten I suppose, ten or eleven and I was there until about the age of 13. I have quite happy memories of Effingham Central School. Mr. Hewitt was the Headmaster. There were allotments alongside the school nearest to the road, there was a driveway which led to The Lodge where we used to go swimming; we had permission use the swimming pool. It was a tree-lined drive – chestnut trees, I remember conkers and things like that and to the left of that was a football ground where we played football and just at the back of the football field was an asphalted playground and to the left of that was more grass, a sort of a field, where we used to play shinty and we had running and [on] sports day it was used for general sports.

This was in the 1940s, the war years. Now during those years, the war years, I only had half a day's schooling because the afternoon was taken up by the Strand School which was an evacuated school from London so we had the morning, and they had the afternoon, so I probably missed out on quite a bit of schooling there. I enjoyed it – I enjoyed the time off! The school holidays were about five weeks – it seemed a lifetime at the time so we were back on the Common playing.

When the bombing came, some were dropped and landed on the Common, unexploded, and Jeff Warnham and myself were collecting up these incendiary bombs. I suppose they were about a couple of feet long with fins and unexploded and we used to collect them all up and pile them up and we were hauled in front of the class in assembly and given a right ticking off by Mr. Hewitt and I believe the local police came along because we'd been warned about these bombs. I remember they actually buried these bombs at the side of the road between Mallaby-Deeley and Effingham Station on that straight bit of road there on the right hand side of the road.

A landmine landed at Mr. Garnett's farm which is at the back of the Common [Brickfield Farm, now Huckamoor]. There was a cinder path which went past our cottages, past the railway sheds and right at the end is a right turn and go on as far as on the left was a big gate. And I used to deliver the church magazine down there and a landmine landed there.

On the cricket ground, leading up to the War, was a searchlight unit so after the War it all had to be got up to scratch and converted back to a cricket ground and we had the help of prisoners of war to do this, cutting down all the long grass and landscaping it and getting it back into some playable condition. Dr. Sutton, he was the President of the club, got a friend who was a very good artist to come down and painted a picture of the workers cutting down the grass with scythes and the picture is either up on the walls of the cricket club pavilion or my nephew or somebody may have it. I don't know where it is. I have a copy of it.

There was no pavilion and the first one we had was a wooden shed type building with a pull-down front flap where we had lemonade and a copper tea urn where tea was obtained. The tea urn had to be filled up from a tap in Adrian Estler's land at the back where he kept a cow and on a number of occasions when we had filled this tea urn up with water we were chased by Estler's cow which was very funny at the time! We had a marquee with trestle tables where the actual teas were laid out.

Toilets were non-existent. I think we did have some corrugated iron arrangement. Estler went through a period where he had a bit of a dispute with our president Dr. Sutton over something or other and he allowed his horse to tread all over the wicket and we arrived one day to find there were hoof prints all over the ground and there was a bit of a to-do about that. He and Dr. Sutton didn't get on very well.

Adrian Estler was a character. He didn't mince his words, he didn't take to fools kindly, he wore a straw panama hat and when he went in to bat, he had this straw panama hat, open necked shirt, loose sleeves undone, no socks, no pads and scruffy work boots and he used to go in at number eleven. He did make a few runs at times and he also knew the rules of cricket. He made a very good umpire and we had a bit of a row with one of the teams because he no-balled a bowler from the square leg position. How he could see from that position I don't know! But it caused a bit of a kerfuffle with the opposing team. Estler also was very keen on making home-made damson wine and he used to invite some of us round to his kitchen and on a great big oak wooden table he used to get out a great big hunk of cheese, set the glasses down, get the bottles out which incidentally were still fermenting in some cases, pour out the wine and half the bottle would turn white so we could only drink the top half and then he used to carve up the cheese and that was that.

Of course he had his Rolls Royce van with the bolted door; we used to have to climb over the door to get in. He had all his tree-cutting material and tools in the back because he was a tree surgeon and when there was a local derby, East Horsley for instance, we went in style in his horse and trap but we were covered in horse hairs when we got there. Estler was well known in the village. He was married. I did meet his wife once because we used to go carol singing. I don't know what happened to his wife. He was of German origin and he had a public school education, Oundle College I think it was, and he was very keen on cricket as I say. He always used to call me 'Waller'. 'How you doing there Waller – what are you doing today?' If I was in the garden he always used to stop with his horse and cart and have a chat so he was a well-known character. I used to open the batting sometimes or I would go further down the list a bit, I batted all positions. I used to play wicket keeper as well and I got a nasty bang on the head doing it.

I remember the time over the cricket ground when we had hoards of spectators. All the crowds used to line up down the drive and Harry Trish, the secretary, going round with a collection box and he used to get quite a bit of money. I remember an American getting out of his car while we were batting and saying 'Hey you guys, can I take a photograph of you guys?' I also remember we had an all-day match with a team from London called Ivydeane. We were twelve-a-side. They had a coloured player, a tall chap and I didn't realise he was as old as he was; but he was getting on a bit, and he was in the outfield and a high ball was hit and he went to catch it and it caught him straight in the mouth and they had to cart him off to hospital. It bashed his teeth out. I understood he was round about seventy at the time, so he wasn't a youngster!

We always helped after the game to roll the wicket. It was a big concrete roller, it was heavy, and we had a big Dennis mower which was a devil to start at times and this was kept in the tool shed and we used to stay behind after the game. We used to get the regular helpers and there were others who were more interested in playing and going home after. So we relied on the regulars to help keep the ground in trim. There was always work to be done. During the week there were odd things; practice days were Tuesdays, we had nets down there and we used to have a practice wicket, a concrete wicket. And then of course later the President was Dr. Sutton and he led us to raise all sorts of funds from various people. He'd invite them to become Vice-President and donate some money and we got enough money to build a cedarwood pavilion which we had to build and we had the concrete foundation and when we got to the last end it overlapped the foundation by a few inches so we had to adjust that! Anyway it was all done and we had a celebration on opening night and from then on we had a bar whereas previously we had had to go down to The Lord Howard for our drinks.

Back to 1939 it was the start of the 'phoney war' as they say. I can remember Effingham Station having a gong which consisted of a train buffer and they used to bang this gong, the buffer, as a practice air raid siren. And the LDV [Local Defence Volunteers] was formed which consisted of volunteers; they wore armbands and they used to parade and do practice on Effingham Common to the left of our cottages and us kids used to take the mickey out of them. Later on of course they got uniforms and rifles but they were the Local Defence Volunteers which consisted mainly of railway men.

I remember the railway man who worked in the booking office: Jack Dangey his name was, and Mr. Pottswood who was our next door neighbour at number 2 Station Cottages, he was also a signalman; he worked in shifts with my father. He was a brilliant gardener. You could get to his house from the platform by walking along a path up a few steps under the booking office, the part that used to house all the bicycles at the time and luggage and I could walk up there if I came off a train and not show a ticket because I used to walk in through his garden. He was a very nice chap I remember, he had a dog called Trip.

The house had two upstairs bedrooms; no gas lights – we had to use candles for lighting. Downstairs there was a living room with a range, a cast iron range, which we had to use coal for fires and the oven, where we used to cook our roast dinner. We used to roast chestnuts, and baked apples by the side of the range. We used go out of the living room to the front door where there was a passageway under the stairs where we used to keep cheese and we also kept mice – we used to put traps! Then there was the front room which was used on special occasions. We had a grand piano, two easy chairs and an open fire. We used to have some beautiful log fires, we used to collect logs from the Common and the chimney used to get sooted up. We used to have to sweep the chimney every so often, and the soot would all come down and at some later stage the house had had a bedroom built on at the end, so we had a downstairs bedroom as well. And then we had a scullery with a sink and a concrete boiler and there was a high ceiling and I think my father made a clothes line on a pulley system that we pulled up, and we had a geyser and I think we had a gas cooker and a meter that we had to put money in.

Baths had to be taken in the kitchen in a galvanised bath. The water had to be boiled on the gas stove and just outside the back door, turn to the right, was an outside toilet with an Elsan closet. I used to get trapped in there at times because if anyone came to the back door, I was stuck in there until they'd finished! My father made a shed out of railway sleepers and we had chickens at the bottom of the garden. We grew potatoes, we had vegetables: leeks, Brussels sprouts, roses and a damson tree. Damsons were prolific! We had a damson tree outside the downstairs bedroom and there were also damsons in the hedge at the bottom of the garden.

Before the War, the Walls ice cream man with his three wheel trike used to stop opposite our house, on a Sunday on the other side of the road and my mother used to make a jug of tea for him. He wanted bluebells one time and we collected bluebells for him and he gave us a penny. At weekends we used to get hikers coming down from London, especially Bank Holidays, coming off the trains, but there were people walking about. And people sometimes used to come down to the cricket ground as well and as it was Sunday they may have been coming to church or coming back again. He [the ice-cream man] obviously found it worth while to park his trike there.

During the War years a bomb landed near the station where the line divides, one line goes to Waterloo and one line goes to London Bridge, between them is a sub-station and I think they tried to hit the sub-station, but they didn't. I didn't hear it during the night but when I woke up there was a lump of plaster come off the ceiling and landed on my bed.

Then of course there were the doodlebugs. I can remember a jeep coming over the hill there over the railway full of young men and this doodlebug coming and these Yanks piling out of the jeep and into the ditch using obscene language. I heard the engine cut out and I think it landed at Hatchford, somewhere down there.

Service people especially Wrens or the odd soldier used to catch the last train down from Waterloo and the train used to finish at Effingham, 'cos it didn't go any further it used to go into the sidings, so they used to knock on our door asking if they could stay the night. We used to put up one or two at night time. I also remember a drunk coming off the train lying down in the middle of the road on the far side of the bridge. I was up in the bedroom and I had to go out and chase him off because if a car had come over the bridge it would have run him over.

There was an encampment opposite our house, the army were there, I remember that, we were invited to a Christmas celebration and we had the anthracite stove with the chimney going up through the middle which was lit and it was all very warm and friendly. The British Army this was, I think they were something to do with the searchlight unit on the cricket pitch and they gave us a couple of sausage rolls.

I remember the Canadian Army camp up Beech Avenue on the left hand side, 'cos us kids used to go up there and mingle with them and have dinner with them and they used to give us mince and tatties in jerry cans and they used to give us their pen knives. And also on Effingham Station there were the odd times when the Nestles slot machines were filled up with chocolate and I remember one time they emptied one of them and gave us kids the chocolate. The Canadians were very generous, very generous.

I spent a lot of time in the Memorial Hall with the Boy Scouts and various other sporting activities like table tennis. I didn't camp on the Common but we built a log hut at the back of the hall. I don't know where we got all the logs from but we had that for a time and we used to have some of our meetings at the back of the Memorial Hall.

I was also a member of the Covenanters which used to meet on Sunday afternoons. It was like a Sunday School class; we had a badge. I'm trying to think of the name of the person who ran it. It was run by a chap in Lovelace Close. The Scoutmaster was a Mr. Ingram.

As you come to the crossroads at Effingham Junction, do a left turn and go down the road a bit and there's a house on the right hand side and that's where Miss Poupart lived. She was a well known character, she used to keep the key to the hall and we used to go there to get the key from her to play table tennis – put the gas fire on, gas was cheaper in those days and it used to get nice and warm.

2 Station Cottages, when we first moved there, there were 3 of us, my brother, my sister and myself; three in a bed. And on a summer's night, we used to lie there and listen to the nightingales singing in the woods opposite – a beautiful sound! I actually remember that, I haven't heard a nightingale since, I think.

Jessica Page and Eddie Crouch reminisce together

Jessica

At the time of the beginning of the War, we had just moved to Effingham permanently and I think it was late '38 [or] '39 and we lived in High Barn Road which is on the south end of Effingham going up to Ranmore and we lived in a house called Fiddlers' Green which is still there and still called the same name. My parents lived there for over 30 years. These are my memories of the Common at that time just before the Second World War when I was nine years old and used to play down with some friends in that area, because otherwise we were always up at the Ranmore side to play so these are only rather disjointed, but I have mainly memories of Effingham Common East Court.

My recollection is that it was quite close rather nice grass which had been obviously browsed by sheep so it was really rather close grass and to begin with it was really rather pleasant and I think I can even remember seeing some harebells. And it had large may bushes and blackthorn all over it. But by 1939 the bushes were getting more and more huge and there was less and less grass in between and you really had to thread your way through. And we used to come down to play sometimes with some other children and the Lee Brook then, wasn't a straight line, but it was reasonably straight from the corner of Leebrooke Farm and it went roughly along the north boundary of the cricket pitch and ended up where there is a pipe under the road, and I imagine that's always been there, and it goes on to Norwood Farm and ends up in the water at Norwood Farm. We used to once or twice paddle in it, so that late spring there was plenty of water in it and I don't remember if it dried out in the summer, but I think possibly not, I think there was more water.

It was definitely more of a stream and it was very attractive. The whole Common looked quite different because it was so overgrown rather attractive, but I do remember thinking, 'Oh it's a pity that these bushes are now getting so big you can hardly get through'. Then the War came and I remember seeing these big machines on the Common and they just tore everything up and I am particularly talking about Effingham Common East Court because we didn't seem to go up to Hooke Common. I actually lived in High Barn Road which is at the top part of Effingham and it was a long way away so we only saw it when we came down to play with friends who lived down here and if we were going to the station. But I do remember the machines all over it and it looked so different because the whole thing was flat and open. It was then ploughed and for the rest of the War it was used for Dig for Victory and there were various crops.

Eddie
I came to Effingham in 1946, and Effingham Common as I knew it then had been cultivated during the War and leased to a farmer called Skinner who continued to farm it for a number of years – not all of the Common as we see it today was cultivated. Merely the bit if you're travelling towards the Junction on the left hand side beyond the cricket field. Other areas to the south of that and on the other side of the road were still usable by Commoners if they wanted to, although a lot of those bits have been sold off to different owners and there was always a bit at the front at the northern end of the Common which was reserved for those Commoners who still had rights to be exercised.

Jessica
When the War began, the War Agricultural Department commandeered land for the Dig for Victory and when the Effingham Common was grubbed up and ploughed the contract was given to a farmer called Murrells who lived at Leewood Farm and had fields in that area. He took over the farming but there was another farmer called Hinde who came from Bookham and he felt that he should have been given the contract and so there was bad blood between them which resulted in all sorts of misdeeds which I'll leave Eddie to tell you about.

Eddie
Well Hinde used to ride his horses over Murrells' farmland which upset him no end, as a result of which Murrells got his

tractor and drove it at Hinde on the Common one day – luckily everyone escaped unhurt but because of this Murrell tried to put some fencing round the Common. But a Brigadier Flaviell [lived at Huckamoor] and Adrian Estler used to go out at night and cut this fencing for two reasons: they had Common Rights and being a Common it couldn't be fenced, and ultimately, Murrells was forced to take the fencing down.

There was another story concerning Hinde and Murrells in that Hinde was aware that Murrells was paying far too much attention to Hinde's wife and as a result of which Hinde and his sons chased Murrells round the Common with a horsewhip.

Jessica
I'll just say a few words about Adrian Estler who lived at Leebrooke Farm and is very much bound up in the history of Effingham Common. He was a commoner and Leebrooke Farm is just beyond the cricket pitch and he at that time very early in the War was married and had a daughter, but that marriage broke up and for most of the time he was on his own. He had a horse called William which was a piebald and he grazed this horse on the Common, mostly on East Court; I think only between Wise Folly and the road and sometimes on the other side nearer The Willows.

Eddie
My recollections of Adrian are bound up with the cricket club. Cricket has been played on that part of the Common reputedly for more than 100 years. The site was given to the Cricket Club by the Parish Council [actually by the Lord of the Manor] and of course it continues to be used today. Adrian was a great supporter of the club and he played for them and he used to give us transport to away matches. This transport was in the form of a very battered and ancient Rolls Royce the doors of which didn't open, and I can't remember a top, but there might have been one. Anyway we had to climb over the doors to get in it and we also had all the kit in it as well. There was usually about half a dozen of us in this ramshackle vehicle and if you can visualise Adrian being a somewhat tall man, never immaculately dressed in any shape or form and wore an enormous hat, and we'd turn up for away matches in this ramshackle vehicle. Adrian was quite a good cricketer and in home matches we'd turn up with wives to do the teas and children to be amused and when we were batting, Adrian used to get hold of the horse, William, and most of the, well certainly all my children and most of the other player's children had rides on this horse during the course of the afternoon.

Talking about the Cricket Club, it's reputed to have been there for 150 years, but I'm not sure of this, but I played there from the late 40s to the early 60s when the ball was hitting me more than I was hitting it. But to have a half day's fielding in the outfield at the beginning of the season was quite hard work and you needed a good day's rest afterwards and I remember also fielding one day and a kestrel caught a vole and came and perched on one of the stumps, not one of the cricket stumps, one of the fence stumps within a few yards of me and religiously ate it while I was trying to concentrate on the fielding. It's just one of those things that happen.

It was very boggy in the outfield. We later had it mole drained which was a bit better but it was pretty sticky stuff early in the season. And it was also a while before we got the square into any sort of proper condition, bearing in mind we didn't wear helmets, in those days, you had to duck and weave quite a bit if a fast bowler was on.

The pavilion in those days was just a hut. We did get planning permission later on to build what is virtually there now with a bar and changing rooms with running water inside instead of a cold tap, would you believe?

We had nets in those days. And the sight screens – in the good old days, the Denbies Estate had their own estate cricket team but with the demise of the Estate they had sundry things left over and that's where the Effingham team acquired their sight screens.

Jessica
The Cricket Club had considerable problems because as it was common land they couldn't fence the whole cricket pitch off. They had a fence of sorts round two sides and some posts along the cricket pitch road. And the problem was we got horse riders who totally disregard any proper horse riding paths. There is only one Bridleway which runs along the edge of the Common and they used to ride across the cricket area and out on to the Common. This was eventually stopped because the County Council put in a stile and proper fence across a footpath which runs along the back of the pavilion which stopped the horses going through. Also I believe they had trouble with motor cycles who even rode across the square and as it was very soggy, even after the mole draining, there was considerable damage done.

While we were talking about the Common, we quite forgot to mention that there was a pound for straying animals which was situated just above the village pond which is on the Effingham Common East Court on the south end and we don't know the exact location but we think it was between the pond and what is now Lower Farm Road. Also there was a gate, the Common was gated at both ends and we think the gate was in the pond area, possibly slightly to the south of the pond. There was another gate, we have an old photograph which shows it quite clearly and it was just before Effingham Junction Station. When we come on later to the battle for Effingham Common, one of the people who gave evidence there said that as a young boy, he remembered opening the gates for the gentry to go through to the station which was a wonderful link with the past.

In 1965 the Government had found that many Commons and Village Greens were being lost to development and they decided that it would be a very good thing to have all these tracts of land registered and so they passed an Act; the Commons Registration Act in 1965 whereby all these pieces of land should be registered and claimed for perpetuity. Effingham PC registered Effingham Common. All Commons and Greens are nearly always owned by a private owner and Effingham Common was at that time owned by a Mr. Charles Calburn who was the Lord of the Manor. He did not support the claim; he said that he rejected the claim and that it was no longer common land, so we had to go to court and we had solicitors and a QC and we had to raise £6,000 which for a small village like Effingham was an enormous amount of money.

Eddie
One can't let the story of the registration of the Common pass without reference to the work of Dora Worthington. Dora Worthington was a Parish Councillor at the time who lived in Byway Cottage, Heathview which although it has a Horsley address is in Effingham and in fact backs on to the Common. She was tireless in obtaining written statements of evidence from various people researching this and that and helping with the briefing of solicitors. In fact the greatest credit goes to her that the Common is now in the safe status that it is and I hope the village will be forever grateful to her for all she did.

Jessica
We finally got the acknowledgement that we had won our Common's rights and our rights for our Commoners in 1976 and there was much celebration. This restored the rights that Adrian Estler lost over William in 1959 so the four Commoners were; Leebrooke Farm which was at that time Adrian Estler so he won his rights back, Slaters Oak, Huckamoor and The Willows.

It is interesting to note that the Commoners' Rights go with the property not with the owner of the property so the four properties have the rights in perpetuity and the fact that the properties have all changed hands since those days has no significance whatsoever.

In recent years the Calburn family have sold off most of, retaining a little piece we think. The bulk of it is owned by the Borough Council and the rest by people whose property fronts on to the Common and we think there may be 6, 7, 8 different owners.

One of the more serious consequences of this sell-off and buying by different individuals pieces of the Common was the land bought by The Willows on either side of Lower Farm Road. Unbeknownst to them they bought the land because they had polo ponies but they also bought the road and this gave them the opportunity to see if they could make some money in charges for people who lived in Lower Farm Road and whose deeds were not so clear as some of the older houses. Lower Farm Road had been part of the Easton Estate and had been sold off in the 1920s and 50s.

Eddie
There was a company called the Surrey Land Development Company who owned all the spare frontages and part of the old Denbies Northern Estate. I remember back in the 50s would you believe it at £5.00 per foot frontage. That estate has now changed hands and the original freeholders no longer exist, but Lower Farm Road is a private road. There was an attempt of the freeholders of the road trying to obtain access fees from the freeholders of property in the road.

Jessica
The road itself is owned by Peter Skinner who at one time after the War had the managership of the Common and farmed the Common for the Calburn family. He also put manure on either side of Lower Farm Road to the horror of the residents as it was particularly unpleasant stuff. Anyway he owns the part of the road from the houses down to the end and he owns the fields beyond and he made lakes in the fields beyond. The Willows bought the front piece from the road to where the houses begin and there was quite a problem for some people whose deeds were not clear and who wished to move and were forced to pay quite considerable sums of money to the family who owned The Willows so that they could get their title to pass over this piece of Common land. This had been going on up and down the country and the government were horrified at some of the prices that were being charged and the passed a law saying that people

in these houses could establish their own right and this put a stop to this ransom for the access.

The Common in my mind has always been associated with a good deal of colourful characters. We've mentioned a good deal about Adrian Estler. I believe he was educated at Eton but he spent most of his life as a tree surgeon.

In The Willows there was a woman called Miss Meacock, and she had on her grand piano a picture of her with her Prince of Wales feathers where she'd been presented at court and she was a very large lady as I remember her. She rode a white horse which was rather highly strung and on several occasions it used to go all over the road carrying on, with traffic building up on either side and Miss Meacock rather red in the face but well in control.

Then opposite her in Lower Farm was Miss O'Hagan who unfortunately was a bit of a drinker and she owned a shot gun and in her worst moments, if anyone turned up in her drive, she used to fire on them with the shot gun so she was someone people fought shy of. She managed though, Lower Farm house was in very poor condition and she managed to get the Borough Council to allow her to build a very small two up two down house at the back of her property. This over the years has become a very large mansion. Anyway when she moved from one house to the other and then died people going into Lower Farm opened the cupboard doors and were covered in empty gin bottles which fell out on them and also round the house, various doors were peppered with shotgun pellets.

Ivor Gillespie

The Common was cleared during the War to grow food; before the War there was none of this openness at all, it was all scrubland with bushes and so on.

When I came [in about 1968] there were a lot of nightingales and there haven't been any in recent years, until last year – [when I was] coming home from town – there was a nightingale singing in the carpark at the station, and this year I have heard one once. They're around but the other thing of course that's gone – well a lot of things have gone – but I haven't heard any cuckoos this year. And also what has gone are the swallows. I had swallows nesting in my stables when I came, but they disappeared about ten years ago. I had martins and there aren't any martins this year for the first time, until yesterday it so happened I saw a pair of martins flying across the stable yard, but that is the first one this year. Swallows and martins are much less frequent as are peewits – lapwings. There were a lot of lapwings flying up and down on the Common and of course there used to be a lot of skylarks; there used to be a lot of skylark song. All of that is diminished. I don't hear any skylarks' song now although they tell me there are still skylarks on the Common. Everything is diminishing, noticeably the sparrows. They used to rise in clouds when I first came here but now they've disappeared completely until this year when they are back in small quantities – half a dozen sparrows hopping round the yard; the most I've seen for a long time – I suppose these things come and go for a bit.

Leebrooke Farm was occupied by Mr. Estler, Adrian Estler. He was a character. On one occasion he said to me (this must have been about 1970), he said 'Well, my wife left me in 1935 [1945?] and I haven't done any housework since'. He lived a very casual life indeed. He used to take a newspaper, and I understand he never threw it out and there was a roomful of daily newspapers going back 40 years when he died. But what he didn't do was look after the house, and dry rot got in there and pervaded the house; and effectively that's why it's got to come down, because it will take too much money to put it right. I think it was in '88 he died [it was actually in 1990].

Estler used to be a tree surgeon but he wasn't very good for business for himself, really. I got him in to look at a tree one day that needed some attention and he said 'Oh I'd take the whole thing down', and walked away. He was a very amiable pleasant neighbour although he did feature in the newspapers some time in the 60s, might be 70s, when he had a row over Bill, his horse, with another local resident who lived in Great Lee Wood somewhere. And I remember coming home on the train one night and opening the *Evening Standard* and reading headlines about this because it had ended up in court. The other fellow had taken a whip to Bill and to Estler, that sort of thing. Other locals will remember this, but I found Estler a very pleasant amiable eccentric.

[During a subsequent discussion in January 2011, Ivor recalled that Adrian had lived with his brother Mervyn Estler (who predeceased Adrian); the two brothers were not on speaking terms and used to watch the cricket matches on the Common while sitting on opposite sides of the pitch.]

I remember Hooke Common because originally that piece there [pointing to a map] was called Hooke Copse. Now when I was a child in Ireland, I used to sometimes hear the British news and there was a fellow called Ludwig Koch. He was a German and he was very much into birds and he recorded and broadcast the Surrey nightingale and he was recording it in Hooke Copse. It [the copse] is now gone because it was knocked down and this is the back of Heathview in East Horsley now. I was surprised when I discovered this because I read somewhere it was Hooke, but in the Ordnance Survey Map (and they're wrong) my house is spelt Hook without an 'e'; but my house is spelt with an 'e' because it was named after Hooke Copse and Hooke Common of course.

Next door of course that is the pond / lake, call it what you will, on the left hand corner of the road going down the hill towards Effingham village. That was tarted up by the council in 1977 in honour of the Queen's Silver Jubilee and I don't think anyone's lifted a finger to it since, but it did look smart then. And along here is the entrance to Tunnicliffe's place; Leewood Farm. Tunnicliffe died. There is a very ancient moat there which was inhabited until 1232 or thereabouts and you can still walk through and there is a ditch still there. And I thought one day when somebody knocked and said could they do some metal detecting? And I thought 'Well there's that moat there,' so I said 'Yes you can check on that field there.' And I sat back and I waited. And they turned up with their findings – a whole lot of horse shoes and a cannon shell which they said was from a Spitfire – but nothing from 1232. But that moat is one of the original antiquities of Effingham.

Tunnicliffe died six or seven years ago. He was 93 or 94 when he died. You could always tell when Mr. Tunnicliffe was coming because the Effingham Common Road would be empty suddenly and then eventually he would come along going at ten miles an hour with 500 cars behind him! And he always did that, he drove in the middle of the road, very nearly in the middle of the road, very slowly and to hell with all the cars behind him. Nice old man.

I don't remember where the gates were on the road. The [Effingham Common] road was tarted up between 1956 and '68. I know that because I was in Horsley at the time and I remember people talking about it at the time, but I don't remember what it was like.

I've heard it said that the fair and the circus used to come, but I've never seen it. The nearest approach I've seen to that sort of carry on is that for some years (and there may have been a deal, I don't know) there used to be vehicles parked on the Common just around Derby Day. Now whether they were there by agreement with the Lord of the Manor or not I don't know but there was never any fair.

Booklist

The History of Effingham in Surrey
Compiled by Monica M. O'Connor.
First edition published 1973 by Effingham Women's Institute
© Originally Monica O'Connor and Effingham Women's Institute; now Effingham Parish Council.

Effingham – A Surrey Village Remembered
Mary and Simon Rice-Oxley, 2006.
ISBN 0-955 2785-1-1

Some Account of the History of Effingham North Common
©Bryan Sherwood, 2008. [Unpublished report to Guildford Borough Council]

Some Account of the History of Effingham North Common
©Bryan Sherwood, 2011. Revised, corrected & enlarged.
[Limited availability: details from Effingham Local History Group]

Websites

Websites come and go. The following are current at time of going to press.

http://www.surreycommunity.info/effinghamparishcouncil/

A slideshow about the Epsom Derby on the BBC website is at
http://news.bbc.co.uk/local/surrey/hi/people_and_places/history/newsid_8719000/8719836.stm

The *Gypsy Roma Traveller History Month* home page is at
http://www.grthm.co.uk/index.php

List of Illustrations

Many of the historic photographs in this publication have been scanned and post-processed by Liz and Chris Hogger. This has helped sharpen and even rescue fading images in a way that has sometimes seemed miraculous. If you have historic photographs that you would be prepared to lend to the Group for sharing with the village, they would be very carefully looked after.

Illus. 3-8, 10 and 19 are reproduced here, by kind permission, from the Mary Rice-Oxley Postcard Collection.
Illus. 25, 31, 32, 34, 36 and 37 are reproduced here, by kind permission, from the archives of Effingham Parish Council.
Illus. 24, 27, 29, 41-46, 48-49 and the one on the back cover are reproduced here by kind permission of Dan Harvey.

Front cover (also appearing as Illus. 5)
Pollarded trees near Tyrrells, early 20thC.

What is a Common?
1. Map of the Common showing the properties with rights.
Produced by Chris Hogger, based on information provided by Brian Hendry and Guildford Borough Council.
2. Huckamoor.
Reproduced by kind permission of Fran Parton.

The Parish Council and Effingham Common
3. Effingham Common Road viewed from the railway bridge.

Picturing the Common
4. Indian Farm, c.1909.
5.-8. Views near Tyrrells, early 20thC.
9. Diagram showing camera positions for Nos. 5-8.
Produced by Chris Hogger, based on research and drawings by Martin Smith.
10. Timber wagon on Effingham Common Road.
11. Man scything the verge, 1936.
Preparations for mains-laying at Effingham Common between April and August 1936. Transco plc. 1936.
- Wandsworth and District Gas Company - FILE - GMO249.
12. Last flight of a Concorde, viewed from Effingham Common, in 2003.
Photograph kindly donated by Diana Smith.

Mapping and the changing landscape of the Common
13. Map adapted from the 1871 Ordnance Survey map.
14. Locations of the Station Cottages.
15. Map showing Brick Field in 1871.
16. Paths around Brick Field.
17. The Station Cottages (detail from Illus. 3).
18. Maps showing the Station Car Park, adapted from various Ordnance Survey maps.

The pond, the pound and the Common Keeper
19. The pond by Effingham Common Road, early 20thC.
20. The pound as marked on the 1919 Ordnance Survey Map.
21. The pound as marked on the 1934 Ordnance Survey Map.

Gypsies and the Common

22. Gypsy encampment on Effingham Common, c.1904.
Reproduced here by kind permission of Ann Wilson.
23. *Time* magazine cover showing Augustus John, 1928.
Public domain image, from the internet.

'An account of the sad, splendid lawsuit of William of Effingham'

24. Mr. Adrian Estler, formally attired.
25. Leebrooke, when Mr. Estler lived there.
Reproduced from *The History of Effingham* by Monica M. O'Connor.
26. Cricket match on Effingham Common, September 2010.
Photograph kindly donated by Liz Hogger.
27. William the (1st) Horse with Denis Harvey.
28. Article from *The Times*, 23 June 1959.
29. William the (1st Horse).
30. Effingham Common, 2010.
Photograph kindly donated by Dave Putland
31. Slaters Oak, 1970s.
Reproduced from *The History of Effingham* by Monica M. O'Connor.
32. Effingham Residents and Ratepayers Association notice, 1973.
33. Album cover of *The Kinks are the Village Green Preservation Society*, 1968.
34. Letter from Mr. Estler, 1975.
35. Flowers at entrance to Effingham Common, 2010.
Photograph kindly donated by Liz Hogger.
36. Mr. Estler on Commoners' Day, 1986.
37. Ray Davies with donkey on Commoners' Day, 1996.

William the 1st, William the 2nd and Adrian

38. William the (2nd) Horse (Bill).
Photograph kindly donated by Martin Smith.
39. Drawing of Bill by Holly Henry.
Kindly donated by Martin Smith.
40. Bill being fed a snack.
Photograph kindly donated by Martin Smith.
41. Bill grazing.
42. Reverse side of the (framed) photograph shown in Illus. 41.
43. Cover of Denis Harvey's book, showing Bill.
44. Mr. Estler's home, Leebrooke, on Effingham Common.
45. Mr. Estler's home, Leebrooke, on Effingham Common.
46. Mr. Estler holding a painting.
47. Obituary for Mr. Estler by Denis Harvey, April 1990.
48. Bill frisking.
49. William the (1st) Horse.

Back cover

William the (2nd) Horse (Bill).

Sources referred to in the text

Page 19
The 5th Survey of Surrey: *A topographical map of the county of Surrey in which is expressed all the roads, lanes, churches, ...&c, the principal observations, by the late John Rocque, topographer to His Majesty,...&c.*
Published in nine sheets by his wife Mary Ann some time after his death in 1762, possibly 1768.

Page 34
Memories by A.M.C.
This booklet is available at the shop of F. Conisbee and Son Butchers, Poulters and Graziers, Park Corner, Ockham Road South, East Horsley. Profit from sale of the booklet goes to charity. It incorporates two publications of reminiscences written down and first published towards the end of her life by Agnes Mabel Conisbee (1862-1945), who lived in the Horsleys from about 1894:
Memories of our Village and W.I by An Old Inhabitant, and
A Few More Memories of our Village

Page 36
Extracts from *Augustus John: The New Biography*, by Michael Holroyd, published by Vintage Books, 1996. Reprinted by permission of The Random House Group Ltd.

Page 46
Extract from *Letters from London*, by Julian Barnes, published by Pan Macmillan, London
Copyright © *Julian Barnes, 1995*

Page 76
The Gypsies: Waggon-time and After
Denis E. Harvey, 1979
B. T. Batsford Ltd., ISBN 0713415487

Vertical Foundat

The physiology, biomechanics and technique of explosive vertical jumping

By: Joel Smith, MS, CSCS

Cover Design by Jake Clark

Illustrations by Jake Clark and Joel Smith

Disclaimer

The information in this book is for educational purposes only. The reader should be cautioned that there is an inherent risk assumed by the participant with any form of physical activity. Those participating in physical training programs should check with their physician prior to initiating such activities. Anyone participating in these training activities should understand that such training initiatives may be dangerous or harmful if performed incorrectly. The author assumes no liability for injury from the adverse effects or consequences from the misuse of the information presented in this text.

Created in the United States of America

ISBN: 978-0692287415

Table of contents

Introduction: A new light on vertical jump training   i

Chapter 1:   Success factors of the explosive vertical athlete   1

Chapter 2:   The nervous system, skill acquisition and motor learning   9

Chapter 3:   Muscle actions and roles in jump performance   15

Chapter 4:   Principles of applying instruction in jump technique   39

Chapter 5:   Biomechanical and sequential considerations of jumping   51

Chapter 6:   Individual training differences: Speed vs. force dominant   55

Chapter 7:   Standing vertical jump technique and biomechanics   71

Chapter 8:   Running jump principles and biomechanics   81

Chapter 9:   Running double leg jumping technique and training concepts   89

Chapter 10:   Running single leg jumping technique and training concepts   103

Chapter 11:   Measuring vertical jump skill in the laboratory   117

Chapter 12:   Exercises and programming for various jump styles   125

Acknowledgements: 135

Introduction

A new light on vertical jump training

Of all athletic skills in the world, one in particular seems to turn the most heads, drop the most jaws, and generate the most highlight replays. That skill is a vertical jump. Amongst the sporting movements of pitching, kicking, tackling, or even sprinting, no athletic movement is chased with more ferocity by athletes than that of escaping the pull of the earth. The vertical jump is one of the most distinctive ways by which athletes define themselves, as the ability to separate one's self from the pull of gravity is perhaps the most noticeable feat in all of athletics.

With vertical jumping comes a variety of training methods revolving around strength, speed and plyometrics. The exercises, and combinations of exercises designed to improve leaping ability are nearly endless. Although much of an athlete's improvement in vertical jump comes from these training means, an intimate knowledge of the physiology and biomechanics of jumping can help any training program become that much better.

Coaches and athletes seeking better jumping ability can learn much through looking into the sea of track and field knowledge. Track and field is an area of sport where events are, literally, down to a science. Coaches and researchers have strived over the years towards perfect technique, optimal training and methods of instructing proper form in the sprinting, jumping and throwing of track and field athletes.

Vertical jumping in the arena of team sports, on the other hand is a bit different. It is more individualized based on one's own strengths and movement strategies. Athletes jumping as high as possible in team sports, off of one or two legs, have at their disposal an optimal, individual style with its own path of maximal development. It is the individual movement of team sport which has kept jump technique training from really catching on amongst sport coach professionals, as instruction often falls on deaf ears when it doesn't match the strengths and ingrained movement patterns of the athlete.

To give better cues and instructions, coaches can arm themselves with the general biomechanical principles perfected through the sport of track and field, and combine this with a better knowledge of individual differences amongst athletes. This combination leads to a variety of cues, instructions and exercises that can maximize the performance of any athlete, and leave no stone unturned regarding technique in the process.

Vertical jump technique is not as easy as telling an athlete to bend their knees more or less when they jump; the process is more involved based on the mechanical principles of jumping, along with an athlete's physiology, strengths and weaknesses. In addition to cues that fit their jumping style, many athletes need to spend time working on specific strength qualities that back proper vertical technique, others just need to improve their global athletic skill-set, and some just need simple instruction. A primary purpose of this book is to define the physiological and biomechanical benchmarks of jumping to allow athletes and coaches to bring about maximal potential in the pursuit of vertical excellence.

Becoming aware of the biomechanical and physiological mechanisms behind an expert jump will help you gain an appreciation and greater knowledge of the muscular actions that set up jumping technique. Through this book, you will also become aware of the physical movement classifications that will determine why an athlete's strength is in standing or running jumps, as well as why two foot jumpers don't often jump well off of one foot. You'll learn the useful cues and instructions that can help an athlete get the most out of their individual style, as well as the times where instruction is liable to set back an athlete's progress. To cap it all off, I'll make sure that you understand the fundamental differences in training that reflect the demands of one or two leg jumping and provide programming samples for either style.

When it comes down to it, sporting excellence is based off of effective *movement*. Often times, we try to paint over a lack of fundamental movement knowledge and ability with the paint-roller of barbell strength. Don't get me wrong, strength is critically important to an athlete's success, but behind the strength must always be that base and reinforcement of proper movement. The athlete winning gold medals aren't always the ones with the highest squat max, after all, but those with the most complete mastery of their event.

Athletes training vertical jump deserve the best knowledge, research, and most importantly, experience based application out there in educating themselves on how to train smarter and more effectively. This is precisely why I have written this book. I wanted to give coaches and athletes a *definitive* source on the roots of athletic movement in relation to vertical jumping, an area that is so often muddied by inexperienced personal trainers and marketing experts. I trust that this book will be your guide in the technical aspects of yourself or your athletes reaching their highest skill and success.

Chapter I

Success factors of the explosive vertical athlete

If there is an over-arching theme to vertical leap ability, it would be that an athlete's ultimate result is the product of two things: Jumping skill and athletic power[1].   Often we only think of jump training in terms of strengthening relevant muscle groups, but this is only half the equation. Jumping is a skill, and even a slow, weak, genetically lacking athlete can still become *great* at the skill of jumping and pull off a better jump than a genetically gifted athlete with a low jumping skill.

The other half of the equation is becoming *powerful;* an athletic beast. How strong, fast and powerful one's jumping muscles are indicates the true ceiling of jumping potential. It is skill that tells those muscles when and how to fire properly. The difference between skill and power is that the skill of vertical jumping can be attained (therefore bringing rapid gains) in a short time, but the process of becoming an athletic beast, the strongest version of one's self physically, is a lifelong process that will span an entire athletic career.

Figure 1.1: The critical components of vertical jump success: Skill and power.

Breaking things down further, there are also subsets of jumping skill and athletic power, such as: Coordination, maximal strength, explosive strength, technique, mental strength, speed and mobility. Ultimately, a vertical jump comes back to the two factors of power and skill, and one shouldn't get too far away from them to maximize their abilities. The focus of this book is on maximizing the skill end of the equation. Only focusing on raw power, as many books and manuals do, doesn't allow for the fundamental knowledge

[1] Baggett, Kelly. *Vertical Jump Bible 2.0*. 2012.

of one's own jumping style and the specific paths of strength and plyometric work that exploit that style while strengthening weak points. Learning the proper mechanisms and technique of jumping will also help athletes to potentially gain vertical jump inches in a short period of time, as well as maintaining the their integrity of movement over the course of their training and career.

Jumping and Skill Development

Jumping is a skill. What is a skill? A skill is a *learned* movement, produced by the motor cortex of the brain. Anything you learn in life is a skill such as: writing, eating, tying your shoe, running, throwing or lifting a weight. Anything "athletic" is a skill and must be learned. This may surprise you (sarcasm), but nobody "instantly" becomes a master of a skill. Not only this, but the more complex the skill, the longer it takes to master it! We are typically not talking a matter of weeks when it comes to a skill, but a matter of *years*.

Figure 1.2: *Jumping high is largely a product of skill. Photo Credit Maria Lavelle.*

Now, as far as athletic skills go, the vertical jump certainly isn't the most complicated. Things like pole vaulting, or serving a tennis ball are much more complex than jumping off of the ground. This is why anyone who has excelled in something like pole vault typically has had a knowledgeable and involved coach, and has also studied their technique in comparison to other successful athletes. On the other hand, vertical jumping is a more "primal" skill. It is one that is picked up naturally by many athletes, particularly those with good natural coordination and lots of global athletic practice.

Athletes with a stellar vertical typically don't have a "vertical coach", nor have they read books on jumping biomechanics or technique. Vertical jumping is a skill that can and does come naturally, but athletes who haven't played sports requiring a decent volume of vertical jumping such as volleyball or basketball on a regular basis will have some catching up to do in refining their technique. Even athletes who do jump regularly will often have something to improve, and watching the majority of athletes jump, there is nearly always some aspect of their performance that is holding them back by an inch or two, and sometimes much more! Chances are that athletes who are good at jumping haven't completely maximized their skill.

In regards to athletes who have catching up to do, I have seen some powerful swimmers and tennis players make a vertical jump look like the most awkward thing in the world. If these guys actually played volleyball or a related jumping sport, their jump would increase several inches in a matter of weeks through playing that sport alone. As athletes begin to practice jumping, their brain puts together a "program" over time, using that athlete's individual strengths, to help them achieve maximal lift.

The reason that most people can't jump very high does not lie entirely in their muscle composition, but rather in the fact that they just haven't really developed their skill of jumping. Multiple research studies on vertical jumping ability will tell you that the majority factor in how high a person can jump is actually more related to their *technique* than their power. *To optimally develop any movement, many thousands of repetitions are required.* Most people aspiring to jump higher fall far short of the number of repetitions needed to perfect that skill and instead, start looking for other exercises to "fix themselves", when in reality, they simply need more dedicated practice to jumping itself.

Key Point

Many aspiring athletes tend to look at great jumpers, thinking that they reached their level of performance due to special training or exercises; that perhaps they found a special training program that few knew about. This is rarely, if ever, the case. Talented athletes have good genetics, strong mindsets, addictive personalities, and lots of specific, high-intensity practice under their belt to back it all up. Some lift weights or do plyometrics, but some don't. The key common area is the addictive and deliberate practice of their primary sport movements.

The best way to improve in *any* skill (remember, jumping is a skill!) is to *practice* that skill consistently and with a high level of focus. People who are good at any skill: tennis, baseball, basketball, golf, etc. did not get that way by casually practicing every now and then. They became experts of their skill of choice by years and years of driven practice, encompassing many thousands of repetitions. Here is something to think about: *If someone hasn't practiced at least several thousand jumps in their athletic career, they still have significant room to improve somewhere in the way their body propels itself off the ground.*

Think of the highest jumpers you know, or the best dunkers you see on television or the internet. I can tell you that one thing they all have in common is *not* a special training program or series of exercises. What these athletes have in common is the number of jump repetitions they have performed during their lifetime. They also likely have a strong base of global athleticism through a myriad of hours of team sport play, sprinting, skipping, tumbling and just playing around.

Many great vertical jump athletes, such as dunkers whose exploits are captured on the internet have training programs that consist of nothing more than dunking on a daily basis for up to several hours or more. This principle of repetition is also often times true in the world of track and field jumping. Legendary high jumper, Stefan Holm (Holm leaped a record 59cm over his own head) began jumping over a mock high jump bar at the age of six. He has said that he has probably taken more jumps over the course of his life than anyone else on this earth[2]. He might just be right. The truth of the matter is that the majority of the highest jumpers in the world don't even have what we would call a "training program". Far less have a degree in sports science or have even opened up a book on training. How many college graduates with degrees in exercise science or kinesiology carry with them a 40" vertical jump? Granted, genetics is a huge factor, but I can tell you the answer is not many. Great athletes have acquired the skill of their craft through 1000's of repetitions and unmatched dedication and desire.

Jumping and Athletic Power

Once an athlete is reasonably skilled at the process of jumping, future gains will primarily be the result of the body's ability to rapidly recruit as much muscle as possible into the jump. The manner in which muscle is recruited is somewhat specific to standing and running jumps, so specific power training is always a factor based on what one is trying to improve. Improving

---

[2] Epstein, David J. "Chapter 1." *The Sports Gene*. 26. Print.

athletic power means recruiting more motor neurons (nerves controlling groups of muscle fibers) into the movement, as well as laying down new myofibrils into the working muscle fibers of the jump. Things like squats, deadlifts and plyometrics do a great job at facilitating these adaptations, as well as everyday sporting movements, such as repeated, deliberate practice of maximal jumping, accelerating, cutting and decelerating.

To become a powerful athlete, strong muscles and tendons, along with a well-tuned nervous system make all the difference. We all have different genetics, but absolutely anyone can become a more powerful athlete through the proper channels. In modern training, this includes jump practice, general weightlifting, specific weightlifting, specific plyometric and speed work. In order to maximize skill and power, as well as performing the best when it counts, it is important to address both these areas of training.

The Mental Side of High Performance

It is not athletes with the biggest muscles who win sporting competition (unless we are talking bodybuilding), but rather those athletes who can harness the explosive power of their muscles in the correct manner. This takes a perfect harmony between the brain and body of an athlete. Anyone can perform better by learning to improve what is going on between their ears.

Usually we associate mental training with team sport performance, such as warding off "choking" on a last second shot, or how to get out of a slump, but I'll tell you that mental training is an important factor in becoming a stronger and more explosive athlete. Knowing how to get oneself in the ultimate training zone, and stay there as long as possible is a must for optimal strength and power development (and it certainly won't hurt your sport play either!).

Strong mental skills will help an athlete better acquire jumping skills, and it will also help them to grab every last ounce of power out of their system. Mental skills will help improve motivation, reduce stress, allow the harnessing of adrenaline, make training more fun and reduce burnout. After coaching for many years, I have seen the power of the mind rob an athlete of vertical performance, and also give those who can harness it massive gains in the midst of competition. Our thoughts can alter our physiology, and it is reflected by the attitude an athlete carries in their effort towards training.

How much can working on ones mindset improve vertical jump? It is hard to say exactly, and it is different between athletes, but I strongly believe that it can help jumping ability by several inches, depending on the athlete in question over the course of their career. A critical link to performance, the mental ability, drive and motivation of the athlete, should not be overlooked as it may be the number one factor on whether or not a training program will reach its ultimate success!

A Comprehensive View of Performance

Training, technique and mindset are the most important three factors that instantly come to mind when we think of training to acquire better performance, but there are a great number of factors that exist that determine exactly how powerful an athlete can become and how high they will jump. Reaching ones ultimate level of performance is the result of many pieces working together. Building athletic power relies on the fine-tuned physical state of the body, which is the product of many elements outside of the training program. These include:

- Stress levels
- Nutrition
- Sleep
- Social support
- Competition and expectations
- Body fat percentage
- Training environment
- Motivational factors
- Hormonal profile

There are also un-changeable factors at play such as age and genetics. It is important to consider that each of these areas hold the potential to raise ones performance by 1-2%. Alone, these areas might help a little, but by striving to maximize them all, one can raise their performance *considerably*! I'll admit that an athlete can get their biggest initial gains by having a good training program, optimizing their jump technique, and having a driven mindset and training environment, but an athlete will never reach their genetic limit unless each of these factors is accounted for.

An advantage of performance manuals that are written to improve vertical, strength and speed is that many of the better ones will typically encourage proper recovery protocols spanning nutrition to sleep. Some athletes need to watch their nutrition and recovery more than they do their training program, so even though the programming may not be optimal in these types of programs, they have an advantage in creating a total awareness of the training result.

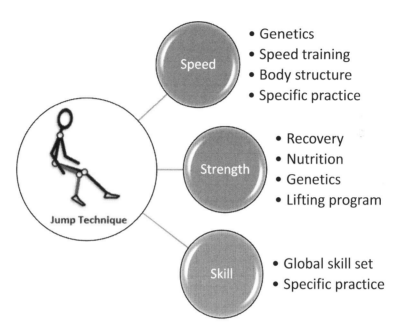

Figure 1.3: Chart of factors determining jump technique.

Building an athlete's vertical jump to its highest level is *not* just the result of a training program, but many factors. When it comes to training, the root of an athlete's jumping ability is the technique they use to propel themselves to maximal vertical. Coordination (skill), speed and strength make up what an athlete's jump technique will ultimately look like. See figure 1.3 above for an illustration of this concept. The process of improving vertical leap is an integrated one, as strength changes in the weight room can have an effect on the technique displayed on the field of play. Because of this integration, giving simple cues or instructions alone to an athlete, in order to improve their jump height is not the optimal path. In order to maximize vertical training, a synthesis of technique and strength is required. Reading this book will give insight to optimize the *total* process.

Chapter II

The nervous system, skill acquisition and motor learning

A perfectly executed vertical jump is a testament to our amazing bodies. Neural impulses travel at lightning speed, signaling muscles to contract with extreme force upon tendons that magnify the velocity and power of the effort to the skeletal frame. The skeleton translates it all to movement that is precise, fast, and powerful. This all happens in tenths of a second, in a very specific and intelligent coordination, all relative to the limb lengths, muscular layout and neural tuning of the athlete. Everything in a jump is controlled by an organ that processes information exponentially faster than the most powerful supercomputers in the world called your *brain*. The result: The human body lifting upwards and breaking the bonds of gravity for a brief moment before returning to the earth.

A vertical jump is a lot more than strong muscles contracting to push an athlete skywards. It is the harmony of different limbs, moving at different speeds at precisely the right time. During a vertical leap, an athlete will lower their center of gravity by bending at the hips and knees as their muscles and connective tissues lengthen and store energy. The joint flexion results in a fast stretch of the muscle tissues of the calves, quadriceps, hamstrings, glutes and spinal erectors. This rapid stretch triggers an involuntary reflex through the spinal cord, signaling rapid contraction that is far more powerful and efficient than what an athlete could pull off via conscious contraction. In an instant, the muscles transmit force to tendons which stretch and recoil, using stored energy to propel the athlete skyward.

The specific and controlled sequence by which this happens has been stored in the cerebellum of the brain. The brain is the ultimate controller of human movement, and any skill relies on precise nervous system control. Even performing actions like squatting or deadlifting a maximal weight is a skill. Squatting and deadlifting (and other forms of lifting) are very useful for jumping higher, but always remember that they are *separate* skills than jumping. An athlete can have the power in their muscles to squat a 400lb weight, but only be able to manage 300lb simply because they haven't nailed down the squatting skill quite yet. This is going to be the case with many elite jumpers you have seen who haven't touched a weight in their lives. These athletes have the power in their muscles to squat heavy weights, their brain just has no clue how to put together the best motor program to do that. Their systems are not used to the specific neuromuscular groove required to perform maximal squats and deadlifts!

There will be times during the course of training where programming will favor a good portion of moderate to heavier weightlifting, but there are also areas of the training scheme when the volume of heavy weightlifting will be reduced in favor of lighter and faster work. When an athlete moves to quicker, more specific training, the volume of the lifting may be reduced to the point where the squat or deadlift 1RM will temporarily go down simply because it isn't being given the attention to maintain itself in terms of *skill*.

Key Point

There are those few athletes whose jumping style and nervous system gearing allows their vertical leap to respond extremely well to doing only weightlifting for periods of time, but this is reflected primarily in standing and slow moving vertical leaps, and not so much running jumps. Barbell focused training will often degrade single leg leaping ability for its duration.

During these times of reduced lifting, the muscles may have more power than ever, which is reflected in a jumping and speed increase! The lifting max just went down, however, because the body moved away from the slow speed, high force skill of squatting for a short time to direct all adaptation reserves towards the speed and power capabilities of the athlete. How high an athlete is currently capable of jumping (or the specific sport skill they are training for) is determined by a fancy term called "level of physical preparedness" which simply refers to how powerful the specific muscles and motor patterns, relative to jumping, currently are. Being able to lift more weight in a squat or deadlift doesn't always mean a higher level of physical preparedness towards jumping (although often it does). Being able to lift more weight on the bar may, at times, just mean that the body had to go "out of its way" to adapt a motor pattern specific to lifting more weight, and chances are to do this it had to drop some adaptations that would have helped out jumping or sprinting!

Early increases in lifting and strength training maxes are almost always useful for athletes, especially those of novice to intermediate training levels. Since athletes can literally put more weight on the bar every time they walk in the weight room for their first several training sessions, it doesn't tax the adaptation reserve of the body to improve these lifts, and this process can also help out vertical jump power, and even key aspects of technique, as we will learn later. It is the deliberate *overemphasis* on the process of strength training that can throw things out of balance, particularly for those athletes who are beyond the intermediate stage of training. Lifting is critically important to the long term success of 90% of vertical jump trainees, but it needs to be done smart and correctly.

There are times that the human body needs to shift its emphasis in skill acquisition to reach the highest levels of performance. The nervous system is very plastic, and will form itself to the primary training means of the time, regardless of the size and power within the muscles. As an example, world class track and field triple jumpers, in their most important competition period of the season, will actually find themselves at a place where their relatively slower standing triple jump and standing long jumps go *down* in order to allow their higher velocity, full approach triple jump to peak out and reach maximal performance. Whatever the exact phase of training, any vertical training program should revolve around improving the skill and power of the exact style of vertical jump via the nervous system *first*, and the size/strength/endurance of the muscles *secondly*. Spending too much time focusing only on raw athletic power without the accompanying *specific* skill will limit results.

Practice Makes Perfect

No great leaper has only been jumping for one or two years; they have played in sports since childhood, developing a level of global athleticism, and also developed a basic set of jump related skills. Most of them *grew up* jumping and striving for maximal speed and vertical jump height. The capacity to increase vertical leap is a bit different than other dynamic exploits such as sprinting. You have probably heard the old school coach statement say: "you can't teach speed". To an extent, this is true. An athlete can only improve their time in the 100m dash by a limited margin; experts will say that a developed male not specifically trained can drop around 10% in their 100m dash time, *at best*, through long term training. This means a physically mature athlete, new to track and field, who runs an 11.5 in their first race, can at best, hope to run around 10.5 down the road of their career. Don't start worrying quite yet about the ceiling on jumping though; there is less room for improvement in sprinting compared to jumping due to the ground contact time and window of force production involved in sprinting. Sprinting allows for ground contact times of a tenth of a second or less, which give athletes very little time to apply force. The short and powerful forces that are applied during sprinting are a product of some of the following factors:

- Fast twitch fiber proportion
- Muscle fascicle length
- Tendon length and pliability
- Tendon insertion and moment arm of key joints (such as the ankle)
- Nervous system strength and speed (central drive)
- Skeletal structure aspects (femur length)

Although many of these same qualities determine how high an athlete can ultimately jump, *vertical jumping is much more trainable due to the fact that there is significantly more time that the athlete spends on the ground*, allowing more room for various styles of jumping that capitalize on the strengths and weaknesses of the individual. Vertical jump training will typically allow up to a 20-30% boost on the vertical jump of a mature athlete in a relatively untrained state, and sometimes more. Vertical jumping is often more trainable than sprinting because many athletes grow up with more accelerating, sprinting and cutting practice than they do jumping practice within the scope of most sports.

Key Point

Athletes who want to jump higher need to practice often. Spend time watching elite jumpers and be aware of how they perform. Practice a variety of jumps in a high-octane environment. Spend time feeling the rhythm and sequence of various parts of jump technique.

Unlike sprinting, which carries with it one basic technical model (a technical model is considered the "ultimate technique" by which a skill is performed), successful jumpers may carry with them a range of technical models and abilities depending on their strengths and weaknesses. This is true for both single and double leg jumpers, and represents the beauty of training vertical leap: even athletes who are not genetically "gifted" still can find ways to leave the pull of the earth. With vertical jump training, there is much to be gained, and the process of reaching ultimate development is both consuming and rewarding. Bottom line: No matter where an athlete is in their journey towards a higher vertical leap, they can still find improvement. The key to mastering the skill of jumping, and finding one's highest level, is a base of proper movement and deliberate practice repetitions.

Although simply practicing a movement may seem routine and boring, there are incredible adaptations that take place on the level of the nervous system, just from specific practice. Know that athletes who are the best in any event area got that way through a mastery of the simple things, and not spending all their time on the latest training fad. I would like to think that you will believe me when I say that a critical ingredient in long term improvement is practice, but I'll also tell you why this helps on a neurological level. The following are three adaptations which happen during the repetition and practice of vertical jumping itself.

1. **Muscular coordination:** Muscle coordination happens on two levels: Coordination between various muscle groups, and coordination within the fibers of individual muscles. Coordination within the muscle, or "intra-muscular" coordination, will allow increases in the strength and power of an individual muscle. This means more muscle fibers fire, and do so in a more synchronized pattern than before. The brain will now wire more power to each muscle involved in a skill. Coordination between muscle groups, or "inter-muscular" coordination refers to muscles learning to work in a better sequence with each other during a skill. For example, in a vertical jump, the glutes, quads, hamstrings, spinal erectors and calves will learn to fire in the best possible order to give maximal vertical lift. If every muscle involved in a vertical leap fired maximally at the exact same time, you would probably end up not jumping very high, and shortly thereafter be on a trip to the hospital!

2. **Myelination of motor neurons:** Myelination is one of the most exciting aspects of repetitive movement. When an athlete practices a skill repeatedly, nerves conducting signals from the brain to the muscle will thicken their coating of a substance known as "myelin". The thicker the myelin coating, the faster the signals from the brain to the muscle travel and athletes will now be able to perform that skill quicker and more powerfully. A great example of this would be nerves running to the hands of a skilled piano player, as they are covered in a significantly greater amount of myelin than a novice player, allowing for faster and more precise striking of the keys.

3. **Motor learning:** Your brain is essentially a computer that stores all sorts of "programs" of human movement. When you practice jumping and special strength exercises similar to jumping, your brain will continually *perfect* that jumping program. Most athletes are not running a "perfect program" and still need plenty of deliberate practice. There is also a high chance that several exercises one may be performing are detracting from that perfect motor program due to conflicting nature of stimuli. Aside from this, the use of various specific exercises, resisted, and lightened work can help the brain to be able to develop a motor program that allows the body to exceed previous performances.

In conclusion, there are many factors that contribute to athletic performance, but ultimately, the number one piece in jumping higher is teaching the nervous system to perform as powerfully as possible in a manner specific to the type of vertical jump that an athlete is trying to build. Realize that jumping off of one and two feet are different motor skills, and there are different routes to peak physical preparedness for either skill. Even within jumping off of two feet, athletes will use different strategies to defy gravity, such as relying on muscular force, or utilizing momentum through the skeletal frame. Because of these differences, it makes good sense to get a handle on the key elements of the muscular contributions to each of these jump skills to be able to maximize both technique and training.

Chapter III

Muscle actions and roles in jump performance

The relationship between the nervous system and muscles of an athlete is of highest importance in improving athletic performance. Muscles by themselves are useless unless they have a controller. In addition, muscles do much more than simply contract and tug on tendons when activated, but carry with them a variety of "actions".

A muscle action is a way that a muscle contracts, which is either by lengthening, shortening, or staying the same length. Not all muscle actions are created equally. They all have different tasks, and there are different ways in which they must be trained and applied to explosive athletic development. It is helpful to understand how muscle contractions work, as this shows up in reinforcing the technique that is applied to jump technique, and also powerful exercises such as the depth jump, squat-drop jump, or even a kettlebell swing. There are four ways in which a muscle can contract (many people usually describe three). These four phases are:

- Eccentric
- Isometric
- Explosive Isometric
- Concentric

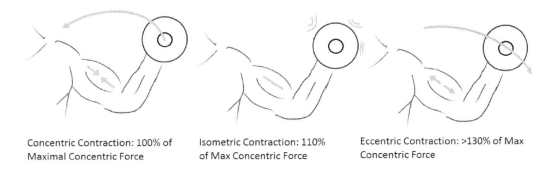

Concentric Contraction: 100% of
Maximal Concentric Force

Isometric Contraction: 110%
of Max Concentric Force

Eccentric Contraction: >130% of Max
Concentric Force

Figure 3.1: Illustration of eccentric, isometric and concentric muscle actions.

Concentric Muscle Action

A concentric muscle contraction is one where a muscle shortens and positive work is done such as lifting a weight. As you take your arm from a straight position to a flexed one, squeezing your bicep along the way, your bicep is contracting concentrically. When we speak in terms of strength training, such as "I can bench press 200lb", what we mean from a muscle phase point of view is: I can concentrically lift 200lbs off of my chest. Although this is the only phase of muscle contraction where real work is done, it is also the weakest of the four. If you can bench press 200lb, chances are you can isometrically hold 210-220lb for a second or two at your "sticking point" in the lift, and lower 250lb or more under control to your chest from the top of the lift. The strength and quality of the concentric contraction is highly influenced by the quality of the two phases that happen prior to it, especially in fast, athletic movement.

In terms of jumping, concentric muscle actions are most important when moving from a dead start position, such as when sitting on a box and then leaping up. It can also play a primary role in standing vertical jumping when performed with low skill. Most training programs don't revolve much around building the concentric strength and power of the muscles alone (although concentric "starting strength" may be an auxiliary focus in a jump training program). Athletes who are extremely strong, but can't jump very high will often be good at jumping from a dead stop in comparison to their normal vertical jumps that involve a dip down and reversal upwards. Of course, this type of slow, concentric dominated jumping is not very useful for sport play.

Isometric Muscle Action

The isometric phase of muscle is one where the muscle is under load, but not changing length. If you walked up to a barbell loaded up with 1,200lbs on the floor and tried to lift it for all you had, every posterior chain, rear extensor muscle in your body would be undergoing an intense isometric contraction, not changing length, but tensing very hard none-the-less. This all happens while the 1,200lbs stayed glued to the floor despite the redness accumulating in your face. The isometric phase of muscle contraction is capable of more muscle tension than the concentric phase by about 10%. For example, if you could arm curl 100lbs from a dead hang, you should be able to at least hold 110lb for a few seconds at the halfway point of the lift.

The isometric phase of muscle contraction is crucial to jumping as it forms the brief moment which occurs between the descent and ascent of the jump. This phase must be as strong as possible to allow maximal energy transfer through the reversal of downward force to upward force. The isometric phase that we encounter while lifting weights is *not* very similar to that encountered in jumping, however, due to the lack of explosion and rate of force development found in its strength training versions. It is for this reason I have listed the closely related "explosive isometric" phase after the eccentric phase which will be described in the next section.

Isometrics performed in the right context have use in athletic power development programs. A strong benefit of isometrics is that they allow for brief moments of extremely high muscle tension; higher than what is going to be found in typical up/down strength training repetitions. They also help to build the stiffness of the muscle-tendon complex, which increases the efficiency of the jumping process. The isometric training that is best suited for this is of a brief nature, however, such as a 2-5 second hold at the bottom of a squat, or a squeeze at the top of a calf raise. Long isometrics (over 10-15 seconds) don't have a whole lot of effectiveness when it comes to training vertical jump[3] as they are so neurologically different than what actually happens in a normal jump process. Isometric training can improve squat jump performance without using the stretch shortening cycle, but this isn't the type of jumping most athletes are interested in improving. Using isometric training alone without any sort of concentric work is a mistake, as this type of training can actually decrease vertical jumping ability.

The best way to use isometrics in a weight room setting are those with a rapid loading phase and short but intense isometric holds. Rapid loading isometrics (such as a squat where an athlete drops aggressively into the bottom position, and then holds it for time before ascending back up) are much better at replicating the isometric phase of sport because of the high rate of force and tension development. These rapid, short duration (2-5 second) holds, done as part of a full lift, are a more effective way to integrate tension into strength work. The best variations of these for improving vertical jump are done with front squats, back squats and split squats.

---

[3] Kubo, Keitaro, Hideaki Yata, Hiroaki Kanehisa, and Tetsuo Fukunaga. "Effects of Isometric Squat Training on the Tendon Stiffness and Jump Performance."*European Journal of Applied Physiology* 96.3 (2006): 305-14.

Eccentric Muscle Action

When muscle is lengthening under load, it is contracting eccentrically. It is in this eccentric phase that the most energy can be stored and the highest forces are possible. This is very important to keep in mind when we talk about plyometric training. For a basic illustration of an eccentric contraction, let's say you bring an arm curl to the top of the movement, near your shoulders. The eccentric phase is you slowly lowering the weight towards the ground under control. Your muscles are lengthening under tension as your arms extend. In the arm curls, let's say again that you have a max of 100lbs. Muscles are capable of creating over 130% tension eccentrically than they are in a concentric contraction, so theoretically you should be able to lower, under control, around 130lbs or more in this manner.

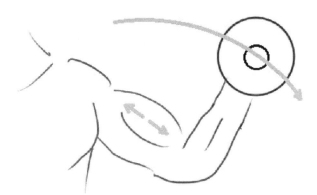

Bicep lengthens under load

Figure 3.2: Eccentric muscle contraction.

The bicep example is a great way to show how the eccentric phase works in a slow, static weightlifting movement, but the eccentric phase works a bit differently in ballistic sport movements. The "storage" of energy during the eccentric phase of jumping, sprinting, throwing, or other ballistic activities is both the result of increased muscle activity, as well as the body storing energy through the elastic tissues that surround and even integrate themselves into the muscles themselves. The exact distribution of how much each mechanism contributes to a jump is not known, but it has been suggested that jumps relying on countermovement and the stretch-shortening cycle (standing and particularly running jumps) rely more on momentum and gravity to produce tension and force, where static jumps from a dead start rely entirely on the muscles to generate power[4]. This is why eccentric training is closely associated with plyometric work, as plyometrics are based on

---

[4] Anderson, Frank C., and Marcus G. Pandy. "Storage and Utilization of Elastic Strain Energy during Jumping." *Journal of Biomechanics* 26.12 (1993): 1413-427.

momentum, and the limiter on strength training is the concentric phase of the lift. Bottom line, *the faster the running start or downwards dip leading into the jump, the more the jump relies on elastic energy.*

Knowing this, one can see how training that replicates the rapid and explosive loading of both the muscles and connective tissues is crucial in helping athletes to reach their highest vertical ability. The effectiveness by which the body stores energy in the eccentric phase is going to directly transfer to how much energy is released in the upwards part of the jump, and ultimately, how high the athlete will go. Again, much of this occurs on a neurological level, so catering training too heavily towards slow strength and barbell means can push the sequence of jumping out of balance in favor of static strength development.

Explosive Isometric Muscle Action

The explosive isometric phase of muscle contraction occurs when a muscle is sent directly to the isometric phase without a preceding eccentric phase. How does this happen? Look at a single leg jump. An athlete plants on a slightly pre-bent takeoff leg that "gives" very little the moment the plant foot hits the ground. In fact, in a single leg jump, the less the leg moves after planting, the higher the jump will be. This "isometric" is performed in a rapid, violent, and explosive manner due to forces of over 5x

Figure 3.3: Single leg jumping relies heavily on "explosive isometric" muscle action in the plant leg.

bodyweight accumulated in under 1/10th of a second. Talk about rapid loading! Clearly this is a radical and violent activity, and is impossible to replicate in places like the weight room. Even many running two leg jumps generally involve at least one leg that is sent to the isometric phase extremely quickly. This rapid force development in the isometric phase can be called, the "explosive" isometric phase, and it is this phase that may even be more important, and relevant than the eccentric phase in determining sport power.

Research can back this type of muscle/tendon action apart from the other three phases. Studies have shown that in the calf muscles of subjects who performed a jumping push of their foot against a force plate, the muscle fascicles stretched, and then held an isometric contraction while the *Achilles tendon* changed length[5]. In simple terms, when the subjects "jumped", the muscles of the calves quickly stretched (eccentric phase) and then locked up isometrically while the tendon did the mechanical work! This means that our muscles work in drastically different forms during running, jumping and any other stretch-shortening cycle movement than they do in the weight room. This concept shows the importance of specificity and technique in any sporting movement.

Another interesting phenomenon regarding the explosive isometric phase is that there will be significant "pretension" in the associated muscles of a jumping, running, or sprinting movement. This means that the body will turn on associated leg muscles *before* an athlete's foot even hits the ground when planting to jump. This pretension is necessary to facilitate a fast takeoff. If the muscles "waited" until the foot hit the ground to become tense, the reversal of movement to vertical speed would take much longer, and momentum and vertical stiffness would be lost. The explosive isometric phase is one that is trained both generally though strength training, but more importantly, specifically through plyometric and jumping exercises.

Muscle Roles in Various Vertical Jumping Styles

Athletes and coaches interested in jumping higher will invariably ask: "What muscles are the most important for jumping?" Usually the topic of the calves, quads, and glutes will come up, but it is important to know how and why each muscle group is used in different types of jumps to optimize training programs. The quads are important for jumping, but they don't play nearly the same role in a standing vertical jump compared to a running jump off of one leg for height, or for distance for that matter.

---

[5] Kawakami, Y., T. Muraoka, S. Ito, H. Kanehisa, and T. Fukunaga. "In Vivo Muscle Fibre Behaviour during Counter-movement Exercise in Humans Reveals a Significant Role for Tendon Elasticity." *The Journal of Physiology* 540.2 (2002): 635-46.

Knowing which muscles do what in regards to jumping is important from the perspective of selecting strength and weakness building exercises in a program, as well as knowing which muscles to work on, and *not* to work on. Ultimately, vertical jumping (and any sport skill for that matter) is about movement patterns, and not muscles, but because the question is so often asked, we'll quickly get into which muscles are responsible for various vertical jump skills and patterns.

Key Point

Ultimately, training movements is much more important than laboring about which muscles are being trained. Although true, knowing which muscles are important for various styles of training has implications for barbell exercise selection.

Firstly, the easiest way to determine which muscles are responsible for a particular type of jumping from an individual standpoint is to do the following drill: Pick a jump of choice, and do it 100 times with less than 3 seconds rest between each jump. At the end of the drill, you will quickly know which muscles worked the hardest by a strange "burning" sensation in those muscles! You'll also likely be reminded the next day which muscles you used! Although this simple method can be eye opening, as well as practical, let's take a look at the muscles of a jump from a scientific standpoint.

Calves

The calves are the muscle that are often the most associated with jumping from a lay perspective. Looking deeper, their role in jumping is important, but having big calves doesn't mean that an athlete will automatically be a great jumper. Calves are of themselves, not the primary mover in a jump, and they are more force "amplifiers" than movers. This means that they take the force produced from the arms, trunk, hips and quads, and transmit this down into the ground through the foot. In addition to having a "transmitter role", the muscles of the calves themselves are not even as important as the strength and elasticity of the Achilles tendon. The Achilles is actually responsible for a large amount (around 73%) of this force transmission[6], so just doing calf raises focusing on the size and strength of the muscle isn't going to necessarily make a person a better jumper. This being said, calf raises do often help athletes to jump a little higher due to general increases in strength around the ankle, but they aren't revolutionary. The Achilles tendon principle also helps answer the question as to how athletes with skinny looking calves can still jump very high! Again, athletes must train the calves and lower legs specifically to get the best result in regards to jumping, and not just focus on the role of the muscles themselves.

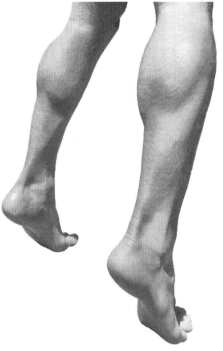

Figure 3.4: The calves, and particularly the Achilles tendon, provide an important force transmission role in jumping.

Although this may seem to sell the calves short, their role is critical in building a top notch jump. Strong calves that are used to create a stiffness in the lower legs and feet effectively turn them into a "pogo stick" that can make jumping both efficient and effective. Optimally training the calves for this task is based on the threefold system of traditional strength, functional isometric strength, and elastic/plyometric training. Much of the training for specific training for calves happens in the course of plyometrics, sprinting and team sport play, so some athletes may have to worry about this aspect of training more than others based on their current level of proficiency.

The Feet and Toes

Many coaches and athletes consider only the role of the calves when looking at jumping, but few look at the role the foot carries in athletic prowess. The foot is the absolute end of the line when it comes to jumping and sprinting, and is ultimately responsible in transmitting force from the body into the

---

[6] Farcy, Nordez, Dorel, Hauraix, Portero, and Rabita. "Interaction between Gastrocnemius Medialis Fascicle and Achilles Tendon Compliance- a New Insight on the Quickrelease Method." *Journal of Applied Physiology*(2013)

ground. When it comes to the foot, the prime area of concern is going to be the *big toe*. The faster an athlete can direct force from the lower leg to the big toe, the more powerful athletic movement will be.

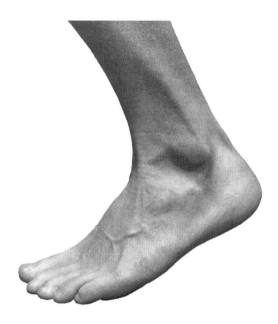

Although training the feet isn't something that is often thought of in the weight room, athletes can often benefit by some barefoot training or specific foot strengthening. This can be done in a variety of ways; anywhere from isometric big-toe squeezes, to towel based foot crunches, to actually squatting barefoot and keeping the pressure of the lift directed into the toe. Any of these methods can be effective for improving the function of an athlete's feet. Big toe strengthening in particular has been shown to increase vertical and horizontal jumping ability significantly vs. controls in untrained athletes[7]. We must always keep in mind that research involving subjects of a low training level is not going to mean that foot training is effective for all athletes, but it certainly can't hurt.

Figure 3.5: The foot is a vital link in athletic performance.

Together, the feet and calves bring up the tail end of what happens in jumping. The faster and more forceful the takeoff of the jump, such as running one leg jumps, the more important this area of the body becomes. Without strong and efficient calves and feet, an athlete will never be able to jump well off of one leg, and will struggle adding significant approach speed into their two leg efforts. Even standing jumps can be improved by maximizing this part of the body. Know that there are athletes who have naturally strong and efficient feet and ankles, so some will benefit from training more than others, but none-the-less it is a part of training that shouldn't be taken lightly.

---

[7] Unger, Caroline L., and Michael J. Wooden. "Effect of Foot Intrinsic Muscle Strength Training on Jump Performance." *Journal of Strength and Conditioning Research* 14.4 (2000): 373-78.

Quadriceps

Where the calves tend to be transmitters of energy in vertical jumping, the "quads" and knee joint are one of the main power sources. For many athletes, the quads are a prime source of propulsion in a jump, especially standing jumps, and for others, they are used just enough to transmit force from the hips down to the Achilles tendon and the foot. The role of the quads can differ in standing jumps, based on the strength of the athlete. Raw power in a standing jump is going to come largely from one of two areas to an athlete: the knee (quads), or the hip (glutes). When muscle force is high in one of these areas during a standing jump, it is lower in the other[8]. The standing vertical jump is where we can easily see the division between "knee dominant" and "hip dominant" athletes. Although this is an effective classification to individualize, assess and train athletes, another useful and perhaps more important distinction will be discussed in chapter 5.

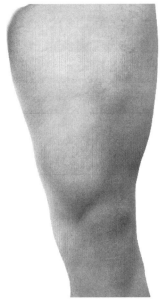

Figure 3.6: The quadriceps are a particularly important muscle in standing vertical jumps.

Despite the individual differences of hip and quadriceps dominance, most of the athletes performing that test of "100 jumps in minimal time" with standing jumps, are going to be feeling their quads burning. The power of jumping must run through the quads in some way, shape or form within the scope of two footed jumping, some athletes emphasizing them more than others. The common injury, "jumper's knee", didn't get its name for nothing!

Knowing the importance of the quads in a standing jump, it is a good reminder that athletes who are strong in the barbell squat are also going to be able to jump well off of two feet. A big squat means that strong quads can produce a lot of force over a long period of time, and send it down the kinetic chain. Of all the lifts directly related to standing

---

[8] Vanezis, Athanasios, and Adrian Lees. "A Biomechanical Analysis of Good and Poor Performers of the Vertical Jump." *Ergonomics* 48.11-14 (2005): 1594-603.

vertical jump, the squat is the highest, and particularly, the deep front squat. The deep front squat is a great exercise for improving two leg jumps due to its heavy reliance on the lower quads, as well as its biomechanical similarities to a vertical jump where force is put into the ground for an extended period of time.

In running jumps, the role of the quads becomes a little different. For mechanically optimal two footed running jumps, they are still vital, but their role changes to more of an eccentric and elastic force transmitter. In quad dominant jumpers, they are often still the primary movers, regardless of technique. In single leg jumping, the quadriceps group are again important for eccentric force transmission. When single leg jumps fail, it is almost always at the knee joint, characterized by a "buckling" where the quadriceps were not strong enough to deal with the eccentric force requirements of the potential leap.

As jumping moves from the vertical to horizontal variety however (such as long jumping), the role of the quads is reduced. The quadriceps are a *vertical* muscle group because they help an athlete position the leg to convert energy *upwards*. They are still important in long jumping and sprinting from a vertical stiffness standpoint, but they are not as important as more vertically oriented jumps off of one leg. An interesting note in the size of the muscle on the thigh is that good squatters and jumpers off of two legs will tend to have good muscle development in the *lower* thigh, particularly the teardrop muscle called the "vastus medialis". Selective size increases around the lower leg are functional responses to lots of deep squatting, and this transfers well to quadriceps based jumping. Athletes who are not so strong in the squat, but still adept jumpers, will tend to put more muscle mass on their upper thighs and hips, respectively speaking.

Glutes and Hamstrings

Where some athletes use their quads to drive the primary force of jumping, others emphasize the muscles that control and extend the hip. These hip extending muscles are the glutes and hamstrings and, of these two, the glutes are the most important for jumping. In fact, the glutes are a vital muscle for virtually any athletic movement where the feet are on the ground. The hamstrings, which do contribute to jumping, also work with the glutes to extend the hip, particularly the upper fibers, although their greatest importance is in high velocity movements, such as top-speed sprinting.

You can typically distinguish an athlete who relies on glute propulsion in a vertical jump by a pronounced forward bend at the hip during the eccentric loading phase. These athletes also tend to have well developed glutes, and fairly skinny lower thighs. Although the quads are used a bit less in this scenario, respectively, they are still important to the ultimate result. Where the quad dominant jumper feeds into barbell squatting movements, hip dominant jumpers are usually good deadlifters, as the deadlift resembles the powerful "hip hinge" action of the jump. Although the deadlift feeds into the hip hinge action of jumping, both squats and deadlifts must be used for glute dominant athletes to reach their full jumping potential.

The function of the glutes in jumping becomes larger as more speed is brought into a jump, regardless of whether the jump is off of one or two feet. This is because fast jumps carry with them a horizontal element, and it is the horizontal element of jumping that relies heavily on the hips, glutes and upper hamstrings. As a general rule, fast approach jumps place a high priority on the hips and ankles, and slower two footed jumps rely more on the quads. Athletes without strong hips will typically struggle in adding speed to their jump, and athletes with weak quads generally don't do well in standing jumps. In each of these athletes, specific strength development must accompany approach cues and instructions to allow them to reach their highest potential.

In training, athletes seeking jumping improvement don't have to worry much about specifically increasing the mass and strength of their glutes, as this will happen in proportion to the athlete's jumping style through the course of traditional barbell and plyometrics strength training. Athletes who are seeking improvement in horizontal jumping ability, particularly track and field long and triple jumpers, will want to ensure that they utilize glute specific work, such as hip thrusts and single leg deadlifting variations to improve the force production capacity of this particular muscle group. Although athletes may not need huge glutes to jump high, they do need to ensure that they are at least activating them well through the process of the jump. In this regard, a battery of remedial and isometric exercises may prove useful in giving the athlete a greater connection with his or her posterior.

Arms, Shoulders and Spinal Erectors

The last set of anatomical landmarks important to vertical jumping are the arms, shoulders and back. The arms are the first joint in motion when it comes to vertical jumping. They have a dual function of transmitting force down to the hips, and also finishing the jump by swinging into a position where they raise an athlete's center of mass at takeoff[9]. Force and momentum from the arms and shoulders is transmitted through the postural muscles of the spinal erectors and core, down to the hips. At the end of the arm swing, the arms end up in a position above the head, which raises the athlete's center of mass. Between these roles, the action of the arms adds about 10-20% more height in a vertical jump compared to a jump with no arm swing.

How much the addition of the arms adds to a vertical jump relies an athlete's level of coordination. Having an athlete perform a vertical jump with and without an arm swing can be an interesting test in this regard. When watching athletes of low jumping skill give their best vertical effort from a standing position their arms often look like they are locked in handcuffs until the later phases of the jump.

Figure 3.7: The vertical medicine ball throw is a great way to train the action of the hip hinge and concentric arm swing in jumping.

---

[9] Lees, Adrian, Jos Vanrenterghem, and Dirk De Clercq. "Understanding How an Arm Swing Enhances Performance in the Vertical Jump." *Journal of Biomechanics* 37.12 (2004): 1929-940.

Encouraging athletes to use a proper arm swing will help improve this portion of jumping, although it may take some time before athletes become familiar enough with this skill for it to make a noticeable improvement on their jump. Strength training can increase the strength of an athlete's arms and shoulders, but since the role of the arms is largely of pure speed and low resistance, upper body strength training won't make much of a difference in this part of a jump. The best training to link the upper body to the lower body for increased jumping power is through various medicine ball throws utilizing a full body, catapulting mechanism. See figure 3.7 for an example of a vertical throw for height, a staple medicine ball exercise for jumpers.

The faster an athlete is moving in their jump approach, the smaller and more compact the arm swing needs to be. A fast jump approach combined with a big arm swing will only slow down the takeoff. On the other hand, a standing vertical jump needs a large arm swing for an athlete to properly take advantage of the added force this motion brings to the table. Coaching the amount of arm swing an athlete uses in a jump is one of the easiest and potentially effective instructions that can be given, as it is a conscious, early-chain fix that improves unconscious movement later in the kinetic chain; namely the established motor patterns of the knees and hips.

Hip Flexors: Friend and Foe to Vertical Jumping

The hip flexors are an important muscle in sprinting, jumping, and nearly any other athletic movement imaginable. Although there are plenty of muscles that flex the hip, the primary ones of concern in jumping are the psoas and iliacus, or "iliopsoas" group. The central quadriceps muscle (the rectus femoris) is also a powerful flexor of the hip in addition to its role in knee extension. Aside from jumping, the hip flexors are a critically important muscle group in the body, as they have many functions in hip stability and power transmission, as well as any movement that involves lifting the knee (virtually anything athletic). They are just as important in sprinting and forward movement as the glutes and hamstrings, and also power the swinging leg knee drive that is present in single leg jumping. Strong and functional hip flexors create greater stability in the hip joint and therefore allow for greater power transmission from the upper to lower body. Many issues in sprinting or gait can be narrowed down to dysfunction in the iliopsoas group.

Many athletes are functional in the hip flexors naturally through a high level of global athleticism, particularly team sports involving sprinting, kicking, or quadruped, ground based movement such as crawling. Over time, athletes can become dysfunctional in this group through extended periods of sitting, lack of global sport performance, and general lack of attention to their well-being. It is in this case that specific strengthening and stretching can go a long way in allowing the hip flexors to stabilize movement, and in the process allow more power to be routed to the legs via the glutes and other primary movers of the hip.

Where the hip flexors can be a "foe" to vertical jump efficiency is when they are too tight. Unfortunately, in average populations, particularly in the Western world, the hip flexors are often both weak and tight from long periods of time sitting at desks, where instead they

Figure 3.8: One of many hip flexor and quad (rectus femoris) stretches.

should be mobile and strong in a healthy, functional athlete. Tight hip flexors act as an "antagonist" to the hip extension (their action is opposite of hip extension) that drives the initial phases of vertical jumping. If an athlete is tight in the hip, they will not be able to extend their torso as powerfully and effectively as if they had more suppleness in that area.

Several minutes of static stretches in the hip flexor area are a remedy to this plaguing issue for many athletes. Research has shown that performing bouts of 30 second stretches in the hip flexors (iliopsoas) and dorsiflexors of the feet (tibialis anterior muscles) significantly improved standing vertical jump height over controls[10]. Based on this study, athletes would be wise to be aware of the tightness of their hip flexor musculature, and be sure to get static stretching in this area prior to jumping performances. Bottom line, strong and mobile hip flexors are the best way to ensure optimal hip function.

---

[10] Sandberg, John B., Dale R. Wagner, Jeffrey M. Willardson, and Gerald A. Smith. "Acute Effects of Antagonist Stretching on Jump Height, Torque, and Electromyography of Agonist Musculature." *Journal of Strength and Conditioning Research* (2012): 1.

The Stretch Shortening Cycle: Jumping is More Than Muscle

Maximal strength expressed through outlets such as squatting and deadlifting is extremely important to jumping high, but it isn't everything. There are plenty of strong, gravity-bound athletes out there. Here is a trustworthy paradigm when training athletes.

"Everyone who can jump high is strong. Not everyone who is strong can jump high"

Here is one answer as to why there are strong people who can't jump for a lick: jumping relies heavily on the ability of the body to use a mechanism called "the stretch-shortening cycle". The stretch shortening cycle allows muscles and connective tissue the ability to rapidly store and release energy, and its sequence is performed as follows:

1. A rapid stretch is placed on a muscle; i.e. an athlete dips in preparation to jump and the quadriceps muscle is quickly stretched (eccentric phase).
2. The muscle spindles within the quadriceps muscle detect the rapid stretch and send a signal to the spinal cord for the muscle to rapidly contract.
3. The message runs to the spinal cord. All this happens unconsciously, and also much faster than an athlete could consciously manage.
4. The motor neurons associated with muscle contraction are engaged and the quadriceps muscles contract powerfully (concentric phase).

In addition to allowing extremely powerful muscular contractions, a well-developed stretch shortening cycle will add elastic energy immediately stored in the eccentric phase to the upward (concentric) portion of the jump. An under-developed stretch-shortening cycle will cause a loss of this energy, particularly during the eccentric and isometric phases of the jump, which will cripple a vertical leap. *Athletes with poor stretch shortening cycles will be doomed particularly in fast approach jumps* where the quality of the explosive isometric contraction is relied on, rather than in a standing vertical jump where an athlete can still jump fairly high on concentric muscle power.

Even in more general movements, such as weightlifting, the stretch shortening cycle plays an important role. Research has shown that a bench press performed with a pause of one second at the bottom will result in a 55%

loss of elastic energy available from the stretch shortening cycle[11]. Furthermore, the longer a bar is held at the chest at the bottom of a bench press, the more energy is lost, and the less weight an athlete can lift. It is the same way in a vertical jump, just on a much faster scale! The longer it takes an athlete to reverse themselves from the eccentric phase of a vertical leap, the lower the jump becomes from energy leaks. Nearly any movement in sport is going to involve the stretch shortening cycle, and the vertical jump is no exception.

The Stretch Shortening Cycle Applied to a Vertical Jump

Figure 3.9 on page 31 is an illustrated sequence describing muscle phases we just covered, along with their relation to the stretch shortening cycle during a vertical jump. Let's briefly explore each individual phase and its relation to the total effectiveness of the leap.

Step 1. Eccentric Phase/Explosive Isometric Phase

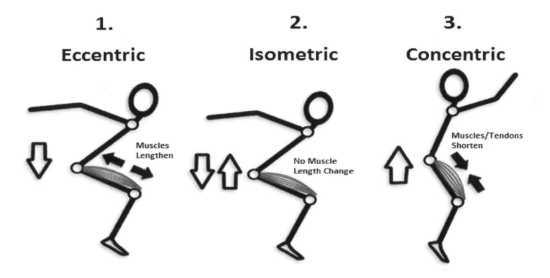

Figure 3.9: Illustrated sequence of muscle phases applied to vertical jumping.

In the eccentric phase of jumping, an athlete lowers their center of gravity, initiated by a rapid backwards swinging of the arms. As the hips, knees and ankles bend, the associated muscles and connective tissues lengthen and

---

[11] Wilson, Gregory J., Bruce C. Elliott, and Graeme A. Wood. "The Effect on Performance of Imposing a Delay during a Stretch-shorten Cycle Movement." *Medicine and Science in Sports and Exercise* 23.3 (1991): 364???370.

store energy in preparation to reverse the movement back upwards. In cases where the athlete immediately finds themselves in the bottom position of a vertical jump, such as a fast running jump, they skip the eccentric phase and move right to the explosive isometric phase of the jump. During this time, proprioceptors called "muscle spindles" are stretched and a nervous signal is sent to the spine indicating a rapid stretch load. Given the signal, the spine shoots back a rapid message for the muscles to contract.

The critical thing to know in regards to a vertical jump is that its potential is determined in the eccentric or explosive isometric phase. The energy that an athlete can store and use during the eccentric phase is going to determine how high, or far, the athlete will go. It is specific jump and plyometric training that maximizes the efficiency of this plyometric phase.

Step 2. Isometric Phase

The athlete hits the bottom (isometric) position of the jump. At this point, the muscles and tendons are beginning to release the elastic energy that has been stored. *A weak or slow isometric phase will rob inches from the jump!* The athlete must be solid through the isometric phase or they will leak energy leading into the rapid reversal of the concentric phase. Something I have noticed about the isometric phase is when instructing athletes through a faster eccentric phase, most initially won't jump any higher. This happens even though this fast eccentric phase is what is required for them to eventually increase the speed and height of their leap. The reason why is they do not initially jump higher is because they are not strong enough yet to handle the increased rate of loading in the isometric phase that comes as the result of a speedy eccentric phase. It takes training to get there!

Figure 3.10: The strength of the isometric phase of the jump is crucial to its success.

The isometric phase is often the phase where most jumps fail. Have you ever attempted to jump when suddenly your knee buckled from under you and you went nowhere? If so, what happened was that another proprioceptor in the muscle (the Golgi Tendon Organ) detected an abnormally large amount of tension buildup, and sent a signal to shut down power in the muscle. The reason that the Golgi Tendon Organ does this is to prevent damage (and for good reason as forces in jumping can exceed ten times bodyweight!). This "shutdown" can be remedied through training which will strengthen connective tissues, as well as raise the threshold (amount of tension) where the Golgi Tendon Organ activates and shuts the jump down. In order to optimally develop the isometric phase of jumping, very specific training is necessary, such as depth jumps (learn more about the depth jump in chapter 11) and related plyometrics. Traditional strength work is actually not the best way to strengthen the isometric phase.

Step 3. Concentric Phase

The athlete releases the energy stored during the descent/isometric phases, and the involved muscles shorten rapidly, creating upward propulsion. The better the athlete stores energy during the eccentric and isometric phases, the more powerful this phase will be. This energy transfer is trained independently of "strength gains" found via the weight room. Lifting weights is great for improving jumping ability, but works largely through a different mechanism than improving the stretch shortening cycle. Significant and rapid gains can be made by optimizing the stretch shortening cycle alone through plyometric and jump training.

Figure 3.11: The concentric phase of jumping is where muscles contract and positive work is done.

If you have done "plyometrics" or jumping exercises before, you may notice that it helped your running jump more so than your standing jump. A running jump relies even more on an efficient stretch shortening cycle and its related physiological adaptation then a standing jump. The ability of plyometric training to improve the quality of the transition between the above phases through the stretch shortening cycle is a big reason that athletes will notice the positive impact that plyometric exercise makes on their running one and two leg jumps. The efficiency of the stretch shortening cycle can only reach a particular level, so training methods other than plyometrics (such as barbell training) are useful, and often required tools in helping an athlete reach their highest performance potential.

The stretch-shortening cycle isn't only trained by plyometrics. It can be improved through speed training, sport play and virtually any movement that involves a quick reversal of muscle phases. Never forget that *playing sports is in itself "plyometric"*, a point which coaches and athletes neglect that can lead to over-training. Many great jumpers do plyometric exercises very well naturally due to good coordination, along with their deep and extensive backgrounds in athletics. Despite this, even the best jumper typically has aspects or intensities of plyometric work that they can improve in.

Key Point

Plyometrics can be referred to as: "Any jumping exercise that emphasizes a quick reversal from eccentric/explosive isometric to the concentric phases of movement". Anything from jumping rope, to skipping, to depth jumps from a high box are all "plyometric", but clearly, some methods are more powerful and effective than others. As an athlete increases in ability, more intense plyometrics are required to increase their leap.

With the complexity of muscle phases and stretch-shortening cycles, it might seem that building a higher jump is tricky business. The physiology behind the mechanisms are indeed complex, but training them is simple, as the brain does a fantastic job at putting things all together *using only simple training exercises, drills and cues*. Using the drills, awareness recommendations and cues given in the jump technique portion of this book, the human mind can subconsciously acquire the programming to create the ultimate leap without needing any complicated technological equipment or personal coaching.

Neuro-Muscular Factors Leading to Vertical Jump Success

Knowing muscle actions and the science of the stretch shortening cycle is nice in order to pass an exercise physiology class, but how does it relate to jumping in terms of what to train for? How should coaches and athletes go about selecting exercises for training? The relation of the muscles to the nervous system, and their implications for vertical jump performance are important to know when it comes to technical and training mastery. In terms of the nervous system, and its ultimate influence on the muscle, tendon and skeletal expression of strength, there are three factors to be concerned with.

1. Strength and speed of muscular contraction (rate of force development)
2. Coordination of muscular contraction
3. Rapid contraction and relaxation ability

The first factor, the strength and speed of muscular contraction, is more commonly known as *power*. When it comes to anything athletic, power is a crucial part of the equation. Being strong is nice, but unless that strength can be utilized quickly and effectively, athletes won't be able to make the play, and get left behind.

Power is simply the product of two things: speed and strength. Raw speed in terms of moving against zero resistance (waving your arm in the air as fast as possible) is genetically set, and not much can be done to change it. Force application (strength), is the side of the equation that *can* be improved. In order to improve power, both strength, and the *rate by which that strength is applied* must be trained.

Most coaches and even athletes are aware of this, which explains why a spectrum of strength, speed-strength, and power training means are applied in modern programming, from forceful squats, to powerful Olympic lifts, to fast medicine ball throws and sprint work. These training means all work together to improve the power and rate of force development that makes a great athlete. Never forget that just training jumping and playing sports are fantastic ways to train rate of force development, so special exercises such as jump squats and Olympic lift derivatives are just some of many tools that will help to get the job done with power.

Strength and speed must also be applied *with a level of coordination* if athletes are to turn their power into athleticism. Some athletes are powerful beyond their levels of coordination, which tends to lead to big weight room numbers and standing jumps, but movements requiring more skill yield diminished performances. Many will give coordination credit for acrobatic athletic moves on the field, but few realize that levels of coordination are also important for optimal muscle sequences in jumping, sprinting, throwing and nearly anything else athletic. All other things being the same, coordinated athletes can jump higher than their uncoordinated counterparts. Although coordination is somewhat genetic, it can be trained specifically for jumping through a variety of drills, movements, and of course, specific jump practice.

The final neuromuscular factor that leads to good jumping is the ability of athletes to rapidly contract and relax their muscles. Think of this concept through the following example: If an athlete is jumping upwards, extending their hips, and the muscles that flex the hip are still contracting, they are fighting *against* upwards propulsion. The same goes for other paired muscle groups in the jumping process, such as the flexors and extenders of the knee joint and ankle joint. Elite athletes, through genetics and repetition achieve incredible rates of muscle relaxation when compared to athletes of lower levels.

Figure 3.11: Rapid tuck jumps are one of many ways to teach fast antagonist relaxation in jumping.

Although the rapid contraction and relaxation required for blazing athletic feats come naturally to many, proper exercise selection can help to improve the contraction and relaxation speed of various muscle groups. Some great methods that can help these rates in respect to vertical jump are:

- Tuck jumps for speed (hips)
- Butt kicker jumps for speed (knee)
- Lateral barrier hops (knee)
- Ankle hops with quick dorsiflexion (ankle and foot)
- Speed squats, foot anchored with emphasized downwards acceleration
- Oscillatory isometrics
- High quality sprinting

Utilizing these exercises together, either as part of a warmup, a jump circuit, or as a super-set with a strength exercise utilizing a similar muscle group are all effective ways to get the most out of this principle. Athletes who are much stronger in the weight room than they are dynamically in jumping and sprinting can nearly always benefit from hefty dose of contraction-relaxation work. This type of work is useful year round, as it helps to form the base of movement that athletes need to reach their highest levels.

Chapter IV

Principles of applying instruction in jump technique

In order to become a technical master of a skill, lots of proper repetition is key. Watch an elite jumper in slow motion and you will notice that their limbs move in a very precise and explosive manner throughout the setup and execution of a jump. Their skill in the jump movement is *always* optimal or close to it. Chances are they have great power, but their movement ability is also close to the highest possible level.

On the other hand, most people who are completely and utterly ground-bound have very little skill in the jumping sequence. They typically don't use their arms or hips well, stay flat-footed, and load the jump slowly, or perhaps not at all. They also typically lack a complete extension of the arms, shoulders and calves at the top of the jump. These athletes can add a wealth of inches just through improving these technical flaws. The skill aspect of jumping alone has more to do, *initially*, with how high an athlete can jump than their strength or power. Strength and power become much more important for long term improvement once skill is established. There are some powerful athletes who may be able to pull off a good standing jump with little skill, but their running jumps will flounder with their lack of coordination. When it comes to sport movement, strength is often used as a shortcut over movement skills to improved performance, but the best way to ensure long term success is to always base training around the quality of movement, and use proper strength work to bolster that technique.

Key Point

Initial improvements in vertical jumping are usually due more to positive changes in the skill of the jump rather than improvements in athletic power.

Guidelines for Making Technical Changes to Jump Technique

When it comes to assessing and refining vertical jump technique, there is a debate that must be clarified: the argument of natural technique. The basic principles of this concept are as follows: Athletes will perform any sporting skill to the best of their current natural abilities and strengths; coaching techniques outside of this natural "fingerprint" of form will lead to sub-optimal results and a limited ceiling. Taking a look at track and field, you will notice that the Olympic performers in any event have *similar* technique on the base level, but each phase of the triple jump, hammer throw, or pole vault is going to be just a little different between each performer. There is no single, absolute technique that each athlete must fall into, and there is a point where athletes must use their own natural strengths to reach their highest performance.

Conversely, few can doubt the importance of technical coaching in any sport. Without a coach, track and field jumpers would rarely, or never, reach their genetic potential. Having another set of eyes on each run, jump and throw keeps athletes on point in regards to important instruction and technical guidance that can lead them through the basics, and all the way to sport mastery. Part of being a coach is knowing how to show athletes the proper technique and form!

There is truth in both these arguments, and they actually work together to form the basic theory on when and how athletes should be instructed in jumping form. In general, beginners and novices need a bit more rigid coaching in order to be brought up to a baseline of technique that takes advantage of basic physics for their event. Once an athlete has this basic technique to a good working proficiency, work from that point is all about their individual "blueprint". This is where the individualistic theory hits in full effect.

Key Point

Many athletes reach an extremely high skill of jumping without ever needing instruction. On the other hand, many beginner and intermediate athletes can benefit from the basic footwork and positioning that leads all athletes to great vertical leaps.

Taking golf as an example, a beginner will be best served by learning how to hold the club, place their feet and align their head early in their development. After a few years of practice, they will not need to be told that their backswing must leave the ground at a 22 degree angle, and that they must shift their hips into the swing .12 seconds before the downswing begins to occur, but rather, they will have learned to focus their attention on certain points of "feel" during the swing, and let their brain and body take care of the rest. Once the basics are in place, it is all about awareness of particular points of one's technique that leads to consistent and effective results.

Before we get into the specifics of jump mechanics, let's go over some guidelines for application. As mentioned above, some athletes don't need to worry much about consciously changing their technique, and trying to correct things will only send them backwards. Believe me, I have seen track coaches screw up athlete's technique and performance by trying to impose techniques on them that killed their natural fluidity and style. Always know this: *Some athletes are already jumping with nearly the best technique that their body can currently and naturally achieve, and over-coaching or over-analyzing will send them backwards.* This can be somewhat of a confusing tightrope to walk then; when to make changes to technique, and when to leave things well enough alone. In order to simplify things as much as possible, there are four rules of thumb regarding applying any sort of instruction for jumpers.

- **Rule 1:** The faster the takeoff, the more technique and coaching needs be applied to the jump.
- **Rule 2:** The less sport and movement experience the athlete has, the more technique practice that needs to be applied beyond what the athlete has managed to put together themselves.
- **Rule 3:** For athletes with a strong athletic background, strengthening primary muscle groups and motor patterns is better than redundant technical instruction.
- **Rule 4:** The more prone an athlete is to either being too cerebral (overanalyzing) or self-judging and critical, the less they should pay attention to concrete technical points.

Rule 1: The Faster the Takeoff, the More Coaching Required

When it comes to vertical jump technique, manuals, books, loads of research and seas of DVD's have been devoted to the development of the high speed jumping technique found in track and field long, high and triple jumps. These athletes *do* need to spend more time on finer details of jump technique due to their high takeoff speeds. *Being in a bad position to jump when moving at maximal (or near maximal) velocity will instantly negate powerful muscles and provoke injury.* In other words, extremely fast takeoffs are going to have one general "style" where slower takeoffs can have a variety of styles. Even within track and field, some athletes need less technical coaching then others. Giving a track and field jumper too much information and coaching at once can be the death of fluid movement and performance.

In terms of takeoff speeds and variation, track and field high jump has a wider range of jumping styles when compared to long or triple jump. There are more ways to set up the high jump, where an athlete might be moving at 6-8 meters each second versus a long jump where an athlete is moving up to speeds of 12 meters per second. Style differences amongst high jumpers (and all non-track and field jumping athletes) can be things like:

- The height of the hips at the plant
- The bend of the plant leg
- The tightness of the swing leg and arms
- The length of time the athlete spends on the ground at the plant (contact time)
- The height of the athlete's center of mass at takeoff (how high the arms, shoulders and drive knee are at point of takeoff)

This being said, there are more athletes out there who are capable of being great high jumpers then there are great long jumpers. This is because, in order to become a great long jumper, athletes must be able to plant and leave the ground in under .12 seconds, which is a fairly genetic trait (fast twitch muscles and good muscle/tendon and skeletal structure). Athletes who cannot accomplish that won't be elite long jumpers, as they can't transfer speed into the plant fast enough to conserve horizontal speed.

Taking off at slower speeds allows for a greater variety of body types and jumping strategies. Since slow takeoffs allow a greater variety of technique, for the purpose of this book, I'll really push only the essential cues that a jumper needs to be aware of in a way that lets them also take advantage of their natural strength and ability. This isn't a book on the technical points of the individual track and field jumping events (although the basic technical principles and training philosophy can and should be applied to track and field jumps!).

Rule 2: Athletes with Low Global Athleticism Need More Coaching

Rule 2 is a simple one. If you are a physical educator, or a coach who deals with young athletes, this concept may be especially exciting to you, as you have a chance to work with those whose slate is fairly fresh in terms of their vertical jumping skill. Coaches often talk about building a training "base", and usually address this from a stance favoring large amounts of running, lifting and conditioning prior to the start of a season. When we are talking vertical jump

Figure 4.2: Athletic skills such as tumbling and gymnastics build greater global athleticism which makes the development of jumping skills easier and more effective. Photo Credit Maria Lavelle.

training in this book, or any other athletic movement, the most important base is that of *athletic movement* that starts from youth.

This base of movement will help an athlete's brain put together the pieces of a good jump from previous, similar movement skills. All of the touch football, dodgeball, tumbling, wrestling, soccer, volleyball etc. that we participated in during gym class, recess, and after school sport provides the neural instructions by which athletes will learn to build tension, coordinate limbs, accelerate, plant, and ultimately jump more efficiently. Just like a child who learned musical theory from a young age picks up the guitar extremely quickly, so will athletes with a wide and varied athletic base pick up jumping with relative ease. These athletes typically don't need the technical coaching breakdown and drilling that their less experienced counterparts require. The jumping technique of these athletes will also mirror their natural form closer than that of an athlete with low levels of global athleticism.

An anecdote that I repeat over and over again is one of the success that being a multi-sport athlete brings to a track and field jumper. I have seen over and over where an athlete who played football and basketball in the fall and winter goes on to have successful spring high school track seasons; often without touching a weight in the process (or lifting, but not having much of a clue what they are doing). The wide variety of speed and power movements gained during sport seasons translate very well into the specific jumping power needed during track season.

Once these athletes get to college to specialize in track, they replace their sport play with a fall training that revolves around longer, slower running and lifting weights. Once these athletes get to their competitive season, they don't have the movement bank they did in high school. For some reason they don't have the "hops" they did before and many times go on to have subpar seasons. Fortunately, good coaches and athletes know how to keep that movement bank full! Global athleticism is key to maintaining good overall movement skill and keeping athletes fresh.

Rule 3: Athletes with Strongly Engrained Movement Patterns Don't Respond Well to Coaching Cues

There comes a point where attempting to change an athlete's technique and alter an established motor pattern becomes extremely difficult, if not impossible to change once it has become enough of a habit. The more fundamental the skill, such as sprinting, the more solidly engrained it becomes over time. One can think of the establishment of technique as taking a stick to a beach, and drawing a line in the sand. The more one practices their current technique, the more deeply they draw that line in the sand. Once this line becomes deep enough, it is nearly impossible to draw it any other way or direction, because the walls have become deep and resistant to change.

This principle is similar when it comes to anything in the athletic world. Experienced athletes have built their basic motor skills to a point where it is difficult and draining to consciously change the pattern. The fact of the matter is that by the time an athlete reaches maturity, their brain has "hardwired" many of the basic athletic patterns they have established. This means that there is a program set in the brain that is difficult, if not impossible to completely change.

A common example of a negative change to an athlete's motor pattern would be taking a football player who is used to running with low hips and low knee action (for better agility), and trying to get them to run a 100m dash like a track sprinter: running tall with their knees high. Football players don't naturally run with a tall, high knee action because if they did, they couldn't change directions easily in the game they have played all their life. Making them run with their knees high will cripple their speed because they are forced to use a pattern rooted in conscious thought, rather than the way they instinctively move. At the same time, having an athlete with an established technique and motor pattern jump in a way that they are not used to (such as using a

Figure 4.3: The more often an athlete practices a particular technique for a fundamental movement skill, the more deeply it becomes ingrained in their system, just like a line drawn in the sand.

deep knee bend when they typically jump with fairly rigid legs) will sideline their performance, as this pattern is one that is slow, mechanical, and not backed by the muscle layout that makes their preferred pattern effective.

In regards to habits, some motor learning specialists have even suggested that rather than try and change an old habit, it may be best to start completely over with a new one. This is often seen in track and field when the technique of a jumper is completely re-worked by new coaches their freshman year of college. During this year, a related drop in performance often accompanies that change. One or two years later, however, the athlete may be setting new personal bests (if the change was warranted and properly administered; often it is not), and it just took a year or two for that technique to ingrain itself where the athlete was no longer mechanical with it. The more fundamental the skill, however, the harder it is to change.

With "slower" team sport oriented jumping, it is often better to "let it be" with certain mechanical cues, due to established patterns, unless the athlete naturally jumps in a way that makes them prone to injury, such as overly knee dominant jumping. The major, unchangeable, pattern in established jumpers is the amount of knee bend in the jump. Athletes will naturally work in a range of knee flexion that meets their current strength and skill level.

Key Point

Learning the technical aspects of jumping also helps us to understand its strength requirements. This knowledge aids exercise selection for strength and plyometric work within training programs.

Athletes who don't bend their knees much in jumping may find that squat oriented strength training routines will actually allow them to jump well with greater knee bend, and eventually higher, without putting any conscious thought into these mechanisms. Athletes who naturally bend their knees a lot in jumping (and therefore typically jump well off of two feet) will find that practicing a quantity of plyometric exercises focusing on small knee bends and stiff contacts will improve their running jumps and one leg jump much more than simply thinking of it when they are jumping. The body simply needs time to adapt and strengthen to accommodate technique.

Rule 4: Don't Let Technique Instruction Lead to Paralysis

Finally, we have rule 4 regarding jump technique, which is to not let any technical instruction lead to over-analysis, mechanical action, and most importantly, not to let over-analyzing technique or a training program interfere with one's ability to just "be an athlete". Of these four rules, this plain and simple advice can easily have the greatest effect. Even if an athlete is far away from the proper technical model of jumping, there are times where giving a variety of instructions that significantly change technique in a jump will not be a good idea in regards to improvement. Commenting on an athlete's jump with a thorough analysis consisting of: "You do this and this and this wrong!" will only cripple an athlete's confidence and take them away from their natural athletic strengths. Rather than judgment and instruction, many athletes are better served by "awareness".

Awareness is asking athletes not to rigidly perform a particular technique, but rather to simply feel rhythm, tension and activation during important athletic actions. Where cues and instruction are based on following a model, awareness is based on feeling, and allows the powerful sub-conscious mind to better sort out technique according to one's strengths. Coaches should generally ask over-thinking athletes to assess how certain aspects of the jump feel rather than how they "must" be done. Asking an athlete to be aware of the rhythm of the last two steps of their two leg jump can go a lot further than asking athletes to position their hips or legs in a particular manner.

Other examples of awareness in jumping can be points such as the length of particular steps in the jump, the activation of certain muscles through the course of the jump, such as the calves, or the amount of arm swing the athlete is producing. A more thorough list of awareness ideas will be given in chapters 9 and 10, where complete technical breakdowns of running jump styles are discussed. Athletes who watch great technique in action, and who are then given awareness points rather than step by step instruction can often find themselves more successful in technical excellence than athletes just following rigid guidelines.

In addition to the use of simple awareness, coaches should look to "external" cues, rather than "internal" cues when they do give instruction. External cues are descriptive, goal oriented instructions, such as "be a spring on your approach for the next jump", where internal cues deal with body parts or related sequences, such as "extend your legs and calves as hard as possible"! External cues have the greatest transfer to the final athletic goal, where internal cues may improve pieces of the movement, but will detract from the athletic technique and the final result[12]. Another way of looking at this is while internal cues may improve the power or efficiency of small parts of the total jump sequence, external cues will typically allow the whole process to happen more effectively and with better total coordination.

---

[12] Talpey, Scott, Warren Young, and Bradley Beseler. "Effect of Instructions on Selected Jump Squat Variables." *Journal of Strength and Conditioning Research* (2014)

Putting it all Together

A vertical jump is fairly innate to any athlete who has been around sports such as volleyball or basketball for some time. I often measure standing vertical for my collegiate athletes as part of the assessment of their daily physical state and have gained several insights through its observation. My athletes who perform explosive vertical skills often, such as track and field sprinters and jumpers, usually perform the standing vertical jump with great technique without much added coaching. This is largely due to the cumulative effect of their training, which requires being maximally vertically explosive in a variety of ways that include, but are not limited to:

- Squats and deadlifts
- Olympic lifting
- Explosive medicine ball and shot throws
- Hurdle hops and other vertical plyometrics
- Bounding
- Sprinting
- Coordination drills

In addition to their training, many of these athletes grew up playing sports such as volleyball, basketball and gymnastics, which added to their global skill set and further improved jump technique.

On the other end of the spectrum are those who have relatively poor skill at standing jumps. Around a quarter of my athletes demonstrate vertical jumping with very poor efficiency, and could easily gain 2-4 inches through improvement of their technique. These athletes may have sporting skill in a variety of movements, but since they didn't play sports requiring vertical jumping or requiring a premium on vertical segmental power during their developmental years, their vertical skill is far behind. These athletes can make maximal use of cues and drills that will allow them to reach a higher leap, just like the golf novice who needs to learn how to grip the club and set their feet properly. Athletes who have poor mechanics due to a lack of exposure can benefit largely from simple cues and instructions. In addition to cues, repetitive drills that work aspects of the correct jumping technique are also an invaluable tool to help athletes perfect their form in early sport skill instruction.

Although building a decent working vertical jump skill comes naturally for many, attaining the absolutely optimal jumping technique for one's body type is a long term investment. Awareness of proper technique, and a feel of one's own mechanics is a vital practice in long term vertical jump development, and literally any sport skill. Bottom line: Beginners are best instructed by cues and drills that back the basic biomechanics of jumping, where more advanced athletes are better served by awareness of jump elements, and the specific strength training that caters to their own individual jumping style.

Chapter V

Biomechanical and sequential considerations of jumping

Biomechanics is a complicated sounding term, but it simply refers to the physics of human movement, in this case, a vertical jump. For vertical jump biomechanics, we'll keep the math simple: It's all about adding speeds of each limb involved in the jumping movement. Alone, one's limbs aren't capable of that much speed, but together, they can produce a lightning fast result. Consider the following analogy to a vertical leap.

Sample Analogy. Think of a whip in the hands of a skilled lion tamer. The tamer brings his arm back to ready the whip and then thrusts it forward at an arm speed of 45 mph. At the end of the movement, the tail of the whip ends up cracking at over 600mph. How did this happen? The answer is that the cord of the whip amplified the speed produced by the tamers arm to the point where one small section was able to reach a speed that broke the speed of sound.

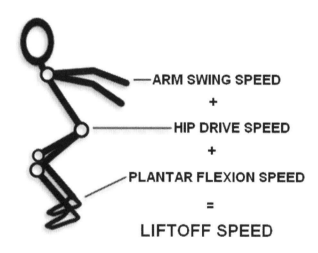

Figure 5.1: Force transmission in jumping starts at the arms and ends at the feet.

Jumping is similar to the whip of the lion tamer. Firstly, jumping is a result of the body adding together the speeds of the arms, trunk, hips, legs and calves. Each of these joints alone don't produce a whole lot of speed, but by adding the speeds together, a very fast result can be accomplished. Effective vertical jumping is the result of "proximal to distal" muscle activation[13], which allows the conversion of the rotational energy of the

---

[13] Bobbert, Maarten F., and Gerrit Jan Van Ingen Schenau. "Coordination in Vertical Jumping." *Journal of Biomechanics* 21.3 (1988): 249-62.

arms, trunk and then knees, into kinetic energy released through the lower legs. You may be surprised how high you can jump when you maximize the timing of your limbs, even if you didn't think of yourself to be a "stellar athlete".

In addition to using the sequential acceleration of limbs to produce vertical speed, jumping uses the thick Achilles tendon as a force "amplifier", similar to the high speed of the end of the whip in the lion tamer example. This means that the calves take the force sent to them from the added speeds of the arms, trunk, hips and knees, and amplify it into speed via the strong Achilles tendon and plantar fascia. One can think of the arms, trunk, hips and knees as the hand of the lion tamer, and the lower legs and feet as the whip, taking the force from the upper extremities of the body and channeling them down into the powerful "speed amplification" of the calves. If you jumped on a pogo stick when you were a kid, (or even now) realize that the lower legs as similar entities to that pogo stick, as they will absorb and powerfully release energy that is put into them from above. For a practical application, try this quick experiment:

1. Perform a standing vertical jump, but keep all your weight on your heels the entire jump, including the takeoff. Jump as hard as possible. How high did you get up? You'll probably claim around 8 inches or so, maybe a foot.
2. Now try a second jump: Jump by using *only* the power of your calves. Don't swing your arms, or bend at the hips, and keep your legs completely straight. How high did you get off of the ground? Maybe 2-3 inches?
3. Add the total height of these two jumps together, and they will fall far short of what your normal vertical is.

This experiment goes to show that sections of the body working together can produce a much greater result than working on their own! The calves move through too small of a distance (about 2-3") to produce any significant lift or speed, but they sure can amplify the force that goes to them from the rest of the body. Likewise, the muscles of the arms, trunk and legs can produce a lot of force, but aren't capable of much speed. By combining the force of the upper body with the speed of the lower legs, they produce a high velocity result that is much faster than the sum of what each part is capable of by itself.

Biomechanics can also be a useful tool in explaining the principles of momentum and levers for running jumps off of one or two legs. In running jumps, legs are used as rigid levers to convert horizontal velocity to vertical speed. Think of the pole vault event in track and field, and how the pole lifts an athlete up and over a high bar. The same principle is present in a single leg jump, except replace the pole with the athlete's leg!

Key Point

Calves are force amplifiers, not producers. Calf raises are a useful initial exercise in working towards vertical jump improvement, but will not yield much results for an intermediate to advanced athlete, who must learn to use their calves and feet effectively with the rest of the body.

From this biomechanical perspective we can see that running jumps are primarily a series of moving levers, adding their speeds together to produce high velocities. Most vertical jumping manuals typically don't spend much time describing jumping biomechanics or technique, but it is a worthwhile venture to maximize all parts of the end product. Knowing the mechanisms that help athletes create vertical speed off of the ground will help lead to a greater awareness of why particular jumping strategies, jumping instruction, special exercises, and weight training regimens may prove useful in the training of an athlete looking to improve their ultimate vertical.

Now that we have the essentials of muscle phases, coaching points, and some basic concepts of motor learning, let's start getting into the individual differences that cause one athlete to jump differently than another. There is a reason that there is no single, "perfect", form for jumping for all athletes, and that some athletes favor single leg jumping to double leg jumping. How athletes move, and respond to training on an individual level is what the next chapter is all about.

Chapter VI

Individual differences in athletic performance: Speed vs. force

Before we dive into the specifics of approach jump technique, we must talk about an important distinction between two primary types of jumping athletes.

- Hip dominant "speed" athletes
- Knee dominant "force" athletes

Without knowing this distinction, we will be tempted to push athletes all into one technique and training mold, rather than considering how they have been wired to move their whole lives. Knowing the movement patterns of an athlete will dictate aspects of training which will help them improve and nurture their instinctual jumping pattern, based on their own strengths and weaknesses. Perhaps more importantly, we will not attempt to impose a jumping technique on an athlete that is not physically able to use that technique based on their strengths and movement history. Let's talk about the differences between these two athletes and start with the hip dominant, "speed" jumper.

Speed Dominant Jumper Characteristics

A "speed" jumper tends to have the following characteristics:

- Hip dominant with strong ankles.
- Respectively weak in the lower thighs.
- Tends to be taller and lankier.
- Looks more like an 800m type runner than a 100m runner.
- Good at Olympic lifts, deadlifts, and most pulling movements.
- Not as good at deep squatting, particularly deep front squats.
- Good half squatters.
- Many shy away from the weightroom completely or tend not to take it seriously.

- Doesn't bend their legs much in standing and running vertical jumping.
- Tends to use a fairly high speed approach when jumping for maximal height.
- Has a much better jump off the run compared to their standing jump.
- Uses the ankles and hips well in the second half of a jump, extends the ankles and hips completely and quickly.
- Knees sometimes cave inwards (valgus) during two leg jumps due to weaker legs.
- Sprints and runs with tall hips and good mechanics.
- Are good plyometric/elastic athletes and tend to naturally favor plyometrics or depth jumps in their training.
- Tend to be decent one leg jumpers if they have learned that skill. A one leg jump is based off of a very fast takeoff, so speed jumping style caters well to this type of movement.
- Often power clean more than they can front squat.
- Tend to need a higher volume of jump and sprint exercises, as well as team sport play to maintain or improve their elastic abilities.
- Often make good track and field jumpers and fast break basketball players.
- Injuries for these athletes tend to be skeletal and connective, such as tendonitis, stress fractures and sprains.

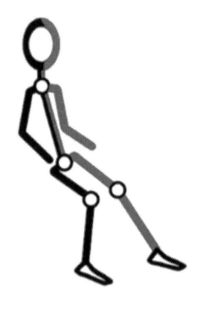

Figure 6.1: Typical speed jumper takeoff position with little knee bend.

Speed Jumper Examples:

James White, LeBron James, John Wall, Michael Jordan, World-class high jumpers

---

The speed athlete operates on momentum. They don't bend their legs much and tend to use their skeletal structure and ability to convert horizontal velocity to jump high. Moving in this manner for the span of their athletic career tends to leave them with strong hips and ankles relative to the rest of their lower body. The dynamic strength gain acquired through this movement also reflects itself in the weight room, making them relatively good at things like half squats, hang cleans and deadlifts due to their hip strength. The full squat is *not* the strength of a speed jumper. Although they rarely get into much of a low squat when jumping or in general sport movement, speed jumpers who are powerful and explosive can still put up excellent squat numbers if they are trained in the weight room consistently.

Speed jumpers will naturally take to plyometrics and plyometric type training programs (plyometric work is based on short ground contacts and little bending of the legs) since that is their preferred manner of movement. Plyometrics also feed directly into their motor pattern and general movement style, allowing them instant improvement with relatively little soreness. A case in point: Straddle high jump world record holder Vlad Yaschenko stated that he never felt like weights really helped him jump higher, preferring plyometric depth jumps as his vertical weapon of choice. Since speed jumpers are often poor squatters and lifters in general, they may also shy away from the weight room for ego reasons.

The standing vertical leap of a hip dominant speed jumper can be somewhat poor. Since these athletes don't bend down into a jump too far, they don't give their body enough time or distance to generate much vertical speed when no horizontal velocity is present (remember, standing vertical jumps are a function of the length of time an athlete applies force into the ground). A speed jumper who doesn't bend much at the hips, and doesn't use their calves well, leaving the heels on the ground for the most of the jump phases, will have the poorest standing vertical jump of any athlete. These athletes will do much better with a running start (provided their adequate skill) since working with rigid legs tends to convert horizontal speed to vertical velocity quite well. *Speed jumpers can still jump well off of two legs,* but they will tend to use fairly little knee bend when they do so, and their jump will usually pale in comparison to their one leg jump.

Speed jumpers are often at varying levels of skill in their standing jump technique, since they may avoid its regular practice, or the strength training that will improve their form.

Figure 6.2 indicates the standing vertical techniques of speed oriented athletes of low and high skill levels. The high skill speed jumper will use a pronounced forward bend of the torso and a big arm swing to transfer maximal force down into their legs. A low skill speed jumper will tend to use very little hip bend, which allows for relatively little loading of the legs, as well as little time to put force into the ground. This skill in a standing vertical has almost zero transfer to a running single leg jump, as they are virtually different skill sets.

Low Skill Standing Vertical   High Skill Standing Vertical

Figure 6.2: Low and high skill standing vertical jump techniques for speed jumpers. The difference is in the hips and lean of the trunk! Speed jumpers will eventually need to learn to apply force over a longer distance with significant trunk lean in standing vertical efforts.

With speed jumpers, it is important to remember that regardless of the changes brought about by strength training, *the technique of jumping with rigid legs is very hard to break*. It is nearly impossible to take a speed jumper and train them to full characteristics of a deep-bending force jumper, who will be described next. The best way to train a speed jumper is always going to be specific to the type of jump they are trying to improve (one or two leg), but in general, speed jumpers will do well with higher volumes of elastic and plyometric work, and slightly lower volumes of strength work (although strength work is still important for the short and long term development of these athletes).

It is often thought that speed jumpers are always going to be hip dominant, and weaker in the quadriceps and knee joint, and although this is often the case, it is not always true. A prime example of which is a national level horizontal jumper I coached who was a knee dominant speed jumper. In standing vertical jumps, he would barely bend his legs and still hit jumps in the low 30's, but he was also capable of a double bodyweight deep squat. In his squatting, or nearly any other movement, his first reaction and movement was always at his knees, which hurt his sprint speed, but his jump off the run was massive; people often commented that they rarely see jumpers with such vertical lift off the long jump board. This is one of the reasons that merely quantifying athletes as either knee or hip dominant has its shortcomings, as the speed and force classification may be more relevant to ways in which athletes move and perform various jumps, sprints and lifts.

A final concept regarding the speed jumper is that *a speed jumper will react to excess weight much more poorly then a force jumper.* This is because the window of time a speed jumper has to produce force is very small, and excess pounds of bodyweight multiplies itself much more quickly in the high rates of force development a speed jumper encounters. For a speed jumper, weight gain is much more negative than for a force jumper who has much more time to produce muscular tension into the ground. It is for this reason that the average Olympic high jumper typically has a height of around 6'5 (1.95m) with a bodyweight of around 160-175lb (70-80kg). Being light is hugely important for athletes who rely on momentum to jump.

Force Jumper Characteristics

Let's switch gears and talk about the other side of the spectrum, which is the force dominant/knee dominant jumper. Not all force type jumpers will fit entirely into this mold, but they will usually gravitate strongly towards it. The "force" jumper has the following characteristics:

- Generally stronger in the weightroom than a speed jumper.
- Strong legs, particularly in the quadriceps/knee extensors.
- Has more muscle mass then a speed based jumper.
- Tends to be on the shorter side compared to speed jumpers.
- More of a 100m type sprinter than 800m type runner.
- Great squatters, often capable of 2x bodyweight deep squats.
- May struggle with Olympic lifts in comparison to their squatting strength.
- Can typically front squat more than their power clean.
- Tends to use a lot of knee bend in jumping, sometimes more than 90 degrees.

- Attains a very low hip position at the bottom of their jumps.
- Often favors using short approaches when jumping, and slow approach speeds.
- Doesn't tend to jump much higher off the run than their standing leap.
- Can struggle with a powerful extension through the hips and calves at the final push of a jump.
- Sprints with fairly low hips. Has trouble sprinting tall.
- Tends to be a poor one leg jumper, as they are used to longer periods of force development, while a single leg jump requires rapid force development.
- Often makes good football, rugby, and athletic soccer players.
- Tends to do better with slightly lower volume training programs due to the high magnitude and muscle contribution of their athletic movements.
- Can do well using only strength training as the primary exercise method for short time periods.
- Injuries tend to be soft tissue, such as pulled muscles, rather than stress issues (except for lower leg issues, which these athletes commonly struggle with).

Figure 6.3: The force jumper displays a trademark low center of gravity during jump performance.

The "force" dominant athlete is named so due to the fact that they go into a deeper knee (and sometimes hip) flexion in their jump, and thus spend *more time producing force* then a speed jumper. They load up a jump very well compared to their speed jumping counterparts. Despite the fact that they go deep into the bottom of a jump, their powerful muscles allow them to reverse it all quickly enough to still achieve a great leap.

Force Jumper Examples

Spud Webb, Dee Brown, Nate Robinson, Gerald Green, Most Olympic Weightlifters

Force dominant jumpers carry with them great standing verticals. Research backs this up, showing that athletes who can put force into the ground *longer* will end up jumping the highest from a standing position[14]. Watch the movement of a force dominant athlete, and you will notice they will naturally bend down to a half squat or lower in preparation to jump, some even to parallel (although going to parallel robs the athlete of some elastic energy). This lower dip gives the athlete more time to put force into the ground, and thus allows them more distance of movement to reach higher takeoff speeds! Dipping down to parallel during a standing vertical is also a characteristic of athletes who spend lots of time in deep squat positions, such as weightlifters and power lifters, to the point that it has become part of their neural movement pattern.

Ask a force based athlete to sprint, and they may be very fast (often faster than speed jumpers, as they are usually very fast twitch), but they will naturally run with lower hip height then their hip dominant, speed jumping counterparts. In track and field, the most efficient way to sprint is with high hips, with the foot cycling down directly under the body. Sprinting with low hips reduces stride length and also causes foot-strike out in front of the body, a recipe for hamstring disaster. Moving with natural lowered hip heights is extremely useful for a variety of sport skills, however, such as defending, short accelerations, cuts and shuffles. Unfortunately, it is not as useful for top end speed, and speed efficiency.

Figure 6.4: Classic force jumper deep-offset takeoff position that often belongs to many jumpers who go over 45" off two feet. This position allows them to take maximal advantage of approach velocity.

Force jumpers tend to set up their running jump differently than a speed jumper, as they naturally move slower into the plant to take greater advantage of their muscular strength, particularly in the knee.

---

[14] Pandy, Marcus G., and Felix E. Zajac. "Optimal Muscular Coordination Strategies for Jumping." *Journal of Biomechanics* 24.1 (1991): 1-10.

Force jumpers, many times, like to "hop" into a two footed jump with the hips square to the direction of the jump, rather than loading with the hips slightly diagonal to the plant (a diagonal plant allows athletes to take better advantage of a rigid lead leg). Loading up with the hips somewhat diagonal to the direction of the leap, is also known as an "offset plant", which is the most biomechanically efficient way to jump off of two feet, but can be difficult for un-coordinated force jumpers to pull off well.

When force jumpers can pull off a running two-leg jump with a solid offset takeoff, these are typically the guys that you'll see highlighting dunk reels or volleyball spike montages. The fast-twitch, force based athlete who has taken on speed based jump characteristics and optimized their approach is generally the most spectacular jumping athlete out there. Chances are high that the force dominant athlete with a fast running approach doesn't spend all their training time in the squat rack. It is years of repeated movement training that allows an athlete to achieve a fast and effective running vertical technique.

The force jumper will nearly always be a more natural two foot jumper than a one foot jumper. Force jumpers will often have poor extension and strength at the final impulse of their jumps (as the legs are straightening) and they struggle with recruiting muscle quickly enough in the rigid leg position that a single leg jump demands. They rely instead on the force they produce at the bottom positions of the jump to achieve jump height. We'll go into further detail on how speed based running jumps and force based standing jumps differ physiologically in the next chapter. A trademark of a force jumper is an inability to jump much higher from a run than from a standing position. Although often labeled under the blanket of "poor reactive strength", this discrepancy is potentially due to a number of factors, such as:

- Lack of practice
- Poor coordination
- Poor technique
- Weak hips and ankles
- Low elasticity and eccentric strength

Of the previous list, poor technique is the number one reason why force athletes will struggle to get up better with a significant run. Remember that technique is influenced by a number of factors, and an athlete with weak hips and poor elasticity is a good candidate to have bad technique due to these two factors. Ultimately, strengthening weak points in conjunction with the improvement of technique through cueing and awareness will bring an athlete to a higher vertical level.

Novice and intermediate force jumpers are often very strong in the legs, as well as hips, but their Achilles heel (literally!) is their lower leg and foot. Many times, these jumpers fail to use their calves and feet well in jumping, sprinting, or any other movement for that matter. Again, just doing calf raises isn't the answer to getting better foot action in a jump, but rather working on the correct cues, and performing the correct special strength and plyometric exercises will help build the strength necessary to achieve a well-rounded athletic state.

Key Point

Force jumpers tend to have great squat numbers that go along with their utilization of a deeper knee bend in vertical jumps. All the jumping repetition they perform over the years induces a "reverse training transfer", which can bring the barbell back squat of an athlete to a very high level with minimal barbell squat practice.

Conclusion of Individual Jumping Styles

Concluding this section, knowing the difference between speed and force oriented jump technique carries with it helpful implications for both technique and training. The following three concepts will assist coaches and athletes in reaching their highest vertical performance.

1. Jumping style determines which jump technique cues athletes should capitalize on and avoid, particularly the amount of knee and hip bending in a given jump. Knowing what type of style an athlete naturally utilizes helps avoid applying a technique that the body will have trouble adapting to, and one that will limit ultimate potential. All athletes have a natural form and style, and when it comes to something like jumping (which can favor multiple styles), it is important to know how those styles work.

2. Knowing the jump technique an athlete favors helps to determine areas to focus on in training that improve weak points of the jumper without compromising their style and motor patterns during preparatory (off-season) training periods. Addressing weaknesses during early and non-consequential training periods can help prevent injury, improve well-roundedness, and set up a base for a new personal best during the more intense training periods that focus on athlete's strengths.

3. Knowing which jumping style an athlete favors helps them to know how to train to *maximize their strengths* during the portions of their training where they want to be at personal best levels. Any time an athlete wants to be at a level where they are jumping record heights, their training must reflect their preferred jumping and movement style. This means that speed jumpers will cater towards speed and elastic training means more in periods of peak performance, where force based athletes may want to cater more towards low volume, heavy strength efforts.

Training Speed and Force in Jumping: Practical Examples

Ultimately, every example of movement and biomechanics should have implications for training and exercise selection. Many athletes achieve excellent results in jump technique improvement from correct barbell and strength training exercise selection, performing effective plyometric exercises and simply practicing jumping often. When it comes to using exercise to maximize an athlete's vertical jump technique, or technique in any power movement situation, the following two principles are of utmost importance:

1. Is the athlete maximizing their movement strengths according to their own individual style?
2. Is the athlete utilizing training methods that improve the type of jumping they are attempting to increase (fast running jumps, standing jumps, etc.)?

Let's talk about a few examples and case studies of how speed and force jumpers can benefit from various exercise programs designed to improve forms of vertical jump in respect to the two points above.

With speed jumpers, their innate strength revolves around utilizing momentum through relatively stiff legs that transfer force well. For this to happen, these athletes need strong feet and ankles, a good ability to utilize the stretch reflex at the knee, and a strong hip hinge ability, particularly for lower speed jumps. Clearly, to jump higher off of two feet, any athlete needs to get better at barbell squats, and largely for the reason that it helps athletes to put more force into the ground for long periods of time. A less common, but very effective training emphasis for speed jumpers that ties directly into their own natural style are exercises that maximize both the distance and power of the hip hinge mechanism. Exercises that help speed jumpers to take advantage of their hip hinge are hip power and force oriented exercises, such as:

- Medicine ball throws (elastic hinge training)
- Kettlebell swings (eccentric hinge training)
- Olympic lifts (concentric hinge training)

These exercises and their variations are a great teaching tool and remedy for speed jumpers who need improvement in their hip hinge. Case in point, I had an online client who started with me with an all-time prior vertical jump best of 36" (he had improved over 10" from the time he started serious training), and who had been training intently for several years on a variety of plyometric and strength oriented programs. In our time of 12 weeks training together, he was able to take his standing vertical best from 36 to 39 inches, as well as significantly improve his running jumps to the point where he could easily dunk a basketball with two hands.

In these 12 weeks, I was not concerned too heavily with his strength to weight ratio, as this had been heavily emphasized before in prior programming, and his barbell front squat was already very good: 300lbs at 175lbs body weight. Strength was not his immediate issue. A problem he had was that his standing vertical looked like the left athlete in figure 6.2. He wasn't utilizing enough distance in his hip hinge to give himself vertical lift. Through utilizing specific power training revolving around the technique of the jump itself and maximizing his natural strengths, we were able to get him to utilize a more powerful and extensive hip hinging action in his jumping and, in the process, bring his vertical up several inches without hammering at his squat max. Improving his natural strengths as a speed jumper also involved improving his ankle strength through a variety of methods focusing on quick contact, submaximal plyometric work.

Figure 6.5: Speed oriented high jumpers require a different yearly approach to barbell training than athletes looking for general improvements in jumping ability. Photo Credit Matt Franz.

Speed jumpers can increase their standing vertical quickly through the proper strength training channels, *but too much strength training can harm their running jumps.* This is true particularly of their one leg running jump if the program does not contain enough elastic strength work, such as plyometrics, sprint work, and most importantly, regular team sport play. As we will learn, the one leg jump is all about the transfer of elastic energy and proper use of the body's levers, so speed jumpers must never move too far away from their innate strengths.

If speed oriented jumpers are trying to jump higher off two feet, this means they will need to attack their weaknesses in the form of deep barbell squatting. Deep barbell squat work is going to help these athletes out immensely in improving their double leg jump, but when it comes to single leg jumping, it isn't always as useful from a skill and technique perspective. Let's take a look at training a high jumper (single leg focus) over the course of entire training season where they need to address their weaknesses, but ultimately play to their strengths.

With a high jumper, it may be useful to infuse the offseason training with some force oriented work, such as power oriented depth jumps, deep squats, deadlifts, and lunges to work on muscle mass in the legs, general strength, and an increase in the motor pool available for jumping. Once the athlete is at the point where they need to be having training sessions at a high level, and especially competitions, the athlete must focus primarily on those exercises which train their hip dominant speed pathway, such as partial squats, short contact plyometrics, speed depth jumps, and sprinting work.

The closer an athlete moves to elite, the more time out of the season needs to be devoted to specific, quality jump practice resembling their natural motor pattern. This is why advanced athletes will typically have shorter "GPP" (General Physical Preparation) periods of their yearly training compared to novices. Advanced athletes need to spend more time maximizing their strengths, where novice athletes need to spend more time in the early season utilizing well-rounded preparation and weakness building.

I have seen dozens of cases of single-leg speed jumpers who bog themselves down with too much strength work, and lose their speed jumping form and ability in short order. Of course, their standing and running two leg jumps will often pick up with the extra barbell work, but it doesn't play to their strength. This is really only a big deal for those athletes involved in track and field, or those who just like to jump off one leg (such as a basketball player aiming to dunk). Any team sport athlete (basketball, volleyball, etc.) would be foolish to turn down extra strength just because it caused them to drop an inch on their running jump in favor of 3 more on their standing leap.

Force oriented athletes also have their own strengths and weaknesses that need to be catered to in the course of their long term jump training. Where speed jumpers will make rapid jump improvements with basic barbell training, force athletes will make the same fast, initial improvements through the utilization of basic plyometric training. Most of the "I gained 6 inches on my vertical jump in 12 weeks of training stories" are from genetically powerful force jumping athletes who utilized basic plyometric training work to improve their technique and reactive strength ability. Although force dominant athletes will gain fast initially from plyometric work, they will do well in the long term to continue to play to their strengths which is training with power movements of larger magnitude, such as barbell squats and deadlifts. Many force jumpers don't have to be quite as picky in the work that they are doing as their speed jumping counterparts, as they will tend to add a force and power element to nearly any training stimulus. They can gain strength and power from weights focused training, as well as plyometric and speed focused training, or just jumping on a regular basis. Ultimately they will always want to be improving their strength to bodyweight ratio in squats and deadlift to make the most of their body's ability.

To demonstrate how this plays out in training, let's first take a hypothetical example, looking at a volleyball player. A volleyball player, who has a force jumping style and loads up her two footed takeoff with significant knee bend and low hips for a running two-leg jump will want to keep exercises in her program that support her jumping motor pattern. This means that a deeper squat will not interfere with the motor pattern she uses when leaping to block or spike a volleyball off of two feet the way it does for an athlete focusing on single leg jumps off a rigid takeoff leg. Her offseason can be a mixture of plyometric, strength and speed work, but the only two variables she truly needs is strength and specific jumping, so in-season, her "hops" can be easily maintained through a basic lifting program and frequent competitive jumping. For the force dominant jumper, significant strength training can stay in the program the majority of the year without interfering with their own style.

Key Point

Speed jumpers need to continually nurture their elastic pathways for long term improvement. Force oriented jumpers will need to make sure they play to their strengths in power oriented barbell work for maximal development.

Let's move to an actual example of training a force jumper, considering their strengths and weaknesses. I worked recently with a client who had a massive back squat (about 400lbs at 165lbs bodyweight), but possessed relatively weak hips (his deadlifting and Olympic lifting were not nearly as good as his squat). In his jumping and general movement, he worked in ranges with a lot of forward knee bend. He also had quite a good vertical jump, as he could nearly dunk at 5'9". Still, his technique was so quad dominant, he couldn't take maximal advantage of his approach speed during the jump process. I put him on a 12 week program devoted to strengthening his weak points (hips, hamstrings and feet/calves) through a battery of special exercises and Olympic lifts. At the end of the program, his movement on the basketball court was remarkably better, but unfortunately, his vertical jump had not increased. The reason why is that he was so deep into the groove of his natural strength (as far as jumping was concerned), that trying to strengthen areas that would fit a speed jumper strategy would not help him jump higher. Eventually he could increase his jump once he overhauled his jumping technique to the point where he was taking full advantage of his increased hip strength; something that would take him longer to do than 12 weeks.

Chapter VII

Standing vertical jump technique and biomechanics

The standing, two foot vertical jump forms a basis for the success of the running two foot jump, as well as many plyometric exercises (such as depth jumping). If an athlete can't jump with any sort of skill from a standing position, they usually won't be much better from a running start. One foot jumping is a little different story, as it is a different motor skill that is based on momentum. There are occasions where athletes with poor skill in a standing vertical jump might be able to perform extremely well in jumping off one leg (this tends to happen frequently in female track and field high jumpers).

Standing jump mechanics are not the exact same for everyone. They are going to be slightly different depending on the loading style of the athlete and whether they have greater strength in their legs or hips. Athletes will also jump differently based on their muscle fiber type and power, as well as their general build. With that said, there are 6 general phases that occur in the course of standing vertical jumping. We'll start with the first phase, the crouch.

Phase 1: "The Crouch"

At the beginning of a stationary vertical jump, the athlete will begin in a standing and fully upright position. Beginning by swinging the arms forcefully behind the body, they will crouch down quickly in preparation to jump. This crouching may be more pronounced at:

- The knee (if the athlete has strong quadriceps)

OR

- The hip (if the athlete has strong glutes and posterior chain muscles)

In the crouch, *the arms must be thrown down and back behind the athlete quickly* in a wide arc to prime the upper body stretch reflex. Also remember that each action has an equal and opposite reaction, so a long, fast backswing of the arms will prime their reversal to be equally powerful, giving the vertical jump a great start. The arm swing in a standing vertical jump is often more pronounced than in running jumps, but athletes with good skill in running two leg jumps may generate a large arm-swing for both styles. During fast single leg jumps, too big of an arm swing can slow the jump process down. Standing jumps, however will always benefit from a larger, faster arm action.

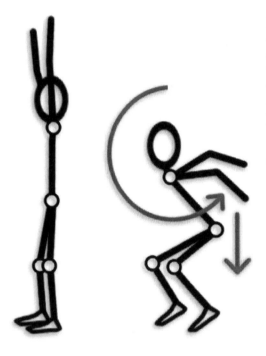

Milliseconds after the arms are thrown back, the athlete bends at the hip and knee. The athlete should crouch downward as fast as possible, perhaps even "throwing" themselves to the bottom of the jump. The speed at which an athlete reaches the bottom position of the jump *is* coachable and improvable in conjunction with strength development. Some athletes will be able to do this more quickly and deeply than others depending on their strength and fast twitch muscle layout. Strong, explosive, fast-twitch athletes load quicker and more deeply than their slow twitch counterparts.

Figure 7.1: The crouching action of a standing vertical jump.

Trying to make a weaker, slower twitched athlete load too deeply for their skill level will not allow for an efficient reversal of elastic energy and can severely impair jump height. Ultimately, the focus of training is to get athletes to load their jumps faster, as rapid eccentric loading is a trademark of elite jumpers[15]. The crouch phase of the jump is reflective of an athlete's ability to load the legs, which carries over to other aspects of sport such as lateral movement and agility. For the crouch phase, an athlete should descend as fast as possible, but only to a depth which allows them to still be fast in the reversal.

[15] Coh, and Mackala. "Differences between the Elite and Sub-elite Sprinters in Kinematic and Dynamic Determinations of Couter-movement Jump and Drop Jump." *Journal of Strength and Conditioning Research* (2013)

Phase 2: Start of the Whip

Keeping the chest up, the athlete leads with the head (signaling the extensor reflex) and begins to swing the arms forward. Keeping the head neutral with the spine is a nice idea from a postural perspective, but this can shut off the extensor reflex that makes a jump powerful. The athlete should start the jump by extending the head and looking up, but shouldn't over-exaggerate this aspect of the process either. Simply looking upwards should suffice. This is a skill and action that comes naturally to nearly every athlete, and will happen unless they have been coached another way.

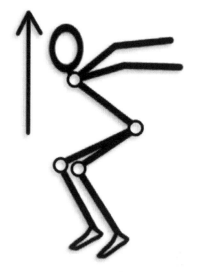

Figure 7.2: Leading with the head.

Phase 3: "The Reversal"

Following the movement of the head, the arms will begin their forward swing, starting a powerful chain of events through the body below. An important idea of vertical jumping that may help the novice athlete is that the vertical jump is more of a "pull" lead by the arms than a "push" from the legs. This is the cue that can be in the conscious thought process of an athlete during jumping exercises. Thinking of pushing with the legs (rather than pulling with the arms and upper body) tends to interfere with the ability of the rotational whip of the upper body to transmit its velocity down to the legs. The push of the legs will happen subconsciously, transmitting force from the speed of the arms and hips. Bottom line: Think of a two footed jump as more of an aggressive pull off of the ground than a push. Additionally, research has shown that one of the main differences between submaximal and maximal jumps is the power of the hip extension[16], and that consciously swinging the arms harder can potentially lead to higher jumps.

---

[16] Lees, Adrian, Jos Vanrenterghem, and Dirk De Clercq. "The Maximal and Submaximal Vertical Jump: Implications for Strength and Conditioning." *The Journal of Strength and Conditioning Research* 18.4 (2004): 787.

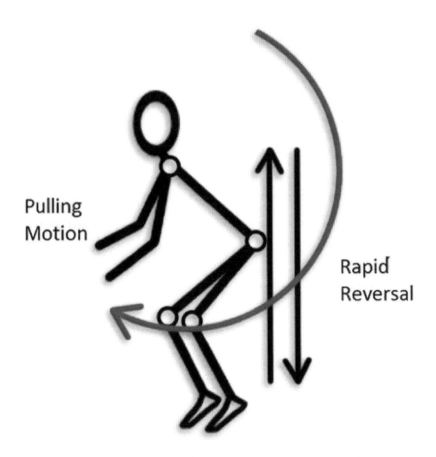

Figure 7.3: The reversal from eccentric to concentric power.

Through the swinging motion, athletes with strong hips can transfer force very well to the legs. This is why hip dominant athletes will often make use of a strong, pronounced arm and torso action to take advantage of this biomechanical mechanism. Athletes who have strong, explosive legs usually won't use their torso quite as much and make this up with a bit more knee bend. To jump high, there must be significant displacement *somewhere* in the jump, either the hips, knees, and in extremely strong athletes, both.

During the reversal, an athlete must only lower themselves through their knee bend as much as they can quickly reverse backwards. "Pausing" at the bottom of a jump, even if for an instant, robs the athlete of elastic energy and severs its efficiency. Slower and weaker athletes should be wary of loading too deeply, but they can still jump well through a strategy utilizing the arms and upper body conveying large forces to fairly rigid legs capable of transmitting it to the ground.

Phase 4: "The Release"

The release phase refers to the upwards explosion which happens after the initial reversal of the jump. If the athlete reversed well, the release aspect of the jump will follow suit. *Remember, the more energy an athlete can store in the eccentric phase of a jump, the higher they will go.* The first instant of upward explosion in a jump can be termed "the release" because within it, an athlete is releasing the energy they stored up during the prior eccentric and isometric phases. The only athletes that tend to crouch and load poorly, and still release well are athletes

Bad   Good

Figure 7.4: Optimal action of the lower legs during the reversal aspect of jumping.

with *huge* weight-room numbers (aka, lots of concentric strength). When the athlete loads well, the release phase will happen smoothly and reflexively.

By the time an athlete is exploding out of the reversal, the power from the upper body has been transmitted down the legs. Through this aspect of the jump, the athlete should be directing force to the balls of the feet. In order for this to happen effectively, the heels should be brought off of the ground, placing the feet around a 70 to 90 degree angle to the shin. This range of placement is optimal for maintaining stiffness and tension in the foot and ankle. If the heel hits the ground in this phase, tension and elastic energy is taken out of the system, and the integrity of foot/ankle complex will be weakened. Staying flat footed during the release phase, hurts the ability of the calves and feet to "amplify" the jump as we talked about before. Some elite jumpers naturally prefer more, or less forefoot emphasis during their jump, but at the minimum, the heels should at least be off the ground (even if it is only by a fraction of an inch). Anecdotally, I have noticed that athletes with longer Achilles tendons cater towards greater forefoot dominance during all stages off a two foot jump.

Of all potential power "leaks" that hurt athletes in jumping, tension in the feet may be the biggest. In any standing jump, the heel should not remain in full contact with the ground aside from a possible brief moment during the eccentric loading phase, and many great jumpers do not let the heel hit the ground *in any capacity* during the jump. In this regard, there have even been case studies of athletes with heel spurs who have 40" standing vertical jumps, credited largely to their ability to quickly transmit force through the forefoot through thousands upon thousands of steps, jumps and sprints primarily directed to the ball of the foot. Again, this is a mechanism that simple calf raises cannot create, *as the ball of the foot mentality is linked to whole body movement*, and not isolated at the ankle joint. Many elite track and field high-jumpers will recommend walking on one's toes. As simple as this recommendation may seem, it can be effective for increasing elastic force transfer and stiffness in jumping, based on the concepts above.

Phase 5: "Final Impulse"

As the athlete prepares to toe-off, the shoulders and arms should be as far away from the ground as possible in order to raise the center of mass. The higher the center of mass at takeoff, the higher an athlete will jump. Think of shooting a cannon straight upwards from a hill vs. ground level for a simple example of why it is important to be as "tall" as possible at a jump takeoff. The upward extension of the shoulders and arms, as well as getting to the balls of the feet early, will result in being "taller" at takeoff, and possibly add 1-2 inches or more to the jump. This skill typically comes naturally if an athlete has been jumping regularly in any capacity, but the cue of being "tall" at the finish of a jump can still be useful for athletes at a variety of levels.

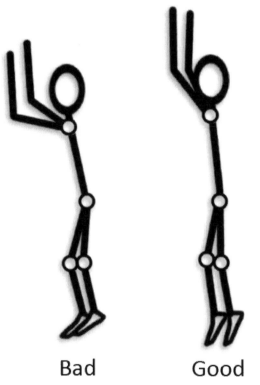

Bad   Good

Figure 7.5: Good and bad downward extension of the feet in jumping.

At the final moment of takeoff, the hips should be violently extended, and brought through so that the angle between the knee hip and shoulder runs at a 90 degree angle to the ground. In Olympic lifting, this has been referred to as "closing the triangle", and this is a reason that various Olympic lifts and medicine ball throws that focus on triple extension will greatly assist a vertical leap, especially those of beginner or intermediate athletes. Finishing a jump without completely extending the body at the hip will result in a loss of 2-3 inches or more on the total jump height. This robs velocity out of the end of the "whip" of the jump.

Figure 7.6: Olympic lifting can help athletes improve the hip (and foot) extension aspect of vertical jumping.

Many athletes whose vertical jumps don't meet their strength and power levels (such as seen in the weight room) often fail to completely extend their torso to vertical, such as the left figure in 7.5. Not only does this reduce the speed of the jump, but it also reduces the peak vertical position of the athlete, costing the athlete between 2 and 6 inches on the jump itself. This situation is often caused by athletes with weak hips, poor foot function, as well as those whose developmental sports did not require jumping with an overhead goal in mind. This situation can be remedied by incorporating lots of triple extension movements, as well as jumping with specific full extension cues, and the use of overhead targets for jumping.

At the end of the final impulse, the feet will continue to push downward and "plantar-flex" into the ground (see this in figures 7.5 and 7.6) through liftoff. The farther beyond the parallel plane of the ground that the foot pushes downwards, the higher the athlete's center of mass at toe-off will be. Complete plantar-extension so encourages a full and powerful downward push of the feet. This aspect of the jump is critically important, and has been recognized as a success factor of vertical jumping[17].

To be able to pull off fully extended plantar-flexion, an athlete needs to have ankles which are flexible enough for the task. I have had a good handful of ground-bound athletes with squats well over 400lbs who only carried vertical jumps in the low 20's, largely due to the fact that they could only lift up on their toes an inch or two at best. They had no "range" in which the calves could amplify the power of the leap, and no matter how strong their calves may have gotten, they still would have lacked the ability to push through a full range of motion.

Phase 6: "Liftoff"

The final stage of takeoff is when the athlete leaves the ground in order to dunk, spike a volleyball, head a soccer ball, block a shot, jump over a car, etc. The efficiency and power of the sequence leading up to liftoff will determine the overall height of the jump. At the point the athlete leaves the ground, nothing more can be done to increase hangtime or jump height. Athletes can flutter their hands or feet all they want, but at liftoff, vertical velocity is firmly determined, and nothing but gravity is in charge of

Figure 7.7: Once the athlete leaves the ground their vertical path is set.

the height and direction of the jump, barring random 100mph gusts of wind. *All this is a lot of information for something that happens in a half second or less!*

Many well-trained athletes do the previous steps very well instinctually. There are common areas, however, that athletes generally struggle in. Inexperienced or weak athletes will typically battle with loading up the jump with a significant degree or knee or hip flexion, and they also tend to get into

---

[17] McErlain-Naylor, King, and Pain. "Determinants of Countermovement Jump Performance: A Kinetic and Kinematic Analysis." *Journal of Sports Sciences* (2014)

this position fairly slowly. Novice athletes don't tend to use the stretch shortening cycle well during their standing jump, as they will "sit" at the bottom position of their knee bend for a split second before reversing it backwards (instead of performing an instant switch from eccentric to concentric). Many athletes don't naturally pick up the rapid downward loading that a high vertical requires, largely due to a lack of practice, aggressiveness, and strength levels.

Key Point

One downside of years of high volume, heavy strength training work is the body routing the transmission of force away from the feet and the big toe, as many of the movements performed in the weight room direct force through the heel or flat of the foot. Strength training is a must for jumping higher for the majority of athletes, but it must be done correctly and in balance with the total program.

A common area that stronger, more experienced athletes do tend to struggle with is the optimal action of the calves and feet through the takeoff. This often comes from a background that is too heavily focused on strength, and low in jumping and elastic activities. Years of squatting through the heels can re-route the nervous patterns of athletes in a direction that robs the feet of their power transmission ability. As with the perfection of any skill, *movement* is the number one priority, and strength training performed out of balance can dominate effective technique.

Standing Technique Summary and Checklist

All of the above information is just for a standing vertical leap. As much info as it is, much more could be written. Hundreds of scholarly research journals, each one being well longer than the last chapter, have been produced in regards to the minutia and individual facets of standing vertical biomechanics. I am a strong believer in minimalism and that athletes should only focus on those bare essentials that contain the greatest transfer to performance. With that in mind, here is quick recap of those basic keys to the technique of a standing vertical jump:

- Use a fast backwards arm swing in order to maximally prime the phases to come.
- Crouch down quickly at the knees and hips, as deep as one can while still able to achieve a powerful reversal. For some athletes, this will not be very deep.
- Lead with the head and keep the eyes up, but don't over-extend the neck. This phase usually happens naturally.
- Reverse the downward motion of the jump upwards as quickly as possible. Staying in the bottom position too long wastes elastic energy and is often a sign of forcing/muscling the jump.
- During the reversal of the jump, use the arms in a "pulling" motion. A vertical jump should be more of a "pull" off of the ground then a push. Pushing tends to take the hips out of the jump, and hurts the sequential action of jumping. This is usually more an issue for quad dominant athletes who struggle with running leaps.
- Get to the balls of the feet as quickly as one can during the course of the jump. Don't let the heels sit on the ground for the duration of the upward phase.
- Completely extend the hips. Think of "closing the triangle" of the knees, hips and shoulders. Medicine ball throws and Olympic lifts are great special strength exercises in this area.
- Finish the jump "tall" with the shoulders and arms raised high.
- Complete the jump with a powerful downward flexion of the calves into the ground.

There isn't a tremendous amount of practice that needs to be dedicated to practicing the standing vertical jump itself, as the implementation of plyometrics and depth jumps with correct form will give an athlete plenty of chances to work on these basic techniques. Basic strength training (especially the Olympic lifts) often assist in standing vertical jump technique through improving the intermuscular coordination of jumping muscles. Standing jumps for maximal height can and should be practiced periodically with a few technical cues in mind (especially if one is preparing for a testing battery such a combine), but athletes will often do better to focus their time on practicing running jumps which require many more repetitions, along with development of specific strength, to master.

Chapter VIII

Running jump principles and biomechanics

Let's shift gears a bit and move past individual styles, into some universal laws of jumping mechanics and optimal technique. Anyone can perform a standing jump well once their strength is there, but running jumps require lots of skill and practice time. Basic knowledge of the mechanics that direct athletes upwards is helpful in understanding the rationale behind various cues and instructions commonly given to athletes to improve their running vertical height. There are six main principles that guide all running jumps for height.

1. Technique is based off of skill and specific strength.
2. A jump is regulated by its weakest link.
3. Speed is equal to force multiplied by the distance that force is applied.
4. Running jumps are a series of moving levers.
5. Forward and upward acceleration of the hips is key to converting horizontal energy.
6. Finishing the jump tall adds extra inches to a jump.

Principle #1. Technique is Based off of Skill and Specific Strength

Many athletes can perform a standing jump well, but far less can perform a running jump with maximal efficiency. Athletes who can't jump much higher off the run than their standing efforts are lousy at running jumps for two reasons:

1. They have very little skill at a running jump because they never practice it.
2. Two, because they never practice it, the physiological adaptations that come with practice, such as strong ankles and feet, are not there!

Athletes who rely on muscle more than elastic mechanisms to move are going to struggle with fast running jumps, because their body hasn't made those elastic adaptations that makes them possible. Athletes who don't have the physical ability to carry out a particular jump technique won't be successful with it, and without specific strength, a running jump is doomed to fail. This is a vicious cycle that needs to be corrected for those athletes who seek better running leaps!

If an athlete's running jump is very poor, they need to improve the quality of their elastic muscle contraction, which means improving the strength and integrity of their connective tissue/tendons, and the ability of the muscle to interact with this tissue. This is accomplished through high volume, specific jump practice (that will improve both skill and specific adaptation) as well as repeated, lower intensity plyometrics. These exercises help to improve the strength that allows athletes to improve their elastic and stretch shortening cycle ability.

Principle #2. A Jump is Regulated by its Weakest Link

In any running jump, very high forces are going to be encountered in the various joints of the body, the highest of which will typically be eccentric forces through the hip, knee and ankle. It is for this reason that athletes who are relatively weak, or have poor motor control will find themselves limited in their ability to carry out a fast running jump with the proper technique and form. An athlete can get immensely strong through the weight room, but that strength will only be useful up to a certain speed of takeoff.

As the speed of the jump takeoff increases, the loading on the ankle and hip joints multiply themselves quickly. The increase in force is so great, during some track and field jumps, athletes will encounter up to 10 times their bodyweight on their jump leg! If you ever get the chance to watch the ankles and lower legs of Olympic high jumpers in slow motion, you will realize just how impactful speedy jumps can be on this part of the body! The key to being a well-balanced jumper is to also keep training in balance. A training breakdown of around 80% jumping, plyometrics, speed and sport play, to 20% resistance training is a good general starting point for many athletes to maintain this balance. *A small amount of weightlifting will go a long way when an athlete is doing a large amount of other explosive work.*

Principle #3. Velocity = Force x Distance

If you have been through any physics class, you should remember the equation: Speed = Force x Distance. This is an important principle when it comes to jumping, after all:

- How high can you jump if you don't bend your legs at all?
- How far could you throw a baseball if you didn't bring your arm back behind your head?
- How fast could you hit a hockey puck without bringing the stick back?

The answers, clearly, are not very high, far or fast! In order to achieve a high speed, there must be a significant vertical distance that the athlete brings their "center of gravity" through during the time they apply force to the ground. Every athlete has this "center of gravity". The center of gravity (COG for short) is the exact center of the body. If you were hanging from an imaginary string, it is the point where you would be perfectly balanced and could spin evenly in any direction. For most people, this point is about an inch under the belly button, and halfway between the front and backside of the body.

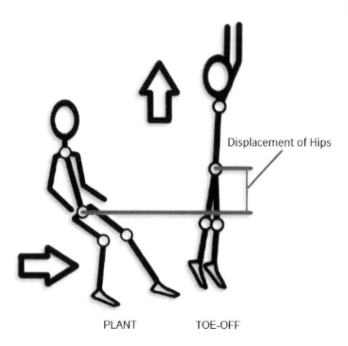

Figure 8.1: Vertical displacement of the hips is an important factor in how high an athlete will jump.

Rather than referring to the center of gravity as: "that point an inch under the belly button and halfway inside the body", we'll just refer to it as "the hips" for the sake of this book. In any jump, there will be a point when the hips are the lowest (bottom of the plant), and the highest (moment of the feet leave the ground) as shown by figure 8.1. The distance between the two heights represents the functional time frame that the athlete is able to accelerate the hips upwards. The greater the distance, the higher the potential for the jump at low to moderate takeoff speeds. It is possible for an athlete to jump very high with less displacement of the hips if they are moving very quickly, such as in a track and field high jump, as external speed becomes a greater factor in accelerating the athlete upwards.

Speed jumpers will prefer a smaller vertical displacement then force jumpers, regardless of whether they jump off of one or two feet. This is an area that athletes will work their jump out naturally given enough practice. Athletes who are in need of more practice, and have low running jump skill will rarely be bringing their center of gravity through enough vertical distance to produce an optimal jump result. Although distance is important in jumping, *it must never come at the cost of speed*. Speed is always going to be the deciding factor in sport play, and if I had to err on one side or the other with any athlete, I would always pick the ability to get off of the ground just a bit quicker. Clearly athletes could set up a jump with their hips less than 18" (45cm) from the ground if they really tried, but the amount that this slowed them down in the process would render the jump worthless in terms of converting any horizontal speed to vertical.

Principle #4. Running Jumps are a Series of Moving Levers

The key to making a running jump work is teaching the body to turn horizontal speed into vertical speed. This is accomplished through hitting proper angles of the legs and torso at takeoff, a task often easier said than done! A standing vertical jump is easy. Take no speed, and turn it into vertical velocity through bending the hips and knees and use the power of the muscle-tendon complex to leap upwards. I have seen plenty of uncoordinated athletes with great standing vertical jumps.

To perform a running jump, *the athlete must strategically place their legs in front of their body prior to the plant in order to form a "lever system" which* adds the horizontal velocity used in the approach to the jump. Figure 8.2

shows a comparison of an athlete using their lead leg as a strong, rigid lever vs. an athlete using their legs as bent, inefficient levers in a running approach. The illustration on the left is the typical position most high flyers off of two feet will find themselves in prior to takeoff (low hips, and a rigid lead leg).

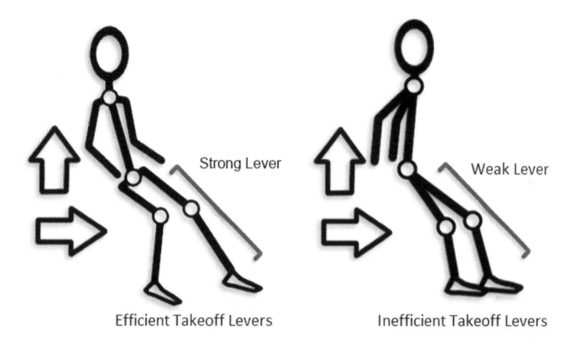

Strong Lever

Weak Lever

Efficient Takeoff Levers

Inefficient Takeoff Levers

Figure 8.2: Efficient vs. inefficient takeoff levers in running jumps.

The faster an athlete's jump approach, the more important it is that their limbs land in a position similar to the left athlete in figure 8.2. Very strong athletes can jump quite high off of two feet without much of an approach, using a strategy similar to the athlete on the right, but once the approach becomes longer and faster their jumps will struggle; the speed and force of the jump makes it too hard to convert the horizontal speed to vertical speed. Even very strong muscles cannot overcome gravity when the joints they are supporting are caught in a disadvantageous position at high velocity!

This rigid takeoff concept applies even more strongly to a single leg jump! Success in single leg jumping, discussed in greater detail in chapter 10, relies on the ability of an athlete to deflect themselves off of the ground through a stiff plant leg. If the plant leg of a single leg jump is unable to maintain rigidity during the takeoff, an athlete won't be jumping very high. One of the main reasons that force jumpers often struggle with one leg jumps is due to the fact that, while they are great in the deep knee bend jump positions, *they often are poor in the tall, rigid leg positions that lead to great single leg jumping.*

In addition to strong levers, an athlete must also demonstrate proper posture through the upper body during a running jump, which is a straight spine, and the head tilted slightly upwards. The bane of a smooth running jump is looking down, or even straight ahead (although it's clearly ok to look straight ahead if you are a long or triple jumper!). Looking upwards provides a steering mechanism for the body to reach its vertical target, as well as triggering the extensor reflex which leads to higher jumping.

Principle #5. Forward and Upward Acceleration of the Hips

In the final approach of a running jump, the hips must do two things:

1. Move from slow to fast
2. Move from low to high

Moving from slow to fast means that an athlete must always accelerate into the plant of a jump, this being the most critical over the last 4-5 steps, if the approach is that long to begin with. Slowing into the plant of a jump will impair the second aspect of a successful jump, which is the hips moving from low to high. *The only way that the hips can move from a low to high position is if speed is maintained into the second to last step.* Slowing down in the last 2-3 steps of a jump will cause an early rise of the hips and cripple vertical efficiency. Both one and two leg jumps off of the run rely on the mechanism of the "penultimate step". The penultimate step is a term coined in track and field, and refers to the second to last step in a takeoff. This penultimate step is the point of the deepest lowering of an athlete's center of gravity (hips). It is facilitated by a *longer* than normal third to last step, which allows the athlete to "sink" without losing much speed.

Key Point

The penultimate step is the second to last step in a jump takeoff, and is characterized by its strong flexion of the knee and ankle, which allows a lowering of the hips. The success of the penultimate is largely a factor of the length of the third to last step.

Lowering of the hips is important in order to allow an athlete to cover more vertical distance over the course of the takeoff, as well as to allow the plant leg(s) to strike out slightly in front of the hips with no loss of speed. This lowering may actually start occurring with 3-4 steps to go in single leg jumps with longer run-ups. Once the hips are dropped through the long action of the third to last step, the last two steps of the jump will naturally come down fast, and in a quick "1-2" rhythm, regardless of whether the jump is performed off of one or two feet. This is key, because most people don't realize how closely the takeoff mechanisms of running one and two leg jumps are related!

Principle #6. Finish the Jump Tall

At the tail end of any jump off one or two legs, there is one final element that can maximize the jump and add an extra inch or two to the result. This element is finishing a jump with the highest possible center of mass, or "finishing tall". At the moment of final toe-off in any jump, there are two biomechanical principles that will determine just how high an athlete will go.

1. Vertical velocity of center of gravity
2. Vertical position of center of gravity

The vertical velocity (vertical speed) of the athlete at the final point of takeoff is going to be dictated by how powerfully they performed the jump. Powerful legs and hips combined with good jumping skill will lead to a fast vertical velocity. Performing the first 5 principles of a running jump well will also help immensely to achieve this goal.

The part of the jump that many athletes and coaches don't often consider is the *peak height of center of gravity* at the moment of takeoff. An athlete can influence how high their center of gravity is by the position of their head, shoulders, arms, and (in a one leg jump) the swinging, non-jump leg. By raising the center of gravity at the point of takeoff, athletes are essentially jumping from "higher ground" than athletes who leave the ground with lower hips. Check out figure 8.3, with the two athletes jumping off of one leg. See how their position at the final point of takeoff influences the highest point of their jump.

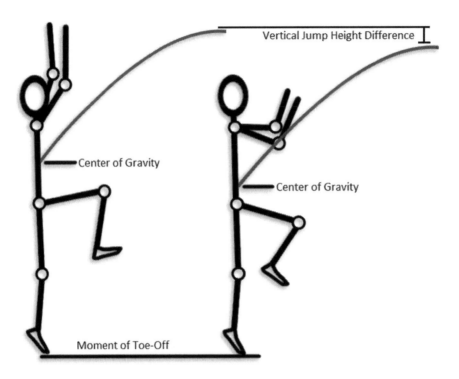

Figure 8.3: Differences in height of center of mass (COM) at takeoff.

When the athlete jumps, they "finish" the jump with their hands, shoulders, and head in as tall of position as possible. The reason for the raised limbs is to elevate the athlete's center of mass just an extra inch or two when the feet leave the ground. Athletes should finish takeoffs with the arms and head high, as well as the shoulders shrugged upwards to maximize the jump height.

Key Point

Jumping is much more than running fast, landing on one or two legs, and using muscle strength alone to catapult upwards. Rather, it involves a specific skill set, combined with powerful muscles to create explosive lift off of the ground.

Chapter IX

Running two foot jump technique and training concepts

Figure 9.1: Running two foot jump sequence with force jumper mechanics.

Most coaches don't look at the fine technical points of running jumps off of two legs. This is probably because the best athletes perform the sequence described in this chapter naturally, and athletes who can't do it well are just labeled as "uncoordinated" or "not very good jumpers". Regardless of where an athlete is at, there is probably something that they can correct or draw awareness to in their running two leg jumps to add extra jump height.

The best way, biomechanically speaking, to set up a fast running two footed jump is to use the *offset plant*, as this is the most efficient model to escape gravity with a bilateral takeoff. Without exception, any athlete under 5'8" (173cm) who can dunk off of two feet will use the offset planting mechanism, and are almost always force oriented jumpers. The offset plant represents the beauty of athletes who have learned to jump naturally, as it is a somewhat complex technique that is usually picked up without coaching. It is also one that is hard, if not impossible to "teach" by traditional means, just as many other sport skills, such as the reversal action of a shot putter or discus thrower. It is a movement style that should happen naturally if all parts leading up to it happened correctly.

Key Point

The offset plant (planting with the hips somewhat diagonal to the direction of the jump) is the most biomechanically efficient way to jump off of two feet from a running start.

Because of the relatively long ground contact time of a two footed jump, a variety of takeoff styles are allowed for, most of which make very efficient use of the body's natural strengths, such as fiber typing or skeletal structure. That being said, the jump-stop is another method of running two foot jumps, but only athletes with incredible strength to bodyweight ratios will find any use of this method, and it isn't optimal from a biomechanics standpoint, so we won't get into it in detail. The jump-stop also isn't very useful when attempting to "get up" at high velocity (athletes who use the jump-stop method favor slow approach speeds). Many athletes who do use the jump-stop would be better served to take the steps to achieve an offset plant, and I have seen instant increases in jump height by setting up better takeoffs according to offset plant principles.

To get an idea of how much proper jumping technique can potentially improve vertical height, take a look at some of your favorite basketball dunkers or volleyball players performing running jumps off of two legs. Freeze the video at the moment the athlete plants to takeoff and observe the low center of gravity, as well as the overall position of the legs and trunk. Now bring up a video of someone less adept at jumping attempting a high leap, and freeze the video at the moment they plant their feet. Note the position of the legs, hips and arms. Chances are there are some big differences in the following areas:

- The height of the hips. The expert jumper likely has lowered their hips more than the novice.
- The formation of the lever system in the plant. The novice is unable to plant their legs out as far in front of their body as they need to in order to direct their momentum vertically.
- Alignment and posture. Torso's of expert jumpers are always tall and erect in the plant, where a novice may be hunched over.

Now do the same thing with an expert vs. amateur jumper, but freeze frame the moment the athlete leaves the ground. Check out the following differences between the two athletes.

- Degree of plantar flexion. Check out how far down the feet of the expert jumper are pointed straight towards the ground, while the ground bound athlete might do well to have their toes pointed down 45 degrees to the floor at the point of takeoff.
- Hip and shoulder extension. An expert jumper will completely extend their hips and shoulder, where a novice might not "close the triangle" between their knees, hips and shoulders.
- Height of the arms and shoulders. The expert jumper finishes the jump with the arms in a higher position.

These are just two differences that separate the amateur from elite, but they are changes that can make for a big difference in total jump height! There is a range of how much athletes may be able to improve by honing in their technique, but the average athlete likely has between 1 and 5 inches to gain by getting things squared away in this department, which makes a total awareness of jump technique vital for getting the most out of any athlete's abilities.

Running Two Footed Jump: The Approach

Ask any track and field coach about the key to a good high, long or triple jump, and the answer is nearly always the same: *a good approach run.* During a two footed approach, only 4-7 steps are needed to provide the athlete with the maximal velocity they need to reach their highest jump height using the offset style, and only 3-5 steps for a jump stop. Obviously, many sport game situations will call for less steps, and even with only a 3 step approach (1 initial and then the double leg plant), the running two foot jump can be 95%+ of the best an athlete can muster with a full efforts. Also, 3 steps is all that is needed to perform an offset takeoff, although this takeoff style becomes even more efficient with more steps and speed leading into it. (At very low speeds, the offset takeoff doesn't offer as many advantages over a squared up takeoff as compared previously in figure 8.2.) Compare this to a single leg jump, which can take at least 3-4 steps to allow an athlete to achieve good jump height, and you can see how double leg jumping is ideal for many sport situations.

During the acceleration phase, the eyes should be kept up at the target of the jump, which will lead the head and spine along into a good posture. The athlete can, and should, run with whatever style they are particularly comfortable with, so long as they are smooth and accelerate rapidly into the final steps of the jump. Over-coaching the manner in which the approach run is carried out can lead to rigidity and a lack of explosiveness. Because the running two leg jump is not dependent on maximal velocity, there are a range of acceptable running styles. Whatever the length of the approach here, there should be an urgent acceleration inside of 6 steps to go, and especially in the last 3.

Running Two Footed Jump: The Plant

The offset takeoff means that an athlete will plant the last two steps of the jump in a staggered "left-right" or "right-left" rhythm with the hips somewhat diagonal to the jump's direction. *Placing the hips diagonally will bring the athlete into a position to better use leverage to their advantage in the rigid forward leg*, and give the rear leg a fuller opportunity to push and produce force. This mechanism is one that no coaches teach, comes together innately, and represents the magnificent ability of the athlete to build a skill off his or her own intuition. There is a spectrum as to how close jumping athletes are to the optimal version of this technique, however.

The motor "program" of the running two footed jump starts with 3 steps left in the process. When an athlete closes down to within 8-10 feet of their takeoff position, their body will automatically begin initiating the final jump sequence, starting with the third to last step. This 3rd to last step is always longer than every other step leading up to it, and can actually be considered a long, low "jump" into the last two steps of the takeoff.

The key word here being *low*, so the "low to high" takeoff mechanism of the hips can work properly. Many times we just look at the last step or two in a jump to determine its effectiveness, but I can tell you that *without a good 3rd to last step, any jump off of one or two feet will be limited*. Check out figure 9.2 on page 93 for an example of the long and low nature of the third to last step.

Figure 9.2: The third to last step is long, low and fast.

As the athlete pushes hard off of the third to last step, the last two steps will come down in a fast rhythm, sometimes landing nearly simultaneously[18]. Typically the second to last step will fall under the hips while the last step rapidly "shoots" out in front of the body to form the rigid lever in which to convert horizontal velocity to vertical (shown on the next page in figure 9.3). This slightly offset step and plant process has been referred to by volleyball coaches as a "step close".

The exact placement of these last two steps is unique to the athlete, and shouldn't be altered by eager coaches or overthinking athletes. As athletes undertake training specific to well-rounded jumping, their placement should fall into place naturally. For training and coaching purposes, it is important to focus on the *rhythm* of these two steps, and not so much the placement. Athletes who favor approaching the jump slowly, and with a jump-stop mechanism, typically won't be able to consciously set up an offset takeoff placement of their feet, and jump with any power. What can encourage this type of takeoff, however, is *forcing the athlete to utilize a faster takeoff than they are typically comfortable with*, as this is a tool that can allow an athlete's subconscious to put together the offset plant. Although the jump won't be as high for these athletes initially (usually), it will come together over time, and also improve as their elastic strength increases.

[18] Kenny, Bonnie, and Cindy Gregory. *Volleyball: Steps to Success*. Champaign, IL: Human Kinetics, 2006.

The foot of the front leg will typically hit a bit flatter than that of the rear leg, as the front leg's job is to deflect the body upwards. Focusing on planting on the ball of the foot will result in "mushing" onto the heel and a subsequent break of momentum. High impact forces of the jump will send the front heel to the ground, regardless of the athlete's efforts in keeping pressure elsewhere. The rear leg will tend to hit more on the ball of the foot, since the rate of loading in this back leg is not quite as high (the front leg deals with instant, heavy loading, while the rear leg has more time to produce power).

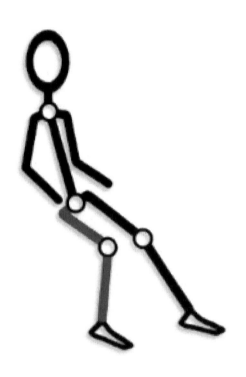

As with the standing vertical jump, an athlete will want to get to the lowest point of the plant as fast as possible in order to make maximal use of the stretch shortening cycle and elastic energy. The athlete should reverse the jump as fast as possible, and if the athlete loaded well and had good eccentric strength, then this phase will happen unconsciously and efficiently. When the athlete begins to reverse the jump, both feet should begin to direct forces through the ball of the foot and the big toe. *The speed at which an athlete can put force through the ball of the foot and big toe is going to often determine who runs the fastest and jumps the highest.* Of all success factors in the running

Figure 9.3: Offset plant leg placement. The hip of the rigid lead leg (solid black leg) is closer to the direction of the jump than the shaded support leg.

two leg jump, the fast rhythm of the last two steps is probably the most critical factor in whether or not the jump will be successful (the rhythm of the last three steps can be thought of as "one...two, three!"). A slow rhythm of the last two steps leads to an inefficient transfer of vertical velocity, and tends to overload the quadriceps and knees as insult to injury.

Athletes will typically finish with their preferred plant leg for single leg jumps as the last step of the double leg jump, this also meaning that it is used for the third to last step. The reason for this is that the lead leg is the "plant leg" and is the one best used as a fairly rigid lever to deflect the athlete upwards while the other leg (the power leg) finds itself bent a bit more underneath the athlete, as shown in figure 9.3, and the left model in figure 9.4.

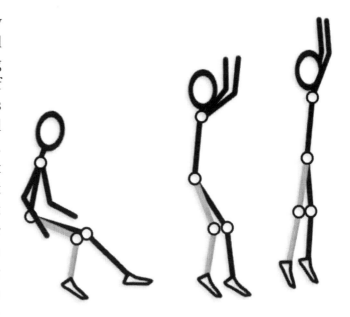

Figure 9.4: The final stage of the running two leg jump happens instinctively and automatically. The goal of the final takeoff is to reach complete hip and knee extension while finishing in a tall takeoff position.

Many athletes will find that the more bent leg of the second to last step is actually stronger in various single leg strength activities such as pistol squats (pistol squats happen to be a fantastic strength exercise for running two leg jumps for this exact reason). When looking at running single and double leg jumps from a mechanical perspective, we find that they are actually very similar in the last few steps, and this also shows that practicing single leg jumps can have a positive transfer for double leg jumps and vice versa.

(Anecdotally, I can say that one of the best periods of two leg jumping ability I had in my early 20's was one where I was doing no traditional barbell strength work, but was working hard on pistol squats and other bodyweight variations. I had tripled the amount of pistol squats I could do in a few months, and my two leg jumps had never felt so effortless. As a natural speed jumper, improving my ability to sustain force for a long period of time in my support leg worked wonders for my two leg jumping ability.)

The takeoff and finish of a double leg jump is nearly the same as its standing version. There is little that truly can be done in the final stages of jumping to increase propulsion, but some athletes may find that directing attention to the feeling of their foot and hip extension may help them to create a longer and faster push through the ground. Focusing on directing force to the balls of the feet quickly, and then pushing the feet into complete extension upon takeoff can result in a more powerful lift for many athletes.

Running Two Leg Jump: Areas of Instruction and Awareness

With the fairly natural skill of the running jump, it is many times more useful to direct athlete's awareness to certain areas, rather than giving hard instruction. Since there is a slightly different optimal technique for everyone, athletes can experiment with different rhythms and speeds of movement that work for them in acquiring better jump form.   When it comes to jump awareness and instruction, there are five main areas to look at.

1. Approach speed
2. Head positioning
3. Rate of the last two steps
4. Loading rate
5. Force transfer and downward extension in the feet

As mentioned before, manipulating the comfortable approach speed of an athlete into their jump can be a useful method to achieve higher jumps. Athletes should have an awareness of their maximal controllable speed, and then allow themselves to practice at speeds just higher than their comfort level for an "overspeed" training stimulus. Many athletes don't reach their two leg jump potential simply because they rarely practiced outside of the slow speed range they were comfortable with.

The second point of the running jump where solid instruction is useful is that of head positioning. Athletes should make it a habit to keep their eyes and head up at the target of their jump. Often times this stops happening once an athlete starts thinking of other aspects of the jump, but this jump action must become a habit, and not be sacrificed in favor of other technical points. Jump with the eyes looking up at the target, and the body will follow; simple as that.

The third piece of the running two foot jump that can be improved is *the rate of the last two steps*. The best jumps happen when the last two steps come down in a fast rhythm. Athletes will be served well by drawing feeling and awareness to the rhythm of the plant, realizing that it should be fast, as the feet hit the ground nearly together. Most athletes will find that the faster these two steps come down, the better.

The fourth area of a jump that can be helped by awareness is that of *rapid loading*. The less time from the moment the plant foot touches down, to the position of maximal knee bend, the better. To optimally load a two legged jump, athletes should think about actively "pulling" down into maximal knee and hip flexion, rather than just "falling with gravity". Rapid loading allows an athlete to take fuller advantage of the stretch-shortening cycle, as well as the strength and elasticity of the connective tissue (tendons, muscle sheaths, titin, z-discs) that is found around and even within the muscle fibers. The rapid loading action also increases the rate of force development and reversal in the primary joints of a jump, and promotes faster takeoffs.

Fast takeoffs in sport are usually far more important than the overall height of the jump. The ability to load a jump rapidly is based largely on skill and elastic strength (and the depth of the loading is regulated by relative strength in the associated muscles), but can be improved quickly with practice and specific plyometric training. When working on this aspect of jumping, it is often useful to start with the standing version of the jump through specific practice, depth jumps, and elastic resistance.

Figure 9.5: Proper plyometric practice can improve the rate of eccentric loading in vertical jumping. Photo Credit Maria Lavelle.

Elastic resisted jumps with a focus on speed of descent may be the best overall method to increase loading strength and skill. This mechanism can also be improved by properly performed kettlebell swings with an emphasis on the downward motion. Kettlebell swings have been researched to have advantages on plyometric exercise in increasing vertical jump, and they do so through overloading the hip hinge mechanism of the trunk, an area that many plyometrics cannot maximize on their own.

The final improvement cues of a running two leg jump are related to the action of the feet and lower legs. This piece regarding the loading portion of efficient two footed jumping must not be neglected! Remember, one of the biggest mistakes that an athlete can make in the plant and toe-off portions of the jump is leave the feet flat until the final action of the takeoff.

Key Point

The kettlebell swing is a great tool for increasing loading rate in the hip hinge.

This habit of flat feet is a plague to defeating gravity, and is often a sign of attitudes of covering over lack of movement quality with strength work. A proper plant and takeoff that makes the most of the energy stored in the Achilles tendon will favor a takeoff with the majority of force going through the ball of the foot, and not the heel. The heel may hit the ground during a running two foot jump, but when it does, it should be for just a fraction of a second during the eccentric half of the jump.

The heel making continual contact with the ground during the concentric (upwards) action of the jump will impede the smoothness and force transfer of the takeoff. If an athlete spends the majority of time in a jump on the back of the foot, massive elastic energy will be lost and cannot be made up! The sequence of transferring weight from the middle of foot to the toe will be different for each athlete, but in general, the faster an athlete can get to the ball of the foot and particularly the big toe, the better.

Many strength training coaches, as well as some common sense, may say not to extend the calves until the hips and knees have extended (such as in Olympic weightlifting), but this is *not* the case in double leg jumping. An athlete must get the heels about 1-2" off of the ground in the second half of the jump, and then *forcefully* point the toes down towards the ground in the last phase of push-off. Optimally, athletes will be able to achieve a subtle feeling of force directed to the big toe during this final action. There are a variety of drills which can teach a connection with the lower leg and big toe, and the simplest ones, such as a calf raise or heel-raised squat, with focus on big-toe tension, are often the best motor teaching tools.

With that, we have the biomechanical series of the running two leg jump. *Although there is a lot of complex information that goes into the jump, there are only a few points/cues that athletes truly need to keep in mind or the process will become over-complicated.* When practicing jumps, focus on only one thing at a time. Paying conscious attention to more than this will tend to result in a paralysis by analysis.

Key Physical Factors of the Running Two Leg Jump

So all of this will clearly beg the question, what will make someone a better jumper off of two legs? Number one, initially, is the skill of the jump which comes through direct practice. An unskilled jumper won't get too high unless they are an incredibly powerful athlete. Outside of jumping skill, a key factor is muscular strength and power. Athletes who are strong in the weight room will tend to be very good jumpers off of two feet, since the longer time to generate force in this style is somewhat similar to the longer time it takes to generate muscular force via strength training. A double leg jump is essentially "throwing" ones-self off the ground using two legs, and since the average athlete weighs 150-225lb, the legs and hips had better be strong to "throw" far!

Another key factor in a two leg jump is the ability to effectively use the lower legs with a strong connection to the foot and big toe. An athlete can be strong, but if this connection doesn't exist, jumping will never be optimal. Athletes can easily build their feet through specific strength training (using exercises such as the "short foot", or performing barbell squats on the balls of the feet while clawing the toe), as well as a healthy dose of barefoot training. There are plenty of ways to strengthen the intrinsic muscles of the feet and the big toe, and they can be very useful in improving athletic speed and movement ability.

Speed is another important factor for jumping off of two legs, but acceleration speed (0-20m) is much transferrable to this skill than top end speed. Acceleration is based more on an athlete's strength then their ability to build up to running at a high maximal velocity. Top end speed, such as 100m speed in track and field has a bit less correlation to the two leg jump due to short contact times.

Ultimately, athletes who are extremely good at jumps off of two feet will have some sort of speed. Nobody who runs 14 seconds in the 100m dash has a 40 inch vertical jump off two feet (or one). In summary, and in order of importance, to be good at running jumps off of two legs, athletes must have:

1. Great power to bodyweight ratio in the quads, and of secondary importance, the glutes
2. Good coordination and skill of jumping
3. Good ability to accelerate (0-20m)
4. A strong connection with the foot and big toe

Cues, Drills and Exercises to Optimize Running Two Foot Technique

I couldn't conclude this section on the technical improvement of running two foot jumps without giving a plan on cues, instructions, and exercises that will help give an athlete maximal lift off of the ground. With that being said, the following figure is a matrix of methods to improve double leg jumping ability and technique.

Cues and Exercises for Double Leg Jumping			
	Approach	**Penultimate**	**Plant**	**Takeoff**
Cues (Beginner)	Tall natural running. Long and low third to last step.	Put last two steps down as fast as possible while staying low.	Keep torso/head upright and get to the forefoot as fast as possible. Full arm swing.	Extend arms and head up high while extending the hips fully and calves down into the ground.
Awareness (Advanced)	What is the speed and rhythm of the approach? How long is the third to last step?	What does the rhythm of the last two steps feel or sound like?	How do the feet, calves, knees, hips or arms feel during the plant?	How do the feet, calves, knees, hips or arms feel during the takeoff?
Plyometrics	Acceleration, Skipping, Sprint Drills	Bounding, Skipping, Acceleration	Single and Double Leg Bounding, Depth Jumps, Accentuated Eccentric Jumps	Band Assisted Jumps, Low Hurdle Hops, Low Box Depth Jumps, Resisted Jumps
Strength	Deadlifts, Glute-Ham, Hamstring Curl, Hip Thrust	Deadlifts, Glute-Ham, Hamstring Curl, Hip Thrust, Skater Squats	Pistol Squats, Front Squats, Back Squats, Forefoot Squats, Kettlebell Swings	Jump Squats, Olympic Lifts, Dynamic Calf Raises, Medicine Ball Throws

Figure 9.6: Cues, awareness and training techniques for running two leg jumping.

Through using figure 9.6, coaches and athletes can determine the best course of action to improve running two leg jump technique based on ability level (beginner or advanced). In addition to cues and instructions, there are also strength and plyometric efforts that work to improve both athletic power and associated vertical jumping technique. It is through utilization of all methods that an athlete can reach the highest level of vertical jumping. This isn't to say that the optimal jump technique can't be achieved through sport play and jump practice alone, but the above chart can certainly create a faster route to an athlete's individual, optimal technique.

In programming plyometric and drill oriented work towards improving vertical jump, realize that a significant amount of repetitions are required to improve the related technical aspect of jumping. Simply performing 1-2

Figure 9.7: The pistol squat is one of the best exercises to improve the quality of the supporting penultimate leg in running two leg jumping. It is also a nice general strengthening exercise for single leg jumpers. Photo Credit Kevin Kuhn.

sets of 10 reps in a given plyometric will often not be enough to encourage the improvement in technical ability. Also useful, but not included specifically for the jump phase technique in figure 9.6, are the myriad of speed based plyometrics used to facilitate rapid switching between contraction and relaxation such as tuck jumps, lateral barrier jumps, and dorsiflexion ankle hops. These exercises are useful for any powerful athletic movement, and especially vertical jumping. We'll get a chance to see how the utilization of these exercises breaks down a bit further when we get to sample programming in chapter 12.

Looking at figure 9.6 from a force vs. speed dominant jumping perspective, realize that initially, each type of athlete will respond well to their weak point (i.e. force jumper will respond very well to plyometric training and vice versa). In the long term of training, athletes should favor the type of training which matches their natural strengths. Speed jump athletes will want to address their weaknesses through strength work, but will find their highest result with plyometric oriented training. Force jump athletes will find their highest result through a combination of specific jump work and strength work, with occasional plyometric work to help with a weakness if they have it. With that, we conclude technique and training applications for the running two leg jump.

Chapter X

Running one foot jump technique and training concepts

Figure 10.1: Running single leg jump sequence.

Jumping off of one leg relies heavily on biomechanics, skill and coordination. An uncoordinated athlete who lacks the technical requirements of a single leg jump will struggle immensely to pull it off. This being said, the majority of the time and skill being equal, jumping off of one leg usually represents the highest an athlete can vertically leave the surface of the earth from a biomechanical perspective. The reason why being that once the skill of the jump is mastered, a single leg jump allows for the conversion of immense amounts of horizontal speed and force to vertical movement.

Jumps off of two legs will always be limited by takeoff speed at some point. Once an athlete is moving too fast, they just can't move their legs and hips into the takeoff position effectively. Two leg takeoffs also can't take advantage of the fast momentum of the swinging free-leg of a single leg jump. It takes a very powerful, forceful athlete to be able to outdo their maximal single leg jump off of two legs given equal practice of both.

A single leg jump will generally have more technical pieces, along with room for potential improvement, than a two-leg jump, as the skill and overall athletic demand is fairly high. A one leg jump has a shorter available period of force application and is generally performed at higher takeoff speeds then its two leg counterpart. Remember, the faster the takeoff, the more attention to technique is generally needed. At high speeds, setting up a takeoff with inefficient "levers" will instantly negate the effect of powerful muscles. Proper biomechanics are very important for a one leg jump to be effective.

Although speed jumpers will naturally jump better off of one leg, force jumpers can make excellent one leg leapers if they take the time to practice the jump and master its mechanics. I have seen a good handful of track and field horizontal jumpers, by nature force jumpers with good sprint speed, improve their running one leg jump immensely through proper coaching and technical progressions. This book would be far too long if I listed a full drill battery for coaching track and field style jumps, but we will at least cover the basis of how athletes jump off of one leg, and key points of awareness for technical improvement. As mentioned before, there is not a great difference between many facets of the running one and two leg jumps. The following aspects of both jumps are actually quite similar:

- The rhythm of the approach
- Acceleration
- Position of the plant foot in front of the center of gravity
- The long, short-short rhythm of the plant

Figure 10.2: Single leg jumping relies more on the speed and rhythm of the approach than jumping off of two legs. Photo Credit Maria Lavelle.

In addition to the above list, both jumps are also asymmetrical in nature, each leg having a different "job" in the jump. Although there are some basic similarities, there are also some critical differences between the one and two leg running vertical jump which are as follows:

1. A single leg jump utilizes a single support at higher speeds, and thus creates an extremely high rate of force development on the plant leg. In a two leg jump, forces are distributed between the two legs over a greater period of time.

2. In a single leg jump, the jump foot stays flat, pre-tensed with energy, during the majority of the plant due to higher takeoff forces. Athletes will not be able to "get to the big toe" and plantar flex during the mid-stance of the single leg jump the way it occurs in a double leg plant, due to the high forces and rapid loading rate in the plant ankle and foot.

3. The second to last step, known as "the penultimate step", works in a rolling, heel-to-toe, fashion in a single leg jump.

4. The plant leg hits very rigidly and works in somewhat of a "sweeping motion" against the ground in single leg jumping. Due to the takeoff angle and sweeping motion of the jump leg, a single leg takeoff is typically more posterior chain (glute, hamstring) driven than the often quadriceps oriented two-leg jump. The ability to sprint fast in a good upright position has a strong transfer to elite performance in a single leg jump due to similar muscle groups and movement patterns.

5. The swing of the free drive knee contributes heavily to the power and vertical position of the athlete at takeoff, where a double leg jump obviously lacks this momentum contribution with both feet planted on the ground.

6. The single leg jump can be performed effectively at much higher takeoff speeds then the two leg jump without breaking stride.

Now that we have the primary differences covered, let's get into each piece of an effective single leg jump, starting with the approach run.

Running One Leg Jump: The Approach

The running jump starts out in a smooth, accelerating manner, similar to the two legged jump. Unlike the two leg jump, where athletes can reach maximal height within 3-5 steps, the single leg jump will typically need 4-8 steps to allow an athlete to get up their highest. Some athletes will employ more than 8 steps, perhaps up to 12 in the performance of elite high jumpers, but anything more than this is unnecessary, and also rather impractical, especially given team sport considerations. Horizontally oriented single leg jumps will have the longest run-ups, at over 20 steps in high level long and triple jumps.

The single leg jump relies more on approach speed then the double leg jump. Just as the double leg jump, the approach should be a smooth acceleration within the athlete's natural running pattern. Overcoaching athletes too far out of their natural stride will have negative results in the long run (and especially in short term results). Whether the athlete runs the first 2/3 of the approach on their heels or toes is irrelevant to the ultimate success of the jump. What *is* important that with 3 steps left in the approach, the athlete should:

1. Accelerate rapidly into the jump
2. Perform the penultimate step (2nd to last step) with the correct rolling action
3. Lower the hips without breaking stride (done through a proper penultimate step)

The athlete must also keep their head and eyes up in the direction of the jump during all aspects of the approach run, just as in a double leg jump. I will note that in track and field horizontal jumping, more coaching can and should be applied to the technique of the run-up, as the meshing of the approach and jump itself is more closely related for this activity. When the athlete nears the takeoff point of the jump, they will begin the sequence of the last three steps. Although many athletes who learn to jump off of one leg do so intuitively, there are many who never pick up on this skill through adolescent development due to lack of specific practice. For these athletes, a concrete knowledge of the last three steps is useful to help them understand what they are trying to accomplish in the process of the jump. The following description of the last three steps are based off of a left footed jump.

Running One Leg Jump: Three Steps Out

When the athlete reaches the point of 3 steps until takeoff (around 10-15 feet from the point of takeoff), the athlete should be accelerating aggressively. If the athlete isn't already moving quickly at this point, they will need to accelerate hard to hit a reasonable speed into the plant. The single leg jump relies heavily on speed and more importantly, acceleration. To start the final takeoff sequence, and begin the third to last step (for a left foot takeoff), the athlete:

1. Keeps the head and torso upright.
2. Pushes hard off of their left foot, taking a longer than normal stride while keeping the hips low.
3. Strides onto the slightly bent and dorsiflexed (heel pointed towards the knee) right leg. *Just like the two footed takeoff, this is a long and low step in the direction of the takeoff.*

Figure 10.3: Third to last stride, single leg takeoff.

Figure 10.3 represents this step. The shaded leg is the plant leg, which is also the "3rd to last" step leg. An athlete may stutter step their way up to this third to last step, and in open, team sport situations, an athlete will usually try and "steer" themselves to the point where they can begin to initiate the final 3 step sequence around 12 feet away from the final point of takeoff. Every step up to this point does not have to be precise or calculated in team sport (as opposed to track and field), but once the athlete hits the 3rd to last step, the motor program that involuntarily controls these last steps takes over, and the athlete will begin to unconsciously set up their takeoff.

Running One Leg Jump: Two Steps Out

The second to last step of a single leg jump is known to track coaches as "the penultimate step". *In single leg jumps, especially those in track and field, the penultimate step is where the process is largely made or broken.* Spending time around the long jump takeoff board of track and field meets, many coaches will mistakenly keep their eyes glued on the athlete's plant step in the jump, and make corrections based off of those mechanics (such as "drive the knee more!", or "put that last step down faster!"). The most important aspects of a single leg jump are actually made are during the 2nd and 3rd to last steps of the jump, because if these pieces fail, the jump goes downhill quickly, and the athlete will fail to reach an efficient position for the final step. If the athlete slows down during the penultimate step, places their foot incorrectly or raises their hips too quickly they will lose jump height or even risk injury. To complete the penultimate (2nd to last) step, the athlete performs the following sequence of events (left footed takeoff):

1. The athlete performs a rolling, heel-to-toe step on the right penultimate foot, which coming off of the long third to last step, effectively lowers their hips in preparation to jump upwards. When this step is performed on the toe, or comes down too far in front of the hips, it usually means that the third to last step wasn't quite low or long enough (each step is linked to the one before it!).
2. The penultimate step is pulled/swept under the body through the force of the glutes and hamstrings. Lack of control of these muscles can cause unwanted braking forces and slow the jump down considerably.
3. Keeping the hips low, the athlete rolls through the right foot and explodes forward onto the plant leg. The more vertically oriented the jump, and stronger the athlete, the lower the dip may be in this phase.
4. During this step, the arms are usually, but not always brought behind the athlete to add them to the force of the jump. The higher the takeoff speed and faster the planting action, the less this becomes a factor, and athletes who naturally use a single arm action shouldn't necessarily be pulled in the direction of a double arm swing by over-eager coaches.

Speed jumpers perform the penultimate step naturally with great skill, while force jumpers often struggle. In many cases, force oriented jumpers will have the bad habit of placing the penultimate step overly dorsiflexed and too far in front of the hips, causing deceleration into the plant and robbing the jump of vertical (and horizontal) speed. In the penultimate step, provided there was good speed coming into the jump, *the athlete's torso will remain vertical, perpendicular to the ground* with the eyes focused on the target of the jump.

Figure 10.4: Penultimate sequence, single leg vertical jump.

In cases where the approach has been slow and more acceleration is needed, the athlete can lean forward a bit into this 2nd to last step, but the torso must come back up to vertical for the last step, at the point of takeoff. Many predominantly two-footed jumpers will habitually lean forward during the plant of a single leg takeoff. This forward lean of the torso diminishes the quality of the lever system that gets them up off of the ground. In a single leg takeoff, good posture, with the chest out and head up at takeoff is important to helping create a tall spine that will deflect forces upwards.

Key Point

The penultimate step is often the most important step in the process of a single leg jump to perform correctly, with errors here reflecting themselves in the takeoff. In high velocity takeoffs, such as track and field, more technical instruction may be needed to ensure the highest efficiency of this step.

Nearly every aspect of the penultimate step in a skilled jumper happens unconsciously and efficiently. Athletes may perform the penultimate step with slightly different styles and alignments depending on their own strengths and weaknesses, but the general concepts ring true across the board. When the penultimate step is performed in the frame of jumping events in track and field, its performance becomes more rigid and tied to one technical model, especially in the horizontal jumps. Team sport athletes who do not have to adhere to one specific technical model may not need the fine tuning of this step that track athletes do, but they still should keep in mind the low, flat nature of the step itself. Through awareness of hip height and jump rhythm, they can find the penultimate step technique that matches their strengths.

Running One Leg Jump: Final Plant and Takeoff

The last step of a single leg takeoff is where the athlete gets to reap the benefits of a good process leading up to this point. If the penultimate step was performed well, speed is sufficient and posture is solid, an excellent jump is in the cards (and possibly a highlight reel play to be shown on TV later). For the final step of a single leg jump, the following sequence is put in motion:

- The left leg comes through low and fast into the plant, the foot hitting the ground around 8-16 inches in front of the hips, landing on the heel with the foot slightly dorsiflexed. (Athletes should think about planting on the flat of the foot, rather than the heel, but a slight heel strike is what ends up happening mechanically.)
- In some cases, to engage the posterior chain to a greater degree while directing the jump vertically, the hip of the plant leg may be projected slightly forward and up immediately prior to, or during the first stage of the plant (note the slight forward shift of the hips in figure 10.5 from left to right).
- The lower leg of the athlete is pre-loaded with energy, and the athlete strikes on the heel but rolls quickly onto the flat of the foot, with the power moving towards the big toe (although the foot typically stays flat until the final stages of takeoff).
- As this is happening, the swing knee drives through and stops at a point where it is parallel (or slightly higher) with the ground.
- The arms are driven up and over the head, and the shoulders shrug upwards to increase the height of the athlete's center of mass.
- The hips, knees, and feet completely extend and the athlete lifts off. The last aspect of the takeoff that the athlete can feel is often the "punch" of the foot pushing off.

Figure 10.5: Takeoff sequence, single leg vertical jump.

Biomechanically speaking, running jumps are the art of deflecting one's self off of the ground, especially the one leg jump. The last step is put down quickly, the leg extended to form a rigid lever. The foot contacts the ground in a rolling dorsiflexed-to-flat manner with loads of tension running through the lower leg. Hitting toe first, instead of rolling, will cause "mushing", as the heel will find itself forced down unless the athlete is running slowly and has unusually strong plantar flexors. When the foot hits flat, the tension runs up the body, as the quadriceps muscles act isometrically on the leg to keep the knee from flexing (although some flexion will happen no matter what, due to high forces).

When the takeoff leg plants, hitting the ground as a rigid lever, a high eccentric demand is placed on the hips and particularly the knee extensors (quads). In the second half of the plant, the hamstrings and glutes contract hard concentrically to provide vertical lift. This mechanism is a combination of a sweeping and pushing action, and helps explain why horizontal bounding exercises are so effective for increasing single leg jump power and total height. *If there is one biomechanical action that can be associated with a single leg takeoff, it is the sweeping, hinging action of the takeoff leg.* This hip driven movement is another reason that force dominant athletes struggle with single leg takeoffs.

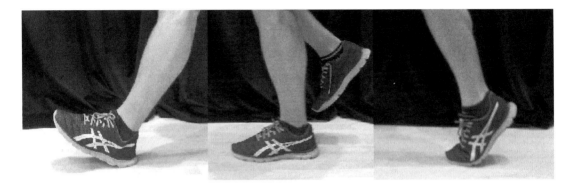

Figure 10.6: Rolling foot action in a single leg jump.

Remember the last two steps of the jump must be put down quickly, *especially the last step*. A slow last step will cause the takeoff foot to fall too far in front of the athlete's hips. This causes a braking effect, and yields an inefficient "deflection" off of the ground due to loss of speed and excessive forces transmitted to the knee. A long and slow last step also is the cause of extremely high forces placed onto the takeoff leg, and can result in injury if performed this way often.

Key Point

The most important aspect of the takeoff phase in a single leg jump is the hinging action of the rigid takeoff leg, a skill that can come easily to speed dominant athletes.

The right leg (swing leg), which is recovering behind the hips of an athlete at the plant, should be held back in its place for a split second to build elastic energy. This allows for a more powerful push when it does swing through and rapidly stop, or "block", causing its momentum to be added to the frame of the body. The swinging rear leg should drive through and stop at a position parallel to, or slightly above the level of the ground at final takeoff. If the swing leg just keeps driving all the way up to the chest, it will allow for a very high vertical position at takeoff, but unfortunately will not add its momentum to the jump efficiently. This is an aspect of single leg jumps that is often incorrectly coached, as many coaches overeager to apply the coaching cue of driving the knee will instruct athletes to "drive the knee as high as possible", rather than to the optimal position of parallel or slightly above.

Figure 10.7: Three amounts of knee drive in single leg jumping. The two on the left are acceptable amounts of drive, where the athlete on the right is not achieving a high vertical position due to lack of drive.

During the plant, the arms also come through and finish high above the head with the shoulders shrugged upwards to maximize the height of the athlete's center of mass and add a couple of "free inches" onto the jump. When this sequence is performed correctly, even a relatively weak or slow athlete can still find significant vertical lift off the ground, as the biomechanics of the jump allow the skeletal frame of the athlete to take the brunt of the involved forces.

Key Factors of the Single Leg Jump

The single leg jump is a slightly different beast than the double leg jump regarding technique and required physical qualities. When it comes to the ability to perform this jump well, skill is again the critical factor. After skill, there are a number of important, and very trainable, factors that lead to single leg success. The two immediate ones that will help an athlete are low body-mass-index and plyometric ability. Having a low body-mass-index, or basically being lean and light, is very important to be a good single leg jumper because of the relatively short time period of takeoff (under .3 seconds), and concept of forces multiplying themselves quickly. Heavier athletes will find an exponential increase in ground contact forces with their increased weight, which are hard to deal with in the shorter time frames of a single leg jump. Remember, good single leg jumpers are typically very light. A 6 foot tall Olympic high jumper will weigh around 155lbs, while females will be even lighter (proportionally) than this ratio.

Strength is very important for a single leg jump in the sense of the high forces the single leg jumper must contend with, but much of the strength gained in the weight room is not entirely useable for a single leg jump. Single leg jumpers must be strong, but they should attain much of their strength through plyometric exercise. Plyometric ability provides an instant boost to the single leg jump due to its improvement of the efficiency of the stretch shortening cycle through quick ground contacts.

Figure 10.8: Explosive bounding replicates the hip action of a single leg jump. Various bounding tests, from standing triple jumps, to 10 bounds for distance are a close measure of an athlete's specific preparedness for single leg jumping variations.

Things such as bounding and hurdle hops are fantastic for improving the single leg jump. Speed is very important for single leg jumpers, and particularly elite single leg jumpers. *On the highest levels, speed is often the factor that differentiates the good from elite.* Elite single leg jumpers are, without exception, very fast. Things like the 100m dash and bounding ability have been some of the primary predictors of success in advanced high jumpers. To be an elite one leg jumper, be fast and have the ability to bound far!

Although weight room strength isn't initially as useful as plyometric strength for unilateral takeoffs, aspiring single leg jumpers will find steady and continual improvement through raising their basic barbell strength levels. Elite single leg jumpers will still look to improve their core lifts such as squat, clean, and barbell step-ups by 3-5% each year in respect to their bodyweight. In this manner, usable weight room strength can be improved alongside the development of good technique, which will prolong ones athletic career and allow for the achievement of maximal results. It is often tempting for coaches to take an aspiring single leg jumper and pack on massive amounts of barbell strength, but this can injure the elastic capability of the athlete in the process, so care must be taken.

In summary, a good single leg jumper should possess the following qualities:

1. Acceleration and running speed
2. Speed jumper/athlete tendencies
3. Strong feet and ankles
4. Coordination and skill
5. Some ability to bound

Cues, Drills and Exercises to Optimize Running One Foot Technique

As with running two leg jumps, I wanted to give a summary of cues and exercises that athletes can use to improve their single leg ability. Since single leg jumping is a bit higher in velocity, and a more complex skill than bilateral jumping, this chart is much more abbreviated than the one in chapter 9.

Cues and Exercises for Single Leg Jumping				
	Approach	**Penultimate**	**Plant**	**Takeoff**
Cues (Beginner)	Tall, springy running. Long, low third to last step.	Put last two steps down as fast as possible while keeping torso upright and hips low.	Keep active tension in plant foot and "pull" with the hip and hamstring of drive leg. Delay swing leg.	Drive arms, shoulders and drive knee high. Fully extend plant leg and foot into the ground.
Awareness (Advanced)	Feeling and rhythm of the run. How long is the third to last step?	What does the rhythm of the last two steps feel or sound like?	Feeling of the quickness of the feet at the plant, and the "tallness" of the head and torso.	Feeling of the drive knee or arms in takeoff. Feeling of the foot in the final push.
Plyometric	Acceleration, Maximal Speed, Sprint Drills	Bounding, Skipping, Acceleration and Maximal Speed	Straight-leg Bounding, Standing Triple Jump, Depth Jumps, High Hurdle Hops	Band Assisted Jumps, High Skips, Medicine Ball Throws, Low Hurdle Hops, Bounding
Strength	Deadlifts, Glute-Ham, Hamstring Curl, Hip Thrust	Deadlifts, Glute-Ham, Hamstring Curl, Hip Thrust, Pistol Squats	Pistol Squats, Barbell 1/2 Squats, Barbell Step-Ups, Barbell Skips, Unilateral and Bilateral Deadlifts	Jump Squats, Olympic Lifts, Calf Raises, Weighted Knee Drives, Barbell Skips

Figure 10.9: Cues, awareness and training techniques for single leg jumping.

With two leg jumping, plyometric, speed and skill work are a bit more important, relatively speaking, than strength work, but a comprehensive approach is best. The single leg jump is one that requires lots of consistent practice and associated elastic strength work to maintain. Trying to improve unilateral jumping by strength means alone (for more than 1-2 months) sends athletes backwards. Utilizing coaching cues, awareness and backing plyometric and strength work will always yield the greatest result over time.

One thing to notice about the difference between the cues and exercises for single and double leg jumping is the depth of the squats, the preference towards unilateral work, and the need for speed and sprint-like plyometrics that the single leg jump demands. Although the jumps set up similarly, once an athlete gets to the plant and the takeoff, the specific strength built for the jumps via strength and plyometric training is very different!

A useful technique when considering the direct practice of single leg jumps is that of shorter approach runs, such as three step jumps, to help athletes master some of the basic principles of the jump. Once mechanics are mastered from a short approach, long approaches become much easier. On top of this, long approach single leg jumps are fairly taxing on the body due to the high loading forces in the takeoff leg, so it can be useful to practice short approaches, as it allows for a greater volume of practice.

Although this type of short work is helpful, it can also be harmful at times for those athletes who depend on fast single leg takeoffs, such as track and field jumpers. Force oriented track and field jumpers, who are naturally great at short approach jumping, will often favor this type of short work to pad their egos, but the technical and elastic strength differences between short and long approach jumps will never allow them to reach their highest potentials if they don't regularly train with high takeoff speeds.

That concludes the technical section of single and double leg jumping. We'll end this book's portion of vertical technique with something that falls outside the realm of instruction, and is definitely more on the science side: Force-time curves of novice and elite jumpers. Force time curves are something that will appeal a bit more to the science-minded among us, but teach us valuable lessons regarding the importance of strong feet and overall "smoothness" when jumping high.

Chapter XI

Measuring vertical jump skill in the laboratory

In my experience working in a biomechanics lab as a graduate student, we studied hundreds of drop-landings and depth jumps using force plate technology. A force plate is essentially an expensive scale that can tell researchers how much force an athlete is producing every 5,000th of a second during the course of their jump (amongst other things). This is a useful tool in studying athletes, as nearly every athlete produces force somewhat differently during the course of their vertical jump or landing. Knowing an athlete's force/speed tendencies, and whether they preferred a one or two leg takeoff taught me a lot about how athletes produce force, as well as where and when they need to be strong to jump well. I wrote this section, not to make deliberate suggestions on what an optimal force-time curve is, but rather to show some general trends in the way that elite athletes display force throughout their movement in various types of jumps. (A force-time curve demonstrates how an athlete produces force over each fraction of a second that they are applying force to the ground in a jump, running stride, or any other form of ground based athletic movement.)

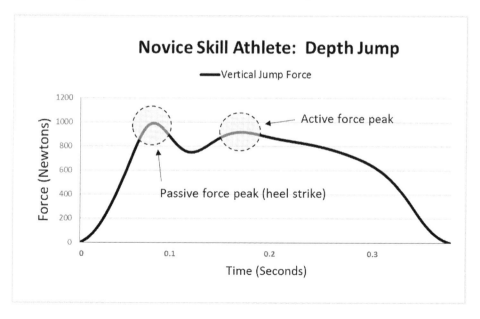

Figure 11.1: Force-time curve of unskilled jumper.

In my studies, the force-time curve of a powerful, but unskilled athlete (as far as jumping is concerned) looked something like figure 11.1. In this graph, the black line indicates the force an athlete produces over the period of time they are in contact with the ground. To set up the jump, they dropped from an 18" box and performed a "depth jump". A depth jump is a plyometric exercise where an athlete drops from a box to the ground, lands on two feet, and jumps powerfully upwards. Before the analysis begins, a few quick notes about the force-time curve in jumping:

- The first "peak", around the .1 second mark, is typically when the heels hit the ground. There is a fast rise in force because the full weight of the body is impacting the ground through the heel. Since this peak is due to the body weight crashing down, and not the force of the muscles, it can be referred to as "passive" force.
- Athletes who have good feet will have a soft, or even nonexistent, curve at the first peak because they can distribute the force of the landing more evenly.
- The second "peak" in force, represents the rate of "active" force development in the jump. For many athletes, the heels will hit for a quick spike in passive force, and then active forces take over.
- The better an athlete's rate of force development, the steeper the second peak of active forces. In the case of figure 11.1, this happens around the .15 second mark.

Figure 11.2: The depth jump is an essential vertical jumping exercise, as well as a useful way to analyze an athlete's force production in lab conditions.

In the depth jump of unskilled athletes, the highest force spike in the jump is always the point when the heels hit the ground. At this point, the forces of the drop landing would be transferred to the skeletal frame, rather than the muscles, and are thus *passive forces*. Unfortunately for jumping performance, when this force transfer to the heels and frame occurs, the muscular "slack" is taken out of the system, and energy is lost. Remember, the best jumps happen when eccentric energy is converted to concentric strength well. High passive forces hurt this transfer and reduce vertical jump height.

The point in figure 11.1 where concentric strength finally kicked in is indicated largely by the second rise in force at the .17 second mark. In a novice jumper, the second rise in force is usually lower and shallower (it doesn't happen quickly). As we will see later on, good jumpers off of two feet will have some passive forces in a depth jump, but they will produce active force *very* quickly to make up for it, and then some! Good jumpers off of one foot will hardly have any passive forces that exist in the jump, as their conversion ability of eccentric force to concentric in a short time frame is a critical aspect of their style.

The goal in teaching any athlete how to jump better is to *smooth out the force-time curve*. You don't need any fancy technology to pull this off (although it can certainly help if available). To "smooth the curve", coaches and athletes should be aware of loud, mechanical jumps. Noise from an athlete's feet slapping down are a good sign of excessive passive jump forces. Teaching jumping, plyometric and landing drills with an emphasis on smooth and extremely quiet movement will go a long way in helping an athlete to express force better, without a need for a 10,000 dollar force plate. Expert track and strength coaches have been doing this for years. I'll often have my athletes perform drills or jump landings where their goal is for me not to hear them move, which ensures a smoother force-time curve. A quiet jump means that the athlete makes good use of the stretch-shortening cycle, and doesn't waste energy. Through studying force-time curves on the plate, I have found that a smoother overall curve means that an athlete is good at transferring forces to the ball of the foot and keeping the heels from crashing to the ground. A basic, rudimentary coaching point in depth jumps is if the heel is crashing down, then the depth jump was from too high! Athletes with smooth and powerful jumps will look more like the graph in figure 11.3.

There are always going to be significant differences in the way that beginner and advanced athletes produce force. A large variance will also exist in the way that skilled single leg and double leg jumpers look in a depth jump analysis. Knowing this has implications for the way that we train, as well as how to instruct athletes in plyometric activities.

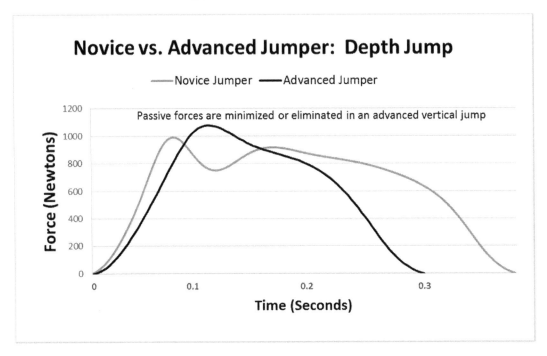

Figure 11.3: Force-time curve of novice vs. advanced jumpers.

Training Implications Based on Force Analysis

In order to jump well off of one or two feet, athletes must become masters of force production. Figure 11.4 is a graph of the force generation patterns of a skilled speed oriented jumper (All-American high jumper) and a skilled two foot jumper (accomplished basketball dunking athlete). This shows that while both jumpers have fairly smooth force curves, a predominantly double leg jumper can still get away with creating some passive forces.

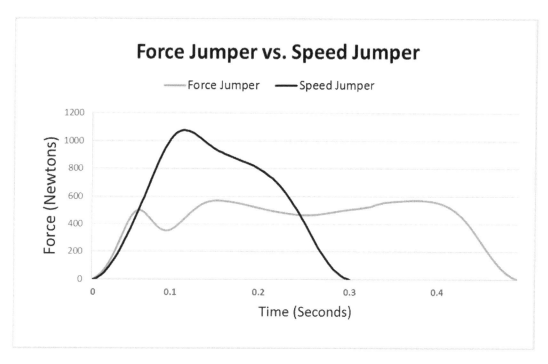

Figure 11.4: *Force plate analysis of a force jumper vs. speed jumper.*

This doesn't mean that it is optimal to put large forces through the heel or flat of the foot when jumping off of two legs, but it won't hurt an athlete jumping off of two legs the way it does in a single leg jump. Of particular note is the long, *smooth* curve of active force production that the double leg jumper displays and the rapid peak in force the single leg jumper achieves. These types of force production are both very distinctive to how the athletes jump in their competitive environments.

The long smooth force curve of the force jumper can be great for two leg jumping, but this habit can also hurt quick jumping, as well as the elastic strength needed for single leg jumps. Force dominant jumpers often make extremely fast gains through the use of a plyometric program with high contact volumes, as this strengthens their ankles and improves conversion from passive to active forces. Barefoot training is a great way to teach athletes the stiffness through the feet that quick jumps and good single leg jumping requires. Anecdotal experience has shown that barefoot style training has led to good increases in single leg jumping ability for those athletes with initially poor foot strength and function.

With long term training, double leg dominant jumpers seeking for continual two leg jump improvement should focus more on plyometric and power drills that allow more time for force expression, such as a power oriented depth jumps, squats and Olympic lifts. Bottom line, force jumpers should spend time on their weak points for quick improvement and well-roundedness, but ultimately they'll need to play to their strengths for long term development.

Key Point

Barefoot and repetitive low to moderate level plyometric work can be a great way for athletes to improve their foot function, and provide an instant boost to their single leg jumping ability.

On the other hand, good one leg speed jumpers have almost no passive forces in a depth jump. They are masters of smooth and efficient force conversion in a short time period. Since these jumpers tend not to produce forces over long periods of time naturally, basic strength training movements such as squats and deadlifts can prove extremely helpful. Strength training will help teach the nervous system of these jumpers to produce force over a longer time period, which nearly always yields nearly instantaneous gains in two leg jumping ability and standing vertical jumps.

Although strength work will yield some quick results to make a speed jumper more well-rounded, strength focused training isn't always the sole key for longer term specialized performance for these athletes. All jumpers should be taught to be smooth, but single leg jumpers need to focus particularly on jumps and drills that focus on keeping good landing stiffness to allow them the continual maintenance and improvement of their single leg ability. Speed jumpers will do well to capitalize on their strengths over time, which are high-intensity plyometrics that include high depth jumps, bounding, hurdle hops, and other forms of shock training.

This isn't to say that athletes can't be equally good at both styles of jumping, because they certainly can. Consistent practice of both types of jumping, being strong in balance, building strong and stiff ankles, and having a good level of coordination allows any athlete to be great off of one or two feet. There is no reason that a two leg jumper can't be great off of one leg or vice versa. This book is all about how to become great at any jumping skill, and even if athletes aren't wired a certain way, they can become much better through knowing the correct way to practice, as well as training techniques that cater to one type of jump or the other.

Conclusion of Jump Technique

Most books written on improving vertical jump or explosive athleticism don't pay too much attention to vertical jump technique, but I feel it is important to know human movement on a detailed level to achieve the highest results. I have written this book for a few reasons. One is to thoroughly clarify the technical aspects of jumping, and give a blueprint of what correct technique off either leg looks like. It is important to understand the similarities and differences between the one and two footed jumping styles in order to understand how to thoroughly train them.

Another, and perhaps a more important reason, is to give a basic understanding of how jumping works so that athletes can have a better feel for *why* they do what they do. The goal is not necessarily to go out and administer loads of drills and positional work emphasizing each of the movements I have shown above, but rather, through awareness, have a better *feel* of the jumping one does, and have a better idea of what allows the best jumpers in the world to go so high. Good coaches never over-complicate things, and respect the individual style and ability of each athlete.

Despite the general principles and knowledge in the pages above, remember that there is no "perfect" jumping technique, but rather, there is you or your athlete's perfect technique. Everybody has their own optimal style, and that style may even change a bit over the years, but the goal is to know the general things that make a good performance and then optimize the small pieces through awareness. That is the true takeaway. Athletes often perform a jump well, but they rarely know why. It is through awareness that we can make those final tweaks to achieve our highest performance.

With the total concept of movement in mind, one can move forward in training with new energy, realizing the purpose of every piece of the program. Each part of the program becomes more meaningful and valuable. In summary, my goals for coaches and athletes to achieve a better ability to coach and achieve better jumping movement and technique are as follows:

- Have a practical knowledge of the general points of correct jump technique.
- Gain the ability to take detailed notice of the different movements of different athletes.
- Know where performance deficiencies can be due to a lack of strength, stretch shortening ability, or skill.
- Perform jumping with an awareness of specific cues and body actions.
- Utilize strength exercises that improve the preferred technique of the athlete.

This book has been about the technical points of jump technique, with some strength associations. Although this isn't a book dedicated to training, I do feel that it is important to tie in some good practical methods by which technique can be backed by strength work, depending on the goal. Knowledge is great, but without experience, the outcome is always compromised. Through seeing programming, the gap between knowledge and experience becomes that much closer, so that is the goal of the next, and final chapter.

Chapter XII

Exercises and programming for various jumping styles

A paramount aspect of any book on improving athleticism is how it relates to exercise selection and training design. When it comes to anything in life, knowledge is nice, but experience trumps all. Ultimately, athletes benefit the most from simple programs designed by coaches who have worked with hundreds of athletes, and have struggled to continually best their own personal records in training.

I realize that most athletes, and many coaches are looking for applicable theory that can be put into practice. Listing facts and highlighting research is a fairly easy thing to do, as these concepts are somewhat rigid. Programming, on the other hand is more fluid and dynamic; one small change in a program has effects that trickle down into every other aspect. A full training program encompassing plyometrics, barbell training, speed training and everything in between is essentially a chess game of various training effects. Bottom line, the only way to program is through the trials and errors of experience.

This is not a book dedicated to programming, but I couldn't write a book without giving the user some insight as to how the ideas in this book make sense in the light of the big picture. With movement skill as the highest priority of athletic excellence, the exercises and dynamics of a program must reflect the end goal: to jump as high as possible (or at least to jump high in the context of other sport demands!). The program should cater to this goal by maximizing the strengths and foundational aspects of each jumping style. We'll cover programming for two jumping styles: The athletic two-foot vertical style, and training for single leg jumping; more of a track and field style programming template.

Basic Program Design for General Jump Training (Two-foot Focus)

Training programs designed to improve jumping ability tend to cater a bit towards that of two foot improvements. The majority of strength and conditioning programs that athletes undergo on a regular basis through high school, collegiate or private training will generally make use of strength, plyometrics and medicine ball throws in a manner that cater towards standing vertical jump improvement, as well as many other athletic qualities, such as short acceleration, agility and athletic size.

Athletes performing strength training and plyometric programs designed to improve their vertical will also notice single leg improvements, but typically not to the level that their two foot jump increases. Two foot jump training teaches athletes to produce larger forces for longer periods of time, a feat accomplished through strength training and plyometric drills that offer some relevance to technique.

The primary deficiency of many modern strength programs is the lack of exercises that allow an athlete to perfect movement technique specific to the biomechanics exhibited in either one or two leg jumps. Aside from strength training, athletes can succeed in increasing their two foot leap through a sufficient volume of specialized plyometrics that cater to improving an athlete's force production in longer windows of time. With most athletic skill development, general barbell training works just fine for improving vertical jumping and athleticism when combined with speed work, but performing simple, specific variations of that barbell work can give any athlete an edge over their competition. The bottom line of program design in respect to athletic technique are the following principles:

- Strength and power training don't always have to be specific, but shouldn't take away from vertical jumping technique either.
- Some specific strength work is useful to back the individual jumping style of the athlete, or to strategically attack their weaknesses.
- All plyometric work should have some aspect of the individual's vertical technique in mind (or whatever other skill is trying to be improved).

This being said, let's jump into some programming samples that are designed to cater towards individual jumping styles, starting with two leg jumping. "Force" oriented athletes will tend to respond better to a program like this than they would a program designed to improve single leg ability, as they are built more for strength work than they are a high volume of bounding and depth jumping. Below is a basic training template for an athlete training strength and power, with a vertical jump focus, in the offseason. The programs listed below only have exercises relevant to vertical training within them, so no upper body training is present (although a strong upper body is useful to jumping, upper body strength work isn't a requirement).

Explosive Off-Season Training: Vertical Leap Focus

Day	Order	Exercise	Week 1			Week 2			Week 3		
			Sets	Reps	%RM	Sets	Reps	%RM	Sets	Reps	%RM
Mon	1	20m Sprints	5	1	97%	5	1	97%	4	1	97%
	2	3 Jumps for Distance	5	1	97%	5	1	97%	4	1	97%
	3	Power Clean (From floor)	8	2	70%	6	2	75%	6	1	65%
	4	Deadlift	2	5	70%	3	3	75%	3	4,3,2	60%
	5	Vertical Med Ball Throw	3	3	97%	3	3	97%	3	2	97%
	6	Glute Ham Raise	4	8	60%	4	6	65%	4	5	60%
Tues	1	18" Speed Depth Jump	4	5	97%	2	10	97%	2	10	97%
	2	30" Power Depth Jump	3	3	97%	3	5	97%	3	5	97%
	3	Eccentric Front Squat (5-0-X)	5	3	75%	4	3	80%	4	2	83%
	4	Pistol Squat	4	4	60%	3	5	60%	3	4	60%
	5	Speed Tuck Jumps	3	12	97%	3	10	97%	2	8	97%
	6	Ankle Hops with Dorsiflexion	3	12	97%	3	10	97%	2	8	97%
	7	Band Assisted Jumps	3	8	97%	3	6	97%	3	6	97%
	8	1/4 Squat/Calf Raise Combo	3	12	60%	3	12	60%	2	8	60%
Thurs	1	30m Sprints	4	1	97%	4	1	97%	3	1	97%
	2	Standing Triple Jump	4	1	97%	4	1	97%	3	1	97%
	3	Power Snatch (From hang)	6	2	60%	5	2	65%	3	3	60%
	4	Snatch Grip Deadlift	2	5	60%	3	3	60%	3	4,3,2	60%
	5	Vertical Med Ball Throw	2	5	97%	2	4	97%	2	3	97%
	6	Kettlebell Swing	3	8	65%	3	8	70%	2	6	65%
Fri	1	24" Depth Jump	12	1	97%	10	1	97%	8	1	97%
	2	18" Single Leg Depth Jump	4	5	97%	3	5	97%	2	5	97%
	3	Barbell Back Squat (1-0-X)	4	5	77%	4	4	80%	3	3	83%
	4	Speed 1/2 Squat	4	5	50%	3	5	50%	3	5	50%
	5	Speed Lateral Bench Hops	3	12	97%	3	10	97%	2	8	97%
	6	Ankle Hops with Dorsiflexion	3	12	97%	3	10	97%	2	8	97%
	7	Band Assisted Jumps	3	8	97%	3	6	97%	3	6	97%
	8	1/4 Squat/Calf Raise Combo	3	12	60%	3	12	60%	2	8	60%

Figure 12.1: 4-Day offseason training program for strength/power with focus on two leg vertical jump.

Specific to the program in figure 12.1 are the following exercises:

- Deep front squats
- Deadlifts
- Olympic lifts
- Explosive "hinging" medicine ball throws
- Specific squat and calf work
- Power oriented depth jumps
- Single leg depth jumps
- Contraction/relaxation plyometrics
- Assisted jumps
- Basic posterior chain strengthening work

As you can see, the program is fairly heavy on strength work and lifting, as some form of lifting is addressed 4 days out of the week. Monday and Thursday are posterior chain oriented days, with Tuesday and Friday being anterior chain, vertically oriented training days. Squats are included twice a week, as these are the most important exercise devoted towards improving two leg jumping. Deep front squats performed slowly on the eccentric phase can be very helpful in improving the ability to load a jump deeper and produce force over a longer window of time. Exercises specific to two leg vertical jumping included in this sample program are as follows:

- Depth jumps from lower (18-24") boxes. Force dominant athletes will do better with lower boxes, as these allow greater power outputs into the jump.
- Single leg depth jumps. These exercises carry with them high forces and long contact times which cater towards bilateral jumps, despite their single leg nature.
- Speed ½ squats. The speed ½ squat, an exercise where an athlete performs rapid half squats with a light load on the barbell, is great for increasing the rate of force development in both single and double leg jumping.
- ¼ Squat + calf raise. In this exercise, an athlete will perform a quarter squat with a barbell and finish with an explosive upward lift onto fully plantar-flexed feet, pressuring the big toe. This exercise alone has the capacity to increase vertical jump by several inches in athletes with poor foot function.

- Contraction/Relaxation cycle plyometrics, including speed oriented tuck jumps, lateral bench hops, and ankle hops with dorsiflexion. These plyometrics allow athletes to work on the speed of contraction and relaxation in each of the main joints in jumping: The hip, knee and ankle.
- Band assisted jump. Band assisted jumps (where an athlete uses overhead elastic bands as a lightened method to jump quicker and faster) are a great way to train the calves in the final pushoff phase of jumping, as well as deliver an overspeed stimulus to the jump itself.
- Vertical medicine ball throw. In this exercise, the athlete will use a hinging action to throw a medicine ball vertically as high as possible, finishing up on the toes with big toe pressure. Another great way to train the upper body, posterior chain and feet all in one move. Force dominant athletes are often weak in this department and can reap great two foot gains here.

Key Point

Remember, "Level of physical preparedness" is a term that can be used to assess the current power and strength of the athlete, relative to the specific type of vertical jump they are trying to improve. Although the level of physical preparedness is related to strength in the weight room, Olympic lift, squat and deadlift maxes are not the sole determinants of physical preparedness for jumping.

This training program is written under the assumption that an athlete is engaging in some form of team sport play and occasional maximal jumping practice over the course of the training week. *Without this element of team sport play and competitive maximal jumping efforts, a training program will generally be less effective.* If athletes are not regularly involved in team sport, a greater volume of specific jumping and submaximal plyometrics can be installed in the program to make up for the elastic qualities lost by the lack of global athletic training.

In the four day training program in figure 12.1, the vertically oriented training days are the most strenuous, with Monday and Thursday having more of a complementary stimulus to the work on their following days. The sample program is designed in a "descending step load" format, meaning each week in the cycle is slightly lowered volume then the one before, with the third week being an intensity oriented de-load. This program design does a good job of managing the fatigue that tends to mask vertical jump gains during the course of many training programs.

A 4-day per week training program can be both demanding, time consuming and require frequent deloads. It is one that can work well for athletes who have the time to spend on it. That being said, a 3-day training cycle can be a bit more effective when looking at the average training frequency of many scholastic athletes, as well as those who have extensive commitments with team sport play, which takes its share of an athlete's ability to adapt to external training loads. Let's look at an example of how this can be accomplished below in figure 12.2.

Explosive Off-Season Training: Vertical Leap Focus

Day	Order	Exercise	Week 1			Week 2			Week 3		
			Sets	Reps	%RM	Sets	Reps	%RM	Sets	Reps	%RM
Mon	1	20m Sprints	5	1	97%	5	1	97%	4	1	97%
	2	30" Power Depth Jump	4	5	97%	4	4	97%	3	3	97%
	3	Power Clean (From floor)	8	2	70%	6	2	75%	6	1	65%
	4	Eccentric Front Squat (5-0-X)	5	3	75%	4	3	80%	4	2	83%
	5	Speed 1/2 Squat	3	3	50%	3	3	50%	3	2	50%
	6	Glute Ham Raise	4	8	60%	4	6	60%	4	5	60%
Wed	1	Deadlift	4	4	65%	4	3	70%	2	5	60%
	2	Push Press	4	5	70%	4	4	73%	4	3	76%
	3	3 Jumps for Distance	3	1	97%	3	1	97%	3	1	97%
	4	Vertical Med Ball Throw	5	3	97%	4	3	97%	4	2	97%
	5	Barbell Hip Thrust	4	5	50%	3	5	50%	3	5	50%
	6	1/4 Squat/Calf Raise Combo	3	12	60%	3	12	60%	2	8	60%
Fri	1	30m Sprints	4	1	97%	4	1	97%	3	1	97%
	2	18" Depth Jump	5	3	97%	5	3	97%	3	2	97%
	3	Power Snatch (From hang)	6	2	65%	5	2	70%	3	3	60%
	4	Back Squat	4	4	75%	4	3	80%	3	4,3,2	65%
	5	1/4 Squat/Calf Raise Combo	3	12	60%	3	12	60%	3	8	60%
	6	Glute Ham Raise	3	8	60%	3	8	60%	2	5	60%

Figure 12.2: 3-day explosive strength and power program with a focus on 2 foot vertical leap. This program is designed under the assumption of a significant volume of team sport oriented practice outside of the training, hence a lower volume of submaximal plyometric work.

Figure 12.2 depicts a program that athletes with lower work capacities or training frequency tolerances may respond better to, as greater recovery is allowed between training sessions. Athletes are given an easier day in the middle of the week on Wednesday, where the training is not as difficult due to a lack of squats and fairly low deadlift percentages. This program still has all of the main elements that make a program for overall athleticism, just spread out over the course of three days. This program comes out with heavy loading on Monday, uses Wednesday as a bit of an active recovery, and then goes hard again on Friday, making use of the two-day weekend to allow the athlete to recover and prepare for the next week. The above example is also given in "reverse step-loading" format, as the first week is the greatest in volume, allowing intensity to slowly increase over the next two weeks and fatigue to stay in check.

Although upper body and core work wasn't listed in the sample programming, its inclusion is important to the total result of a program. Clearly athletes seeking maximal athletic development, particularly in the arena of team sports, will need to pay attention to developing their body in balance and to the size and strength needs of their sport. That being said, more upper body work is acceptable and useful within a training program designed to improve two leg jumping, as the potential increased bodyweight that comes from this type of work will not generally hinder force dominant athletes seeking improved two foot jumping ability.

Speed dominant athletes may want to pay more attention to the amount of upper body work in their training program if it causes them a significant amount of upper body size gain, particularly in the back and shoulders (speed dominant athletes tend to put on size there easily, due to their torso dominant natures). Finally, athletes with weak arm swings in two leg jumping may want to spend some time daily performing seated or standing arm swing drills, working on the development of maximal momentum.

Core work can be useful for improving jump performance for athletes who are weak in that area, but not in the median that it typically used (lots of repeated hip and spinal flexion based work). The best type of core work is generally that which encourages strength in a position of neutral spine and that which ties the upper body to the lower body in a diagonal manner. Core work that is achieved as part of global athletic development is especially useful, such as gymnastic, tumbling and crawling based exercise. Basically, any work that strengthens the hip flexors and ties the body together can be useful for improving any athletic performance, and not just vertical jumping. Watching the practices of many elite jumpers, some of them are also excellent gymnastic athletes.

Finally, realize that the above programs are not as "phase specific" as they could be in terms of fitting into a yearly periodization program. In creating a yearly program, coaches will often funnel specific pieces of the above workout into particular phases. An example of this would be saving assisted band jumps for a phase of training devoted for speed work, and saving eccentric front squats for a phase devoted to strength work. Although the above programs could be more specific based on particular blocks and training foci, they include nearly any training modality available to demonstrate a way to put it all together into one training block. Keep in mind that there are nearly infinite ways to arrange the above training systems, so these are just one of many total program designs.

Basic Program Design for Reactive Jump Training (Single-leg Focus)

Athletes seeking training specifically for one-leg jumping is less common than general training to improve vertical leap, but it does happen, especially in the world of track and field. Speed-oriented athletes will find that routine heavy volumes of force oriented training (such as that found in typical strength and conditioning programming) can throw them out of their speed based motor patterns if they don't get to perform enough plyometric or elastic work. Program design for improving single leg jump must put the demands of the single leg jump as its highest priority.

Since a majority of athletes looking to increase their single leg jumping ability come from the arena of track and field, this book will include a very basic training template that will increase an athlete's single leg vertical *without* the assumption that they are actively training for team sport. Lots of team sport play makes it difficult to regularly perform a plyometric program with enough intensity to overload the single leg jumping pathway. Figure 12.3 depicts a sample 4-day, offseason training program for athletes seeking single leg jump improvement. The biggest differences between the general vertical jumping programming and the single leg program are as follows.

- The single leg program has proportionally more plyometric work and bounding.
- The single leg program uses a high volume of hurdle hops, which carry with them short contact times, similar to a single leg jump.

- The single leg program has depth jumps from higher heights to improve reactive strength.
- The single leg program has a greater volume of sprinting, as well as longer sprint distances.
- The single leg program uses lifting as a means of potentiating the more important plyometric and speed training days.
- The single leg program doesn't utilize as deep of squatting as the general program.
- The single leg program uses the unilateral special strength exercises of barbell step-ups and skipping.

Day	Order	Exercise	Week 1			Week 2			Week 3		
			Sets	Reps	%RM	Sets	Reps	%RM	Sets	Reps	%RM
Mon	1	Power Clean (from floor)	12	1	70%	10	1	73%	4	2	60%
	2	Barbell 1/2 Squat	4	6	75%	4	5	80%	3	3	65%
	3	Speed 1/2 Squat	4	5	50%	3	5	50%	3	5	50%
	4	Barbell Skips (20 meter)	4	1	30%	4	1	30%	2	1	30%
	5	Glute Ham Raise	3	5	60%	3	5	60%	2	5	60%
	6	100m Accelerations	5	1	70%	5	1	70%	5	1	70%
Tues	1	30m Sprints	8	1	97%	7	1	97%	5	1	97%
	2	Specific Single Leg Jumps	20	1	95%	15	1	95%	12	1	95%
	3	30" Depth Jump over hurdle	12	1	97%	10	1	97%	5	1	97%
	4	Alternate Leg Bounding (m)	5	20	97%	4	20	97%	4	20	97%
	5	Single Leg Bounding (m)	5	20	97%	4	20	97%	2	15	97%
	6	Backwards Med Ball Throw	4	5	97%	4	4	97%	3	3	97%
Thurs	1	Split Snatch (from hang)	5	2	65%	4	2	70%	3	3	65%
	2	Barbell Step Ups	5	4	70%	4	4	75%	4	3	65%
	3	Speed 1/2 Squat	4	5	50%	3	5	50%	3	5	50%
	4	Barbell Skips (20m)	4	1	50%	4	1	50%	2	1	50%
	5	Barbell Hip Thrust	3	8	60%	3	6	65%	2	5	60%
	6	100m Acceleration	5	1	70%	5	1	70%	5	1	70%
Fri	1	50m Sprints	4	1	97%	3	1	97%	3	1	97%
	2	Variety Single Leg Jumps	20	1	97%	20	1	97%	15	1	97%
	3	36" Depth Jump	10	1	97%	8	1	97%	5	1	97%
	4	Alternate leg Bounding (m)	6	25	97%	5	25	97%	3	20	97%
	5	Hurdle Hops	5	6	97%	5	5	97%	4	4	97%
	6	Forwards Med Ball Throw	4	5	97%	4	4	97%	3	3	97%

Explosive Off-Season Training: Single Leg Vertical

Figure12.3: Sample training program for single leg jumpers and speed jumpers.

As you can see, there is a significant difference when it comes to training athletes to their highest potential off of either one or two legs. Although the programming above will help athletes to jump higher off of one foot, *speed-jumpers will find that they may be more responsive to this type of work for overall athletic development*, as it complements the elastic and momentum-based manner in which they tend to move. As the general vertical program tends to be effective for athletes seeking two leg improvement, this program can also yield improvements in jumping off of two legs, particularly for speed jumpers, and even for force jumpers with little plyometric background (provided they can survive the training without injury).

The bottom line of putting things together in a total training program is that every piece needs to reflect the outcome goal based on movement and biomechanics. Knowing how athletes move, and the principles by which different types of jumping are based will allow coaches to prescribe programs for maximal effectiveness. Athletes can come up with fantastic technique over time, but the watchful eye of a dedicated coach makes the process that much better. It is my hope that through this book, you will have a greater awareness and understanding of the following:

- The anatomy and physiology that contributes to vertical jump success.
- The types of muscle action that separate dynamic human movement from traditional barbell training.
- Differences in the ways that various athletes move, and the associated pre-dispositions toward various types of jumping.
- How to go about implementing changes to technique, and how to use awareness as the ultimate method of letting the human body do what it is meant to naturally.
- The fundamental aspects of one and two leg vertical jump technique.
- How training programs tend to differ based on the development of either type of jumping technique.

Acknowledgements

Achievement is fairly meaningless without being grateful for those who have helped you along. I would like to thank the dozens of people who, because of their love and passion, each made this book just a little bit better, and my journey in writing it much more enjoyable.

Firstly, a special thanks to Jake Clark. Your design abilities and creativity have pushed me in writing a book that could hopefully compete with your fantastic cover and graphics. Thanks for being adaptive to my constant perfectionism and musings over various features of this long project.

Family

My wife, Emma: Thanks so much for putting up with me writing late into the night, my stressing out over finishing this book, as well as my general obsessiveness with anything involving improving athleticism. Words cannot express my thanks for your love and encouragement through this process.

My parents: Thank you for supporting my dreams. I am sure that not every parent is thrilled when their child goes through 6 years of school to get into a field, competing with 100's of professionals applying for entry level jobs that pay around minimum wage when the hours are considered. Your constant presence at my athletic events was a huge motivation for me to continue pursuing my dreams.

My brother: Thanks for being the best guy to play 1 on 1 basketball with when we were growing up. Sorry for always landing on you when trying to block your shots. Your dedication to your studies and career discipline has been a constant motivation to me in my own life.

Coaches and Mentors

Thanks to the following coaches and mentors whose work has had a massive impact on the way I coach and train athletes, and those whose dedication to their craft has inspired me to keep pushing forward along this path. I also would like to thank those who employed my services as a coach, by which I wouldn't have been given the chance to experience working with athletes each and every day. Without you all, this book would be nothing.

Kelly Baggett, Hank Behrens, Mike Blasquez, Jeff Bolender, Paul Cater, Matt Chisam, Ron Combs, Bret Contreras, John Dagata, Andrew Darqui, Cal Dietz, Nick Folker, Don Fritsch, Josh Hurlebaus, Simon Hunt, Dave Kerin, Tom Kernozek, Henk Kraiijenhof, Jimson Lee, Nelio Moura, Roger Nelsen, Nick Newman, Paul Orchard, Greg Potter, Robert "Raptor" Ruxandrescu, Chad Wesley Smith, Scott Thom, Jack Woodrup, Natalia Verkhoshansky, Jussi Viita, Peter Wright, Mike Young.

Friends

To my friends, you have kept me sane, and my life in balance. Without the ability to turn off the coaching "switch" and live a normal life once in a while, I would be in a tough spot indeed. Each of you have made my life that much better.

Printed in Great Britain
by Amazon

33249400R00084